THE WORLD OF
PETER RABBIT™
Beatrix Potter TM

KNITTING PETER RABBIT™

12 Toy Knitting Patterns from the Tales of Beatrix Potter

CLAIRE GARLAND

DAVID & CHARLES

www.davidandcharles.com

CONTENTS

WELCOME TO

THE WORLD OF
BEATRIX POTTER™

MAY I say, I'm honoured to have been asked to recreate Beatrix Potter's animals in yarn, and only hope I've done justice to the colours and general feel and style of her illustrated creatures.

I, like many others of my generation and many others in post and previous generations, have grown up with Beatrix Potter books by my bedside. Her Peter Rabbit and all her fabulous characters have truly played a very big part in my childhood imagination more than any other author, and without doubt are the reason I have been inspired to make and invent characters of my own.

She has been, is, and will be, a huge influence to all creatives like myself, now and forever.

HOW TO USE THIS BOOK

BEFORE you begin cast your eye over the following information, which will guide you to creating your very own Peter Rabbit, or Jeremy Fisher, or another favourite Beatrix Potter knitted character within these pages.

YARN
To create the colours and textures for the characters in this book I combine different coloured and textured yarns, which are held together to knit.

Within the patterns, the yarn combinations are written as follows:
Yarn ABC means one strand each of yarns A, B and C.
Yarn EEF means two strands of yarn E and one of yarn F.
Yarn J means just one strand of yarn J.

To work with two strands of the same yarn, you can take the second strand from the other end of the ball.

CASTING ON AND CASTING OFF
Cable cast-on and standard cast-off (see Techniques) are used throughout these patterns unless otherwise stated.

STITCH MARKERS
To make things as clear as possible for myself I use different colour stitch markers (see Using Locking Stitch Markers) to indicate each important point in my knitting, and I make a list to remind me what each colour means, for example Nose Seam = Pink.

I highly recommend this approach for ease of following the pattern, especially at the making-up stage. There is a downloadable Marker Guide worksheet available from www.davidandcharles.com for you to keep track of the markers you use for each character.

Using locking stitch markers
I use locking stitch markers to mark points that will be joined, or to show where to pick up stitches. Always put the marker into a stitch rather than on the knitting needle.

SEWING UP
For best results, these are my tips for sewing up seams in both your knitting and when making felt accessories and clothing.
- To sew the seams of knitted pieces, choose a yarn that matches one side of the seam.
- For small seams (for example, around an eye socket), use a single strand of kid mohair.
- For longer seams, use a single strand of 4ply/fingering yarn (or DK/light worsted for patterns knit with DK).
- Many seams need to be eased to get the two sides to fit together. I do this to create the curves of the animal. It helps if you pin these seams before sewing.

- To sew the seams on the non-knitted clothing, choose a shade of sewing thread that matches the colour of the felt.
- For some longer seams it helps if you pin the seams before sewing.
- Felt is very pliable so when you've sewn the seam you can add that little bit more shaping by moulding with your fingers, for example to emphasise the drape at the back of Mr. Tod's jacket or to round the shoulders nicely.
- Felt is very easy to cut and doesn't fray but a good pair of sharp dressmakers' scissors will give a good clean edge when cutting.
- Finally, I suggest using wool felt or felt with a high wool content. The 100% acrylic felts tend to tear and are a little too shiny.

EYES
For most of the projects in this book I have used 'toy safety eyes' which are made of plastic or resin. These come with either metal or plastic washer backs, which you push on to fix them in place.

STUFFING
I use a heavier stuffing, which gives the knitted character more weight and therefore allows it to sit more naturally. It's easier to pose and sculpt too.

How much to use? That depends on which part I am stuffing. For a face I tend to use a bit less to create the gentle bagginess that occurs around the jowls and around the eye sockets. For the body, however, I use more. A top tip is to leave a tiny gap in the very last seam you sew then you can add or remove stuffing as you live with your new friend for a while.

SCULPTING

This is the part that I spend the most time on and it's the most enjoyable and rewarding part of the whole process. I've finished the knitting, I've sewn the seams, stuffed the head and body, added the ears and fitted in the eyes… and then I sculpt. By sculpting I mean moulding the knitted character to make it look as life-like as possible. This means pushing my thumbs into eyes sockets, pulling and bending feet to enhance paw shapes, and squeezing and twisting waists to shape the belly and breast. It might seem quite brutal, but it's worth it for the result.

For finer details, like tiny mouse legs, I dampen the knitting slightly and use my fingers to tease and shape the knitted yarn.

Sometimes I will also add a tiny concealed stitch here and there, to add a bit more definition. This is mentioned where relevant in the patterns.

IMPORTANT: These patterns are not intended as toys for children under three years because of the small parts. However, they could be made for young children if you leave out the hard or sharp parts, and use felt or embroidery for the eyes. You may also want to consider using washable yarns and stuffing.

ABBREVIATIONS

approx.	approximately
dec	decrease
inc	increase
k	knit
k2tog/k3tog	knit two/three stitches together as one
kfb	knit into the front and back of one stitch
LH	left hand
m1	make one (see Techniques)
p	purl
p2tog/p3tog	purl two/three stitches together as one
pfb	purl into the front and back of one stitch
PM	place marker
RH	right hand
RS	right side of work
skpo	slip 1, knit 1, pass slipped st over
st(s)	stitch(es)
WS	wrong side of work
W+Tk/p	wrap and turn knit/purl (see Techniques)
stocking stitch	knit on RS rows, purl on WS rows
garter stitch	knit every row
[ ]	indicates a repeat sequence

UK TO US TERMS

UK	US
cast off	bind off
moss stitch	seed stitch
stocking stitch	stockinette
stuffing	filling
tension	gauge

NEEDLE CONVERSION CHART

UK	METRIC	US
-	2.5mm	1.5
12	2.75mm	2
11	3mm	-
10	3.25mm	3
-	3.5mm	4
9	3.75mm	5
8	4mm	6
7	4.5mm	7
6	5mm	8

TOOLS AND MATERIALS

YARN
These yarns are used in this book, the colours required are specified within the patterns.

- DROPS Alpaca: 100% Alpaca, 167m (183yds) per 50g
- Drops Baby Merino: 100% Wool, 175m (191yds) per 50g
- DROPS Fabel: 75% Wool, 25% Polyamide, 205m (224yds) per 50g
- DROPS Flora: 65% Wool, 35% Alpaca, 210m (230yds) per 50g
- DROPS Kid-Silk: 75% Mohair, 25% Silk, 210m (230yds) per 25g
- DROPS Nord: 45% Alpaca, 30% Polyamide, 25% Wool, 170m (186yds) per 50g
- King Cole Luxury Fur: 90% Nylon, 10% Polyester, 92m (100yds) per 100g

If you want to substitute different yarns, it is important to stick to similar yarn types (for example, a 4ply/fingering yarn for a 4ply/fingering yarn, a fur yarn for a fur yarn), and check your tension using the yarn combinations from the pattern.

NEEDLES & ACCESSORIES
- The patterns are written for straight needles
- Stitch holders or safety pins to hold stitches
- Locking stitch markers (see How to Use This Book: Stitch Markers)
- Tapestry or darning needle for sewing up knitting
- Pins to hold longer seams together while you sew
- Sharp hand sewing needle and embroidery needle
- Scissors

OTHER MATERIALS
Stuffing
I recommend heavy, uncarded, polyester fibre fill/stuffing. Or you can use yarn and fabric scraps, but be sure to cut them into very small pieces.

Toy safety eyes
There are a huge variety of eyes available (see How to Use This Book: Eyes), so take time to find the right colour and iris shape for your character. In my experience, the more expensive ones are better quality.

Felt
Wool felt preferably or a mix with a high percentage of wool – the higher quality the better (see How to Use This Book: Sewing Up). Wool felt is available globally from Etsy.

Sewing and embroidery thread
Coloured sewing thread to match the felt. For the facial features and embroidered details, I use 3 or 4 strands separated from 6-stranded embroidery silk.

Buttons
For the buttons on felt clothes, try hunting on Etsy for 'doll clothes' buttons.

PETER RABBIT™

PETER is the star of Beatrix Potter's most popular and well-loved tale, *The Tale of Peter Rabbit*, which was first published by Frederick Warne in 1902. It tells the story of a very mischievous rabbit and the trouble he encounters in Mr. McGregor's vegetable garden!

FINISHED SIZE
Approx. 24cm (9½in) tall from feet to tip of ears

YARN
You will need no more than one ball of each of:
A: DROPS Kid-Silk shade 01 Off White
B: DROPS Alpaca shade 0302 Camel
C: DROPS Kid-Silk shade 29 Vanilla
D: DROPS Alpaca shade 0100 Off White
E: DROPS Kid-Silk shade 03 Light Pink
F: For the claws and facial features a few
doubled-up lengths of DROPS Kid-Silk
shade 15 Dark Brown
Unless otherwise stated, double strands of yarn are
used together throughout this pattern. The exact
combinations of yarn to be used are indicated by
multiple letters (see How to Use This Book).

TENSION
13 stitches and 16 rows over 5cm (2in)

NEEDLES
3.5mm (US 4) knitting needles

OTHER TOOLS AND MATERIALS
• 3 large safety pins or stitch holders
• 24 coloured locking stitch markers (see How to
  Use This Book: Stitch Markers)
• 2 x 15mm (⅝in) light-brown toy safety eyes
• Toy stuffing or yarn/fabric scraps
• Tapestry or darning needle

PATTERN NOTES
• Use cable cast-on unless otherwise stated
• General knitting abbreviations can be
  found in How to Use This Book

HEAD
Beginning at the Nose.
With yarn AB cast on 10 sts for
Nose Seam.
Row 1: Purl.
Row 2 (inc): Kfb, k4, turn (flip work
over so purl-side faces) to work on
Left Muzzle as follows:

Left Muzzle
Row 3: P6.
Row 4 (inc): Kfb, k4, kfb, pick up and
knit 2 sts into the purl row from Row
1 for Nose, k4 sts across Right Muzzle,
kfb. – 16sts
Row 5: P6, turn (flip work over so
knit-side faces) to work on Right
Muzzle as follows:

Right Muzzle
Row 6 (inc): Kfb, k4, kfb.
Row 7: Purl across all 18 sts (i.e. Right
Muzzle, Nose and Left Muzzle).
Row 8 (inc): Kfb, k6, [kfb] 4 times, k6,
kfb. – 24sts
Row 9: Purl.
Row 10 (inc): Kfb, knit to last st, kfb.
– 26sts
Row 11: Purl.

Cut yarn A, join yarn C, continue with
yarn BC as follows:
Row 12 (inc): K10, kfb, k4, kfb, k10 to
end. – 28sts
Row 13: Purl.
Row 14 (inc): Kfb, knit to last st, kfb.
– 30sts
Row 15: Purl, PM on first and last
stitch for Left and Right Neck Markers.

Divide the Nose from the Cheeks
Row 16: K20, PM on last stitch (20th
stitch) for Right Nose Marker, turn.
Row 17: P10, PM on last stitch (10th
stitch) for Left Nose Marker, turn to
knit-side to work on Top of Nose
and Forehead only as follows (leave
the two sets of 10 Cheek sts on the
needle as you work in between them).

Top of Nose and Forehead
Row 18 (inc): K2, kfb, k4, kfb, k2, turn.
– 12sts
Row 19: P12, turn.
Row 20 (inc): K3, kfb, k4, kfb, k3, turn.
– 14sts
Row 21: P14, turn.
Row 22 (inc): K4, kfb, k4, kfb, k4. –
16sts
Rows 23-26: Beginning with a purl
row, work four rows stocking stitch on
all 16 Forehead sts.
Row 27 (dec): P2tog, p12, p2tog.
– 14sts
Cut yarn and place all 14 Forehead sts
onto a safety pin.

Right Cheek
RS facing rejoin yarn BC to 10 sts on
LH needle for Right Cheek, continue
as follows:
Row 1: Knit.
Row 2 (dec): P2tog, p6, p2tog. – 8sts
Rows 3-6: Beginning with a knit row,
work four rows stocking stitch.
Row 7 (inc): Cast on 2 sts, knit all 10 sts.
Row 8: P10, PM on last stitch for Right
Eye Corner Marker.
Cut yarn and place all 10 Right Cheek
sts onto a safety pin.

Left Cheek

WS facing rejoin yarn BC to 10 sts on LH needle for Left Cheek, continue as follows:

Row 1 (dec): P2tog, p6, p2tog. – 8sts

Rows 2-6: Beginning with a knit row, work five rows stocking stitch.

Row 7 (inc): Cast on 2 sts, PM on first stitch for Left Eye Corner Marker, purl all 10 sts.

Do not cut yarn.

Join Left Cheek, Nose and Right Cheek

Row 1 (inc): Knit across all 10 Left Cheek sts; slip all 14 Forehead sts off the safety pin and onto a knitting needle, k1, skpo, k8, k2tog, k1; slip all 10 Right Cheek sts off the safety pin and onto a knitting needle, k10. – 32sts

Rows 2-4: Beginning with a purl row, work three rows stocking stitch.

Row 5 (inc): Kfb, k9, kfb, k10, kfb, knit to last st, kfb. – 36sts

Row 6: Purl.

Row 7: K14, PM on last stitch (14th stitch) for Left Ear Front Marker, knit next 9 sts, PM on last stitch (9th stitch) for Right Ear Front Marker, k13 to end of row.

Row 8: Purl.

Row 9 (dec): K12, skpo, k8, k2tog, k12 to end of row. – 34sts

Row 10: Purl.

Row 11 (dec): K12, skpo, k6, k2tog, k12 to end of row. – 32sts

Row 12: Purl.

Row 13 (dec): K10, skpo, k1, PM on last stitch for (1st stitch) Left Ear Back Marker, knit next 7 sts, PM on last stitch (7th stitch) for Right Ear Back Marker, k2tog, k10 to end of row. – 30sts

Row 14: Purl.

Divide the Head Back to Create Head Back Seam

Row 15 (dec): Cast off 9 sts for Head Back Seam Left-Side, knit next 11 sts, cast off last 9 sts for Head Back Seam Right-Side. – 12sts

Head Back

WS facing rejoin yarn BC to 12 sts for Head Back, continue as follows:

Rows 16-24: Beginning with a purl row, work nine rows stocking stitch. Cut yarn, place all 12 Head Back sts onto a large safety pin for now.

Join Head Seams

Refer to Body A, **Fig. 1**, in Making Up.

RS together fold the Nose Cast-On Edge from the beginning of the pattern in half and join both halves together with back stitch – join dotted line A to B.
Turn out to RS.

NECK AND BACK

Refer to Body A, **Fig. 2** in Making Up.

Join Left Side of Head

With yarn BC, begin at rabbit's Left Neck Marker, RS facing pick up and knit 8 sts evenly along row ends to the left-side corner of Head Back Seam Cast-Off Edge; slip all 12 Head Back sts from the safety pin onto a knitting needle then from corner of Head Back Cast-Off Edge knit across all 12 Head Back sts.

Join Right Side of Head

Continue to pick up across the right side of the head, all onto the same needle as follows:

Pick up and knit 8 sts evenly along row ends from right corner of Head Back Seam Cast-Off Edge to Right Neck Marker – 28sts – pick up and knit from A to B; knit across from C to D; pick up and knit from E to F.

Row 1: Purl all 28 sts.

BODY
Back

Row 2 (dec): K10, skpo, k4, k2tog, k10 to end of row. – 26sts

Row 3: Purl.

Row 4 (dec): K10, skpo, k2, k2tog, k10 to end of row. – 24sts

Row 5: Purl.
Row 6 (dec): K10, skpo, k2tog, k10 to end of row. – 22sts
Row 7: Purl.
Row 8 (inc): Kfb, k6, kfb, k6, kfb, k6, kfb. – 26sts
Row 9: Purl.
Row 10 (inc): Kfb, k5, PM on last knitted stitch for Left Foreleg Placement, knit next 15 sts, PM on last knitted stitch for Right Foreleg Placement, k4, kfb. – 28sts
Row 11: Purl.
Row 12 (inc): Kfb, k9, kfb, k6, kfb, k9, kfb. – 32sts
Row 13: Purl.
Row 14 (inc): Kfb, knit to last st, kfb. – 34sts
Row 15: Purl.
Row 16 (inc): K13, kfb, k6, kfb, k13 to end of row. – 36sts
Rows 17-23: Beginning with a purl row, work seven rows stocking stitch.
Row 24 (inc): K14, kfb, k6, kfb, k14 to end of row. – 38sts
Rows 25-29: Beginning with a purl row, work five rows stocking stitch.

> *Peter, who was very naughty, ran straight away to Mr. McGregor's garden, and squeezed under the gate!*

Row 30 (inc): Kfb, k1, kfb, knit to last 3 sts, kfb, k1, kfb. – 42sts
Row 31: Purl, PM on first and last stitch of row for Left and Right Thigh Markers.

Join yarn C, continue with yarn BCC (use other end of yarn C ball) as follows:

Hind Legs
Work short rows (see Techniques) for Left Hind Leg:
Short row 1 (inc): Cast on 8 sts, k9, W+Tk.
Short row 2: P2, W+Tp.
Short row 3: K3, W+Tk.
Short row 4: P4, W+Tp.
Short row 5: K5, W+Tk.
Short row 6: P6, W+Tp.
Short row 7: K7, W+Tk.
Short row 8: P8, W+Tp.
Short row 9: K9, W+Tk.
Short row 10: P10, W+Tp.
Short row 11: K11, W+Tk.
Short row 12: P12, W+Tp.
Short row 13: K13, W+Tk.
Short row 14: P14, W+Tp.
Short row 15 (dec): K14, skpo, k33 to end of row. – 49sts

Work short rows for Right Hind Leg:
Short row 1 (inc): Cast on 8 sts, p9, W+Tp.
Short row 2: K2, W+Tk.
Short row 3: P3, W+Tp.
Short row 4: K4, W+Tk.
Short row 5: P5, W+Tp.
Short row 6: K6, W+Tk.
Short row 7: P7, W+Tp.
Short row 8: K8, W+Tk.
Short row 9: P9, W+Tp.
Short row 10: K10, W+Tk.
Short row 11: P11, W+Tp.
Short row 12: K12, W+Tk.
Short row 13: P13, W+Tp.
Short row 14: K14, W+Tk.
Short row 15 (dec): P14, p2tog, p40 to end of row. – 56sts

Row 32 (dec): K2tog, k12, k2tog, k7, skpo, k6, k2tog, k7, k2tog, k12, k2tog. – 50sts
Row 33: Purl.
Row 34 (dec): K11, k2tog, k7, skpo, k6, k2tog, k7, k2tog, k11 to end of row. – 46sts

Row 35: Purl.
Row 36 (dec): K10, k2tog, k6, skpo, k6, k2tog, k6, k2tog, k10 to end of row. – 42sts
Row 37: Purl.
Row 38 (dec): K9, k2tog, k20, k2tog, k9 to end of row. – 40sts
Row 39: Purl.
Row 40 (dec): K8, k2tog, k20, k2tog, k8 to end of row. – 38sts
Row 41: Purl.

Lower Back
Work short rows for Lower Back:
Short row 1: K31, W+Tk.
Short row 2: P24, W+Tp.
Short row 3: K23, W+Tk.
Short row 4: P22, W+Tp.
Short row 5: K21, W+Tk.
Short row 6: P20, W+Tp.
Short row 7 (dec): K6, cast off next 8 sts for Tail Space, knit next 4 sts, W+Tk.
Short row 8 (inc): P5, cast on 6 sts for Under Tail Space, purl next 5 sts, W+Tp.
Short row 9: K15, W+Tk.
Short row 10: P14, W+Tp.
Short row 11: K13, W+Tk.
Short row 12: P12, W+Tp.
Short row 13: K24 to end of row. – 36sts

Row 12: Purl all 36 sts.
Row 43 (dec): K13, skpo, k6, k2tog, k13 to end of row. – 34sts
Row 44: Purl.
Row 45 (dec): K2tog, k7, k2tog, k2, skpo, k4, k2tog, k2, k2tog, k7, k2tog. – 28sts
Row 46: Purl, PM on first and last stitch of row for Left and Right Belly Markers.
Row 47 (dec): Cast off 10 sts for Left Paw Edge, knit next 7 sts, cast off last 10 sts for Right Paw Edge. – 8sts

Belly
WS facing, join yarn ACD to 8 sts on knitting needle.
Row 1: Purl across all 8 Belly sts.
Rows 2-9: Beginning with a knit row, work eight rows stocking stitch, PM on first and last stitch of last row for Left and Right Inner Belly Markers.
Rows 10-15: Beginning with a knit

row, work six rows stocking stitch.
Row 16 (inc): K1, kfb, k4, kfb, k1.
– 10sts
Rows 17-19: Beginning with a purl row, work three rows stocking stitch.
Row 20 (inc): K2, kfb, k4, kfb, k2.
– 12sts
Rows 21-23: Beginning with a purl row, work three rows stocking stitch.
Row 24 (inc): K3, kfb, k4, kfb, k3.
– 14sts
Rows 25-33: Beginning with a purl row, work nine rows stocking stitch, PM on first and last stitch of last row for Left and Right Inner Thigh Markers.
Rows 34-39: Beginning with a knit row, work six rows stocking stitch.
Row 40 (dec): K1, skpo, knit to last 3 sts, k2tog, k1. – 12sts
Rows 41-47: Beginning with a purl row, work five rows stocking stitch.
Cut yarn C, join yarn A, continue with yarn AAD (use other end of yarn A ball) as follows:

Breast
Work short rows for Breast:
Short row 1: K11, W+Tk.
Short row 2: P10, W+Tp.
Short row 3: K9, W+Tk.
Short row 4: P8, W+Tp.
Short row 5: K7, W+Tk.
Short row 6: P6, W+Tp.
Short row 7: K5, W+Tk.
Short row 8: P4, W+Tp.
Short row 9: K8 to end of row.

Row 48: Purl.
Row 49 (inc): Kfb, knit to last st, kfb.
– 14sts
Row 50: Purl.
Cast off all 14 sts for Neck Edge, PM on first and last cast-off stitch for Left and Right Inner Neck Markers.

Join Thigh Front Seam
Refer to Body A, **Fig. 3** in Making Up.

Working on one side at a time, WS together match Inner Thigh to Thigh Markers, match Inner Belly to Belly Markers, work mattress stitch to join Thigh Front Seam so joining Thigh to Belly from Inner Thigh/Thigh Markers to Inner Belly/Belly Markers – join as dotted line A to B.

Remove Inner Belly and Inner Thigh Markers.

Join Belly to Back Seam
Refer to Body A, **Fig. 4** in Making Up.

Working on one side at a time, WS together match Inner Neck to Neck Markers, ease seam together and work mattress stitch to join Belly and Breast Seam so joining Belly and Breast to Back from Inner Neck/Neck Markers to Thigh Markers – join as dotted line A to B.
Remove Inner Neck and Thigh Markers.
At this stage you can add stuffing into the body. Add a little at a time using the stuffing to pad out the shaping at the thighs, breast, belly and back.

CHIN
Return to the Neck Cast-Off Edge. RS and Belly facing, with yarn AD, starting at Left Neck Marker (on your right), pick up and knit 14 sts across row ends and cast-off edge from Left Neck Marker to Right Neck Marker. Remove both Neck Markers.
Row 1: Purl.
Row 2 (inc): Kfb, knit to last st, kfb.
– 16sts
Row 3: Purl.
Row 4 (dec): K4, skpo, k4, k2tog, k4.
– 14sts
Row 5 (dec): P2tog, purl to last 2 sts, p2tog. – 12sts
Row 6 (dec): K3, skpo, k2, k2tog, k3.
– 10sts
Row 7 (dec): P2tog, purl to last 2 sts, p2tog. – 8sts
Row 8 (dec): K1, skpo, k2, k2tog, k1.
– 6sts

Work short rows for Chin:
Short row 1: P5, W+Tp.
Short row 2: K4, W+Tk.
Short row 3 (dec): P1, p2tog, p2 to end of row. – 5sts

Cut yarn, thread end through all 5 sts, pull up to gather and fasten end to secure for Chin Point.

Join Chin to Muzzle Seam
Refer to Body A, **Fig. 5** in Making Up.

Stuff the head a little to make it easier to join the seams.
Find the centre of the Chin Point Edge and mark with a pin.
WS together, match the pin to the Nose Seam, hold with a stitch or two. Remove the pin.
Working on one side at a time join the muzzle to the chin with mattress stitch, easing the seam together as you do so.

EYES
The eyes are picked up and knitted into the row-ends edge above the cheeks, knitted into an eye shape that matches the eye socket, pushed into the eye socket and then carefully joined by over-sewing into the socket space before adding the toy safety eyes.

Left Eye
Refer to Body A, **Fig. 6** in Making Up.

RS and rabbit's Left Eye Socket facing, with yarn D, beginning at Left Eye Corner Marker, pick up and knit 8 sts evenly along the row-ends edge at the top of the left cheek (this is also the lower edge of the eye socket), from your right to your left, across to Left Nose Marker – pick up as dotted line from A to B.
Remove Left Eye Corner Marker and Left Nose Marker.

*Rows 1-3: Beginning with a purl row, work three rows stocking stitch.
Row 4 (dec): K2tog, k4, k2tog. – 6sts
Row 5: Purl.
Row 6 (dec): K2tog, k2, k2tog. – 4sts
Row 7: Purl.
Row 8 (dec): [K2tog] twice. – 2sts
Row 9 (dec): P2tog.**

Right Eye

RS and rabbit's Right Eye Socket facing, with yarn D, beginning at Right Nose Marker pick up and knit 8 sts evenly along the edge at the top of the right cheek (this is also the lower edge of the eye socket) from your right to your left, across to Right Eye Corner Marker.
Remove Right Eye Corner Marker and Right Nose Marker.
Continue as Left Eye from * to **.

Join Eye to Eye Socket Seam

Refer to Body A, **Fig. 7** in Making Up.

Working on one eye at a time, WS together push the knitted eye into the eye socket. Matching the eye to the socket carefully over-sew all around the eye joining it slightly inside the socket.

Push the toy eye into the centre of the knitted eye, from front/knit-side to back/purl-side and secure it in place firmly with the plastic or metal backing.

EARS

Left Outer Ear

Refer to Body A, **Fig. 8** in Making Up.

RS and with the top of the head facing, begin near rabbit's Left Ear Front Marker and with yarn BC pick up and knit 7 sts into the knitted stitches at the top of the head in a straight line across to Left Ear Back Marker – pick up and knit as dotted line from A to B.
Remove both Left Ear Markers.
Row 1 (inc): Cast on 7 sts, purl across all 14 sts.
Row 2 (inc): Kfb, knit to last st, kfb. – 16sts
Rows 3-9: Beginning with a purl row, work seven rows stocking stitch.
Row 10 (dec): K5, skpo, k2, k2tog, k5. – 14sts
Row 11: Purl.
Row 12 (dec): K4, skpo, k2, k2tog, k4. – 12sts
Row 13: Purl.
Row 14 (dec): K3, skpo, k2, k2tog, k3. – 10sts
Row 15: Purl.
Row 16 (dec): K2, skpo, k2, k2tog, k2. – 8sts
Row 17: Purl.
Row 18 (dec): K1, skpo, k2, k2tog, k1. – 6sts
Row 19: Purl.
Row 20 (dec): Skpo, k2, k2tog. – 4sts
Row 21: Purl.
Row 22 (dec): K2tog, cast off 1 st, cast off last 2 sts for Left Ear Top Cast-Off Edge.
Weave the tail end in and out along ear edge.

Right Outer Ear

RS and with the top of the head facing, begin near rabbit's Right Ear Back Marker and with yarn BC pick up and knit 7 sts into the knitted stitches at the top of the head in a straight line across to Right Ear Front Marker – stitches shown picked up and knitted as dotted line from A to B.

Remove both Right Ear Markers.
Row 1: Purl.
Row 2 (inc): Cast on 7 sts, knit across all 14 sts.
Row 3 (inc): Pfb, purl to last st, pfb. – 16sts
Rows 4-9: Beginning with a knit row, work six rows stocking stitch.
Row 10 (dec): K5, skpo, k2, k2tog, k5. – 14sts
Row 11: Purl.
Row 12 (dec): K4, skpo, k2, k2tog, k4. – 12sts
Row 13: Purl.
Row 14 (dec): K3, skpo, k2, k2tog, k3. – 10sts
Row 15: Purl.
Row 16 (dec): K2, skpo, k2, k2tog, k2. – 8sts
Row 17: Purl.
Row 18 (dec): K1, skpo, k2, k2tog, k1. – 6sts
Row 19: Purl.
Row 20 (dec): Skpo, k2, k2tog. – 4sts
Row 21: Purl.
Row 22 (dec): K2tog, cast off 1 st, cast off last 2 sts for Left Ear Top Cast-Off Edge.
Weave the tail end in and out along ear edge.

Left Inner Ear Side 1

Refer to Body A, **Fig. 9** in Making Up.

RS facing, with yarn E starting at the corner of Left Ear Outer Edge pick up and knit 18 sts evenly along rows ends up to the centre of the Left Ear Top Cast-Off Edge – stitches shown picked up and knitted as dotted line from A to B.
Row 1: Purl.
Row 2 (dec): Knit to last 2 sts, k2tog. – 17sts
Rows 3-6 (dec): Repeat last two rows twice. – 15sts
Row 7: Purl.
Cast off all 15 sts for Left Inner Ear Centre Side 1.

Left Inner Ear Side 2

RS facing, with yarn E starting at the centre of the Left Ear Top Cast-Off Edge pick up and knit 18 sts evenly along rows ends to the corner of Left Ear Inner Edge – stitches shown

picked up and knitted as dotted line from C to D.
Row 1: Purl.
Row 2 (dec): K2tog, knit to end. – 17sts
Rows 3-6 (dec): Repeat last two rows twice. – 15sts
Row 7: Purl.
Cast off all 15 sts for Left Inner Ear Centre Side 2.

Right Inner Ear Side 1
RS facing, with yarn E starting at the corner of Right Ear Inner Edge pick up and knit 18 sts evenly along rows ends up to the centre of the Right Ear Top Cast-Off Edge.
Row 1: Purl.
Row 2 (dec): Knit to last 2 sts, k2tog. – 17sts
Rows 3-6 (dec): Repeat last two rows twice. – 15sts
Row 7: Purl.
Cast off all 15 sts for Right Inner Ear Centre Side 1.

Right Inner Ear Side 2
RS facing, with yarn E starting at the centre of the Right Ear Top Cast-Off Edge pick up and knit 18 sts evenly along rows ends to the corner of Right Ear Outer Edge.
Row 1: Purl.
Row 2 (dec): K2tog, knit to end. – 17sts
Rows 3-6 (dec): Repeat last two rows twice. – 15sts
Row 7: Purl.
Cast off all 15 sts for Right Inner Ear Centre Side 2.

Join Inner Ear Seam
Refer to Body A, **Fig. 10** in Making Up.

Working on one Inner Ear at a time, with RS together, match Inner Ear Centre Side 1 to Inner Ear Centre Side 2 and work back stitch to join along both cast-off edges, continue to join the seam along the diagonal row ends up to the Ear Point. Leave the straight edges at the base of the ear inner open for turning through – join dotted lines A to B.
Turn out to RS and trim the tails ends (it's best not to have any stuffing for inside the ears).

Refer to Body A, **Fig. 11** in Making Up.

Fold each ear in half, tucking the inner ear inside the fold so that the ear edge corners meet and mattress stitch to join the base from the corners to the fold – join dotted lines A to B.

Join Ears to the Head
Refer to Body A, **Fig. 12** in Making Up.

Complete the Ear by joining the Ear Back onto the head by curving it around in a kind of arc; the corner of the Ear Back should almost join with the corner at the front of the ear creating a 'petal' shape. Pin in place and, when you are happy with your placement, make a stitch or two to hold the corner of the ear in place and then securely sew down the ear back onto the head, either with mattress stitch or by over-sewing.

Join Head Back Seam
Refer to Body A, **Fig. 13** in Making Up.

WS together, working on one side at a time, work mattress stitch to join the Head Back Seam Cast-Off Edge to the row ends at the back of the head, at the same time adding a little stuffing to pad out the head back. You can also add little bits of stuffing into the muzzle and nose to pad out those too.

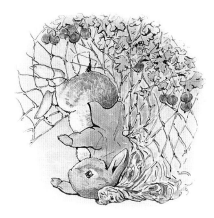

He might have got away altogether if he had not unfortunately run into a gooseberry net, and got caught by the large buttons on his jacket.

HIND PAWS
Refer to Body A, **Fig. 14** in Making Up.

The Left and Right Hind Paws are picked up and knitted along the Hind Paw Cast-Off Edge, knitted into a paw shape, the seam is sewn all along the paw's heel, upper and sole, stuffing at the same time.
The details are embroidered on once the paw is completed.

Left Hind Paw
RS and rabbit's Left Thigh facing, begin at Left Belly Marker, with yarn BC pick up and knit 9 sts along Left Paw Cast-Off Edge from Left Belly Marker to the other corner of the cast-off edge near the rabbit's Back – pick up as dotted line from A to B.
Remove Left Belly Marker.
Row 1: Purl.
Row 2 (inc): Cast on 8 sts for Left Paw Upper, knit across all 17 sts.
Rows 3-7: Beginning with a purl row, work five rows stocking stitch.

Right Hind Paw

RS and rabbit's Right Thigh facing, begin at the opposite corner to Right Belly Marker, with yarn BC pick up and knit 9 sts along Right Paw Cast-Off Edge to Right Belly Marker. Remove Right Belly Marker.

Row 1 (inc): Cast on 8 sts for Right Paw Upper, purl across all 17 sts.
Rows 2-6: Beginning with a knit row, work five rows stocking stitch.

Work short rows for Right Paw Front Outer Edge:
Short row 1: P8, W+Tp.
Short row 2: K6, W+Tk.
Short row 3: P5, W+Tp.
Short row 4: K4, W+Tk.
Short row 5: P3, W+Tp.
Short row 6: K2, W+Tk.
Short row 7: P13 to end of row.

Row 7: Knit.

Work short rows for Right Paw Front Inside Edge:
Short row 1: P8, W+Tp.
Short row 2: K6, W+Tk.
Short row 3: P5, W+Tp.
Short row 4: K4, W+Tk.
Short row 5: P3, W+Tp.
Short row 6: K2, W+Tk.
Short row 7: P13 to end of row.

Rows 8-12: Beginning with a knit row, work five rows stocking stitch.
Row 13 (dec): Cast off 8 sts purl-wise for Paw Upper Inside Edge, purl to end of row. – 9sts
Row 14: Knit.
Cast off all 9 sts purl-wise for Paw Inside Edge.

Join Hind Paw Seam
Refer to Body A, **Fig. 15** in Making Up.

Working on one paw at a time, WS together fold paw in half across the row ends at the heel.
Mattress stitch the Paw Inside Cast-Off Edge to the row ends at the Belly.
Work mattress stitch to join the cast-on and cast-off edges of the paw upper and the row ends that will become the paw front.
Stuff the paw through the last seam at

the heel before closing that seam with mattress stitch.
Flatten the front of the paw with your thumb and forefinger then with a doubled length of yarn F work four lots of straight stitches to create toe sections, pulling the straight stitches as you sew them to make the paw indent a little.

TAIL
Refer to Body A, **Fig. 16** in Making Up.

The Tail is picked up and knitted along the Tail Cast-Off Edge, the under-tail edges are cast on at either side of the picked-up and knitted stitches then the Tail is knitted in its entirety. The seam is sewn all along the tail from tip to cast-on edges. The cast-on edges are then joined to the Tail Cast-On Edge.
Add any more stuffing (also stuff your yarn snippings) through the tail opening.

RS and rabbit's Back facing, return to the Tail Cast-Off Edge. With yarn BC, begin at rabbit's left side (your right side) of the cast-off edge, pick up and knit 9 sts into the cast-off edge, all along from your right to your left – Tail already picked up and knitted as dotted line from A to B.
Row 1 (inc): Cast on 3 sts for Tail Underside 1, purl all 12 sts.
Row 2 (inc): Cast on 3 sts for Tail Underside 2, knit all 15 sts.
Row 3: Purl.

Work short rows for Tail Tip:
Short row 1: K11, W+Tk.
Short row 2: P7, W+Tp.
Short row 3: K6, W+Tk.
Short row 4: P5, W+Tp.
Short row 5: K4, W+Tk.
Short row 6: P3, W+Tp.
Short row 7: K2, W+Tk.
Short row 8: P1, W+Tp.
Short row 9: K8 to end of row.

Work short rows for Left Paw Front Outer Edge:
Short row 1: K8, W+Tk.
Short row 2: P6, W+Tp.
Short row 3: K5, W+Tk.
Short row 4: P4, W+Tp.
Short row 5: K3, W+Tk.
Short row 6: P2, W+Tp.
Short row 7: K13 to end of row.

Row 8: Purl.

Work short rows for Left Paw Front Inside Edge:
Short row 1: K8, W+Tk.
Short row 2: P6, W+Tp.
Short row 3: K5, W+Tk.
Short row 4: P4, W+Tp.
Short row 5: K3, W+Tk.
Short row 6: P2, W+Tp.
Short row 7: K13 to end of row.

Rows 9-13: Beginning with a purl row, work five rows stocking stitch.
Row 14 (dec): Cast off 8 sts for Paw Upper Inside Edge, knit to end of row. – 9sts
Row 15: Purl.
Cast off all 9 sts for Paw Inside Edge.

Cut yarn BC, join yarn AD, continue with the underside of the tail as follows:

Row 4: Purl.
Row 5 (dec): K2tog, knit to last 2 sts, k2tog. – 13sts
Row 6: Purl.
Row 7 (dec): [K2tog, k1] four times, k1. – 9sts
Row 8 (dec): [P3tog] three times. – 3sts
Cut yarn, thread end through all 3 sts for Underside Tail Point.

Join Tail Seam
Refer to Body A, **Fig. 17** in Making Up.

Fold the tail and match the Underside Tail Point to the centre of the Under-Tail Space Cast-Off Edge.
Working on each side of the tail in turn ease the Tail Underside Cast-on Edge and row ends together with the Under-Tail Space Cast-Off Edge Tail edge, join together with mattress stitch, at the same time stuffing the tail a little – but not too much!
Just before closing the seam completely you can also add more stuffing, if needs be, to the body and head.

FORELEGS
The Left and Right Forelegs are knitted independently of the rabbit's body and joined after stuffing onto the Back as directed, using the Foreleg Placement Marker as a guide.
The details are embroidered on once the foreleg is completed.

Left Foreleg
With yarn BC cast on 7 sts.
Row 1: Purl.
Row 2 (inc): Kfb, knit to last st, kfb. – 9sts
Row 3: Purl.
Row 4: Knit.
Row 5: Purl, PM on first and last stitch of row for Shoulder Markers.
Row 6 (inc): Cast on 3 sts for Left Under-Foreleg Side 1, knit across all 12 sts.
Row 7 (inc): Cast on 3 sts for Left Under-Foreleg Side 2, purl across all 15 sts.

Rows 8-11: Beginning with a knit row, work four rows stocking stitch.

Work short rows for Left Knee Joint:
Short row 1: K11, W+Tk.
Short row 2: P5, W+Tp.
Short row 3: K4, W+Tk.
Short row 4: P3, W+Tp.
Short row 5: K2, W+Tk.
Short row 6: P1, W+Tp.
Short row 7: K7 to end of row.

Rows 12-18: Beginning with a purl row, work seven rows stocking stitch.

Work short rows for Left Paw Front:
Short row 1: K5, W+Tk.
Short row 2: P3, W+Tp.
Short row 3: K2, W+Tk.
Short row 4: P1, W+Tp.
Short row 5: K12 to end of row.

Row 19: Purl all 15 sts.
Row 20 (dec): [K2tog, k1] five times. – 10sts
Row 21 (dec): P2tog, purl to last 2 sts, p2tog. – 8sts
Row 22 (dec): K2tog, k1, k2tog, k1, k2tog. – 5sts
Cast off all 5 Paw Edge sts purl-wise.

Right Foreleg
With yarn BC cast on 7 sts.
Row 1: Knit.
Row 2 (inc): Pfb, purl to last st, pfb. – 9sts
Row 3: Knit.
Row 4: Purl.
Row 5: Knit, PM on first and last stitch of row for Shoulder Markers.
Row 6 (inc): Cast on 3 sts for Right Under-Foreleg Side 1, purl across all 12 sts.
Row 7 (inc): Cast on 3 sts for Right Under-Foreleg Side 2, knit across all 15 sts.
Rows 8-11: Beginning with a purl row, work four rows stocking stitch.

Work short rows for Right Knee Joint:
Short row 1: P11, W+Tp.
Short row 2: K5, W+Tk.
Short row 3: P4, W+Tp.
Short row 4: K3, W+Tk.
Short row 5: P2, W+Tp.
Short row 6: K1, W+Tk.
Short row 7: P7 to end of row.

Rows 12-18: Beginning with a knit row, work seven rows stocking stitch.

Work short rows for Right Paw Front:
Short row 1: P5, W+Tp.
Short row 2: K3, W+Tk.
Short row 3: P2, W+Tp.
Short row 4: K1, W+Tk.
Short row 5: P12 to end of row.

Row 19: Knit all 15 sts.
Row 20 (dec): [P2tog, p1] five times. – 10sts
Row 21 (dec): K2tog, knit to last 2 sts, k2tog. – 8sts
Row 22 (dec): P2tog, p1, p2tog, p1, p2tog. – 5sts
Cast off all 5 Paw Edge sts.

Join Foreleg Seam
Refer to Body A, **Fig. 18** in Making Up.

Working on one foreleg at a time, WS together fold Paw Cast-Off Edge in half and mattress stitch to join the two halves.

Mattress stitch the row ends to join the Foreleg Seam up to the Shoulder Markers, so leaving the first five shoulder rows free to join onto the body – join dotted line A to B.

Stuff the paw through the opening at the shoulder.

Remove the Shoulder Markers.

Flatten the front of the paw with your thumb and forefinger then with a doubled length of yarn F work four lots of straight stitches to create toe sections, pulling the straight stitches as you sew them to make the paw indent a little.

Join Forelegs to the Back
Refer to Body A, **Fig. 19** in Making Up.

Find the centre of the Shoulder Cast-On Edge and mark with a pin. Working on one foreleg at a time – and making sure you have the correct foreleg for the side of the body – match the pin to the Foreleg

Placement Marker and hold in place with a stitch or two.

Remove the Foreleg Placement Marker.

Mattress stitch each side of the cast-on edge, working either side of the centre of the shoulder – you're wanting to create a round shoulder shape. Then mattress stitch the few shoulder row ends joining the shoulder to the side of the body/onto the Back.

Complete the seam by joining, with mattress stitch, the Under-Foreleg Cast-On Edge to the body.

FACE DETAIL
Refer to Body A, **Fig. 20** in Making Up.

With a doubled length of yarn F, using embroidered straight stitches work a 'Y' either side of the Nose and along the Nose Seam.

With the same threaded-up yarn then embroider two straight lines along a

small section of the Chin to Muzzle Seam to create a mouth.

Then with yarn E work smaller straight stitches to fill in the nose a little.

PETER RABBIT'S CLOTHES

OTHER TOOLS AND MATERIALS
- Sharp hand sewing needle
- Pins
- Scissors

Coat
- 20 x 20cm (8 x 8in) light-blue wool felt, 1.5mm (1/16in) thick, and sewing thread to match
- Sewing thread in a shade to match the felt
- 3 x approx. 10mm (1/2in) gold bead-type/round buttons and sewing thread to match

Slippers
- Small piece of brown wool felt, approx. 1mm (1/32in) thick, and sewing thread to match

Carrot
- Small piece of orange wool felt, approx. 1mm (1/32in) thick, and sewing thread to match
- Small piece of green wool felt, approx. 1mm (1/32in) thick, and sewing thread to match
- White/off-white embroidery threads to add detail
- Toy stuffing or yarn/fabric scraps

COAT

Trace Peter's Coat (see Templates) and cut one Front/Back on the fold and two Sleeves, all from light-blue felt.

1. Working on one sleeve at a time, fold and match the long Underarm Seam ends together.
2. Either hand- or machine-sew along the underarm seam to join the long ends together.
3. Turn out to the RS.
4. Push the sleeve into the armhole. The underarm seam should lie at the bottom of the armhole.
5. Carefully hand work small back stitches to join the edges of the sleeve to the armhole allowing for roughly a 3mm (⅛in) seam. Repeat for the other sleeve.
6. Sew the buttons on securely in positions shown on the template.

SLIPPERS

Trace the Slippers (see Templates) and cut two Uppers and two Soles, all from brown felt.

1. Working on one slipper at a time, fold and match the Heel Seam ends together.
2. Either hand- or machine-sew along the heel seam to join the short ends together.
3. Place a pin in the centre of the heel of the sole and match it with the heel seam. Work a stitch to hold in place, remove the pin.
4. Place a pin in the centre of the toe of the sole and match it with the centre of the toe of the upper. Work a stitch to hold in place, remove the pin.
5. Carefully hand work small back stitches to join the edges of the upper to the sole allowing for roughly a 3mm (⅛in) seam.
6. Turn out to RS.

CARROT

Trace the Carrot and Leaf (see Templates) and cut one carrot from orange felt and one leaf from green felt.

1. Join the two long edges with running stitch. Turn out to RS.
2. Work a running stitch approx. 5mm (¼in) in from the edge. Pull up to gather and at the same time add some yarn snippings or a small amount of toy stuffing before completely gathering up the top and securing the thread.
3. Mould the shape a little with your fingers to shape the cone into more of a carrot shape.
4. Wrap the straight edge of the green leaf around the gathered-up bundle and work stitches to hold the leaf in place at the top of the carrot.
5. Work in a few white/off-white strands of embroidery thread to emerge at the bottom of the carrot as roots.
6. Work a few embroidered straight stitches as lines all around the carrot to add extra detail.
7. Sew the carrot onto Peter's hand.

BENJAMIN BUNNY™

PETER Rabbit's cousin, Benjamin Bunny, has been a
very popular character since this book's first publication
in 1904. In this tale we hear all about his and Peter's
adventures in Mr. McGregor's vegetable garden, and what
happens to them when they meet a cat!

FINISHED SIZE
Approx. 24cm (9½in) tall from feet to tip of ears

YARN
You will need no more than one ball of each of:
A: DROPS Alpaca shade 0302 Camel
B: DROPS Kid-Silk shade 42 Almond
C: DROPS Kid-Silk shade 15 Dark Brown
D: DROPS Alpaca shade 0100 Off White
E: DROPS Kid-Silk shade 40 Pink Pearl
F: DROPS Kid-Silk shade 01 Off White
G: For the facial features a few doubled-up lengths of DROPS Kid-Silk shade 35 Chocolate

Unless otherwise stated, double or triple strands of yarn are used together throughout this pattern. The exact combinations of yarn to be used are indicated by multiple letters (see How to Use This Book).

TENSION
13 stitches and 16 rows over 5cm (2in)

NEEDLES
3.5mm (US 4) knitting needles

OTHER TOOLS AND MATERIALS
- 3 large safety pins or stitch holders
- 24 coloured locking stitch markers (see How to Use This Book: Stitch Markers)
- 2 x 15mm (⅝in) light-brown toy safety eyes
- Toy stuffing or yarn/fabric scraps
- Tapestry or darning needle

PATTERN NOTES
- Use cable cast-on unless otherwise stated
- General knitting abbreviations can be found in How to Use This Book

HEAD
Beginning at the Nose.
With yarn AB cast on 10 sts for Nose Seam.
Row 1: Purl.
Row 2 (inc): Kfb, k4, turn (flip work over so purl-side faces) to work on Left Muzzle as follows:

Left Muzzle
Row 3: P6.
Row 4 (inc): Kfb, k4, kfb, pick up and knit 2 sts into the purl row from Row 1 for Nose, k4 sts across Right Muzzle, kfb. – 16sts
Row 5: P6, turn (flip work over so knit-side faces) to work on Right Muzzle as follows:

Right Muzzle
Row 6 (inc): Kfb, k4, kfb.
Row 7: Purl across all 18 sts (i.e. Right Muzzle, Nose and Left Muzzle).
Row 8 (inc): Kfb, k6, [kfb] 4 times, k6, kfb. – 24sts
Row 9: Purl.
Row 10 (inc): Kfb, knit to last st, kfb. – 26sts
Row 11: Purl.
Row 12 (inc): K10, kfb, k4, kfb, k10 to end. – 28sts
Row 13: Purl.
Row 14 (inc): Kfb, knit to last st, kfb. – 30sts
Row 15: Purl, PM on first and last stitch of row for Left and Right Neck Markers.

Divide the Nose from the Cheeks
Row 16: K20, PM on last stitch (20th stitch) for Right Nose Marker, turn.
Row 17: P10, PM on last stitch (10th stitch) for Left Nose Marker, turn to knit-side to work on Top of Nose and Forehead only (leave the two sets of 10 Cheek sts on the needle as you work in between them).

Top of Nose and Forehead
Row 18 (inc): K2, kfb, k4, kfb, k2, turn. – 12sts
Row 19: P12, turn.
Row 20 (inc): K3, kfb, k4, kfb, k3, turn. – 14sts
Row 21: P14, turn.
Row 22 (inc): K4, kfb, k4, kfb, k4. – 16sts
Rows 23-26: Beginning with a purl row, work four rows stocking stitch on all 16 Forehead sts.
Row 27 (dec): P2tog, p12, p2tog. – 14sts
Cut yarn and place all 14 sts for Forehead onto a safety pin.

Right Cheek
RS facing rejoin yarn AB to 10 sts on LH needle for Right Cheek, continue as follows:
Row 1: Knit.
Row 2 (dec): P2tog, p6, p2tog. – 8sts
Rows 3-6: Beginning with a knit row, work four rows stocking stitch.
Row 7 (inc): Cast on 2 sts, knit all 10 sts.
Row 8: P10, PM on last stitch for Right Eye Corner Marker.

Cut yarn and place all 10 sts for Right Cheek onto a safety pin.

Left Cheek
WS facing rejoin yarn AB to 10 sts on LH needle for Left Cheek, continue as follows:
Row 1 (dec): P2tog, p6, p2tog. – 8sts
Rows 2-6: Beginning with a knit row, work five rows stocking stitch.
Row 7 (inc): Cast on 2 sts, PM on first stitch for Left Eye Corner Marker, purl all 10 sts.
Do not cut yarn.

Join Left Cheek, Nose and Right Cheek
Row 1 (inc): Knit across all 10 Left Cheek sts; slip all 14 Forehead sts off the safety pin and onto a knitting needle, k1, skpo, k8, k2tog, k1; slip all 10 Right Cheek sts off the safety pin and onto a knitting needle, k10. – 32sts
Rows 2-4: Beginning with a purl row, work three rows stocking stitch.
Row 5 (inc): Kfb, k9, kfb, k10, kfb, knit to last st, kfb. – 36sts
Row 6: Purl.
Row 7: K14, PM on last stitch (14th stitch) for Left Ear Front Marker, knit next 9 sts, PM on last stitch (9th stitch) for Right Ear Front Marker, k13 to end of row.
Row 8: Purl.
Row 9 (dec): K12, skpo, k8, k2tog, k12 to end of row. – 34sts
Row 10: Purl.
Row 11 (dec): K12, skpo, k6, k2tog, k12 to end of row. – 32sts
Row 12: Purl.
Row 13 (dec): K10, skpo, k1, PM on last knitted stitch for Left Ear Back Marker, knit next 7 sts PM on last knitted stitch for Right Ear Back Marker, k2tog, k10 to end of row. – 30sts
Row 14: Purl.

Divide the Head Back to Create Head Back Seam
Row 15 (dec): Cast off 9 sts for Head Back Seam, Left-Side, knit next 11 sts, cast off last 9 sts for Head Back Seam, Right-Side. – 12sts

Head Back
WS facing, rejoin yarn AB to 12 sts for Head Back, continue as follows:
Rows 16-24: Beginning with a purl row, work nine rows stocking stitch. Cut yarn, place all 12 Head Back sts onto a large safety pin for now.

Join Head Seams
Refer to Body A, **Fig. 1** in Making Up.

RS together fold the Nose Cast-On Edge from the beginning of the pattern in half and join both halves together with back stitch – join dotted line A to B.
Turn out to RS.

NECK AND BACK
Refer to Body A, **Fig. 2** in Making Up.

Join Left Side of Head
With yarn AB, begin at rabbit's Left Neck Marker, RS facing pick up and knit 8 sts evenly along row ends to

the left-side corner of Head Back Seam Cast-Off Edge; slip all 12 Head Back sts from the safety pin onto a knitting needle then from corner of Head Back Cast-Off Edge knit across all 12 Head Back sts.

Join Right Side of Head
Continue to pick up across the right side of the head, all onto the same needle as follows:
Pick up and knit 8 sts evenly along row ends from right corner of Head Back Seam Cast-Off Edge to Right Neck Marker – 28sts – pick up and knit from A to B; knit across from C to D; pick up and knit from E to F.

Row 1: Purl all 28 sts.

BODY
Back
Row 2 (dec): K10, skpo, k4, k2tog, k10 to end of row. – 26sts
Row 3: Purl.

Row 4 (dec): K10, skpo, k2, k2tog, k10 to end of row. – 24sts
Row 5: Purl.
Row 6 (dec): K10, skpo, k2tog, k10 to end of row. – 22sts
Row 7: Purl.
Row 8 (inc): Kfb, k6, kfb, k6, kfb, k6, kfb. – 26sts
Row 9: Purl.
Row 10 (inc): Kfb, k5, PM on last knitted stitch for Left Foreleg Placement, knit next 15 sts, PM on last knitted stitch for Right Foreleg Placement, k4, kfb. – 28sts
Row 11: Purl.
Row 12 (inc): Kfb, k9, kfb, k6, kfb, k9, kfb. – 32sts
Row 13: Purl.
Row 14 (inc): Kfb, knit to last st, kfb. – 34sts
Row 15: Purl.
Row 16 (inc): K13, kfb, k6, kfb, k13 to end of row. – 36sts
Rows 17-23: Beginning with a purl row, work seven rows stocking stitch.
Row 24 (inc): K14, kfb, k6, kfb, k14 to end of row. – 38sts
Rows 25-29: Beginning with a purl

row, work five rows stocking stitch.
Row 30 (inc): Kfb, k1, kfb, knit to last 3 sts, kfb, k1, kfb. – 42sts
Row 31: Purl, PM on first and last stitch of row for Left and Right Thigh Markers.

Join yarn C, continue with yarn ABC as follows:

Hind Legs
Work short rows (see Techniques) for Left Hind Leg:
Short row 1 (inc): Cast on 8 sts, k9, W+Tk.
Short row 2: P2, W+Tp.
Short row 3: K3, W+Tk.
Short row 4: P4, W+Tp.
Short row 5: K5, W+Tk.
Short row 6: P6, W+Tp.
Short row 7: K7, W+Tk.
Short row 8: P8, W+Tp.
Short row 9: K9, W+Tk.
Short row 10: P10, W+Tp.
Short row 11: K11, W+Tk.
Short row 12: P12, W+Tp.
Short row 13: K13, W+Tk.
Short row 14: P14, W+Tp.

Short row 15 (dec): K14, skpo, k33 to end of row. – 49sts

Work short rows for Right Hind Leg:
Short row 1 (inc): Cast on 8 sts, p9, W+Tp.
Short row 2: K2, W+Tk.
Short row 3: P3, W+Tp.
Short row 4: K4, W+Tk.
Short row 5: P5, W+Tp.
Short row 6: K6, W+Tk.
Short row 7: P7, W+Tp.
Short row 8: K8, W+Tk.
Short row 9: P9, W+Tp.
Short row 10: K10, W+Tk.
Short row 11: P11, W+Tp.
Short row 12: K12, W+Tk.
Short row 13: P13, W+Tp.
Short row 14: K14, W+Tk.
Short row 15 (dec): P14, p2tog, p40 to end of row. – 56sts

Row 32 (dec): K2tog, k12, k2tog, k7, skpo, k6, k2tog, k7, k2tog, k12, k2tog. – 50sts
Row 33: Purl.
Row 34 (dec): K11, k2tog, k7, skpo, k6, k2tog, k7, k2tog, k11 to end of row. – 46sts
Row 35: Purl.
Row 36 (dec): K10, k2tog, k6, skpo, k6, k2tog, k6, k2tog, k10 to end of row. – 42sts
Row 37: Purl.
Row 38 (dec): K9, k2tog, k20, k2tog, k9 to end of row. – 40sts
Row 39: Purl.
Row 40 (dec): K8, k2tog, k20, k2tog, k8 to end of row. – 38sts
Row 41: Purl.

Lower Back
Work short rows for Lower Back:
Short row 1: K31, W+Tk.
Short row 2: P24, W+Tp.
Short row 3: K23, W+Tk.
Short row 4: P22, W+Tp.
Short row 5: K21, W+Tk.
Short row 6: P20, W+Tp.
Short row 7 (dec): K6, cast off next 8 sts for Tail Space, knit next 4 sts, W+Tk.
Short row 8 (inc): P5, cast on 6 sts for Under Tail Space, purl next 5 sts, W+Tp.

Short row 9: K15, W+Tk.
Short row 10: P14, W+Tp.
Short row 11: K13, W+Tk.
Short row 12: P12, W+Tp.
Short row 13: K24 to end of row.
– 36sts

Row 42: Purl all 36 sts.
Row 43 (dec): K13, skpo, k6, k2tog, k13 to end of row. – 34sts
Row 44: Purl.
Row 45 (dec): K2tog, k7, k2tog, k2, skpo, k4, k2tog, k2, k2tog, k7, k2tog. – 28sts
Row 46: Purl, PM on first and last stitch of row for Left and Right Belly Markers.
Row 47 (dec): Cast off 10 sts for Left Paw Edge, knit next 7 sts, cast off last 10 sts for Right Paw Edge. – 8sts

Belly
WS facing, rejoin yarn BDF to 8 sts on knitting needle.
Row 1: Purl across all 8 Belly sts.
Rows 2-9: Beginning with a knit row, work eight rows stocking stitch, PM on first and last stitch of last row for Left and Right Inner Belly Markers.
Rows 10-15: Beginning with a knit row, work six rows stocking stitch.
Row 16 (inc): K1, kfb, k4, kfb, k1. – 10sts
Rows 17-19: Beginning with a purl, row work three rows stocking stitch.
Row 20 (inc): K2, kfb, k4, kfb, k2. – 12sts
Rows 21-23: Beginning with a purl row, work three rows stocking stitch.
Row 24 (inc): K3, kfb, k4, kfb, k3. – 14sts
Rows 25-33: Beginning with a purl row, work nine rows stocking stitch, PM on first and last stitch of last row for Left and Right Inner Thigh Markers.
Rows 34-39: Beginning with a knit row, work six rows stocking stitch.
Row 40 (dec): K1, skpo, knit to last 3 sts, k2tog, k1. – 12sts
Rows 41-47: Beginning with a purl row, work five rows stocking stitch.

Cut yarn DF, join yarn AB, continue with yarn ABB (use other end of yarn B ball) as follows:

"Then he suggested that they should fill the pocket-handkerchief with onions, as a little present for his Aunt."

Breast
Work short rows for Breast:
Short row 1: K11, W+Tk.
Short row 2: P10, W+Tp.
Short row 3: K9, W+Tk.
Short row 4: P8, W+Tp.
Short row 5: K7, W+Tk.
Short row 6: P6, W+Tp.
Short row 7: K5, W+Tk.
Short row 8: P4, W+Tp.
Short row 9: K8 to end of row.

Row 48: Purl.
Row 49 (inc): Kfb, knit to last st, kfb. – 14sts
Row 50: Purl.
Cast off all 14 sts for Neck Edge, PM on first and last cast-off stitch for Left and Right Inner Neck Markers.

Join Thigh Front Seam
Follow the instructions for Peter Rabbit: Join Thigh Front Seam.

Join Belly to Back Seam
Follow the instructions for Peter Rabbit: Join Belly to Back Seam.

CHIN
Return to the Neck Cast-Off Edge.
RS and Belly facing, with yarn DF, starting at rabbit's Left Neck Marker (on your right), pick up and knit 14 sts across row ends and cast-off edge from Left Neck Marker to Right Neck Marker.
Remove both Neck Markers.
Row 1: Purl.
Row 2 (inc): Kfb, knit to last st, kfb. – 16sts
Row 3: Purl.
Row 4 (dec): K4, skpo, k4, k2tog, k4. – 14sts
Row 5 (dec): P2tog, purl to last 2 sts, p2tog. – 12sts

> *One morning a little rabbit sat on a bank.*
> *He pricked his ears and listened to the*
> *trit-trot, trit-trot of a pony.*

Row 6 (dec): K3, skpo, k2, k2tog, k3.
– 10sts
Row 7 (dec): P2tog, purl to last 2 sts,
p2tog. – 8sts
Row 8 (dec): K1, skpo, k2, k2tog, k1.
– 6sts

Work short rows for Chin:
Short row 1: P5, W+Tp.
Short row 2: K4, W+Tk.
Short row 3 (dec): P1, p2tog, p2 to
end of row. – 5sts

Cut yarn, thread end through all 5 sts,
pull up to gather and fasten end to
secure for Chin Point.

Join Chin to Muzzle Seam
Follow the instructions for Peter
Rabbit: Join Chin to Muzzle Seam.

EYES
With yarn D, follow the instructions
for Peter Rabbit: Eyes.

EARS
With yarn AB for Outer Ears and
yarn E for Inner Ears, follow the
instructions for Peter Rabbit: Ears.

JOIN HEAD BACK SEAM
Follow the instructions for Peter
Rabbit: Join Head Back Seam.

HIND PAWS
Refer to Body A, **Fig. 14** in Making Up.

The Left and Right Hind Paws are
picked up and knitted along the Hind
Paw Cast-Off Edge, knitted into a paw
shape, the seam is sewn all along the
paw's heel, upper and sole, stuffing at
the same time.
The details are embroidered on once
the paw is completed.

Left Hind Paw
RS and rabbit's Left Thigh facing, begin
at Left Belly Marker, with yarn AB

pick up and knit 9 sts along Left Paw
Cast-Off Edge from Left Belly Marker
to the other corner of the cast-off
edge near the rabbit's Back – pick up
as dotted line from A to B.
Remove Left Belly Marker.
Row 1: Purl.
Row 2 (inc): Cast on 8 sts for Left
Paw Upper, knit across all 17 sts.
Rows 3-7: Beginning with a purl row
work, five rows stocking stitch.

Work short rows for Left Paw Front
Outer Edge:
Short row 1: K8, W+Tk.
Short row 2: P6, W+Tp.
Short row 3: K5, W+Tk.
Short row 4: P4, W+Tp.
Short row 5: K3, W+Tk.
Short row 6: P2, W+Tp.
Short row 7: K13 to end of row.

Row 8: Purl.

Work short rows for Left Paw Front
Inside Edge:
Short row 1: K8, W+Tk.
Short row 2: P6, W+Tp.
Short row 3: K5, W+Tk.
Short row 4: P4, W+Tp.
Short row 5: K3, W+Tk.
Short row 6: P2, W+Tp.
Short row 7: K13 to end of row.

Rows 9-13: Beginning with a purl row,
work five rows stocking stitch.
Row 14 (dec): Cast off 8 sts for Paw
Upper Inside Edge, knit to end of row.
– 9sts
Row 15: Purl.
Cast off all 9 sts for Paw Inside Edge.

Right Hind Paw
RS and rabbit's Right Thigh facing,
begin at the opposite corner to Right
Belly Marker, with yarn AB
pick up and knit 9 sts along
Right Paw Cast-Off Edge to Right
Belly Marker.
Remove Right Belly Marker.
Row 1 (inc): Cast on 8 sts
for Right Paw Upper, purl
across all 17 sts.
Rows 2-6: Beginning with
a knit row, work five rows
stocking stitch.

Work short rows for Right Paw Front Outer Edge:
Short row 1: P8, W+Tp.
Short row 2: K6, W+Tk.
Short row 3: P5, W+Tp.
Short row 4: K4, W+Tk.
Short row 5: P3, W+Tp.
Short row 6: K2, W+Tk.
Short row 7: P13 to end of row.

Row 7: Knit.

Work short rows for Right Paw Front Inside Edge:
Short row 1: P8, W+Tp.
Short row 2: K6, W+Tk.
Short row 3: P5, W+Tp.
Short row 4: K4, W+Tk.
Short row 5: P3, W+Tp.
Short row 6: K2, W+Tk.
Short row 7: P13 to end of row.

Rows 8-12: Beginning with a knit row, work five rows stocking stitch.
Row 13 (dec): Cast off 8 sts purl-wise for Paw Upper Inside Edge, purl to end of row. – 9sts
Row 14: Knit.
Cast off all 9 sts purl-wise for Paw Inside Edge.

Join Hind Paw Seam
Refer to Body A, **Fig. 15** in Making Up.

Working on one paw at a time, WS together fold paw in half across the row ends at the heel.
Mattress stitch the Paw Inside Cast-Off Edge to the row ends at the Belly.
Work mattress stitch to join the cast-on and cast-off edges of the paw upper and the row ends that will become the paw front.
Stuff the paw through the last seam at the heel before closing that seam with mattress stitch.
Flatten the front of the paw with your thumb and forefinger then with a doubled length of yarn C work four lots of straight stitches to create toe sections, pulling the straight stitches as you sew them to make the paw indent a little.

TAIL
Refer to Body A, **Fig. 16** in Making Up.

The Tail is picked up and knitted along the Tail Cast-Off Edge, the under-tail edges are cast on either side of the picked-up and knitted stitches then the Tail is knitted in its entirety. The seam is sewn all along the tail from tip to cast-on edges. The cast-on edges are then joined to the Tail Cast-On Edge.
Add any more stuffing (also stuff your yarn snippings) through the tail opening.
RS and rabbit's Back facing, return to the Tail Cast-Off Edge. With yarn AB, begin at rabbit's left side (your right side) of the cast-off edge, pick up and knit 9 sts into the cast-off edge, all along from your right to your left – Tail already picked up and knitted as dotted line from A to B.
Row 1 (inc): Cast on 3 sts for Tail Underside 1, purl all 12 sts.
Row 2 (inc): Cast on 3 sts for Tail Underside 2, knit all 15 sts.
Row 3: Purl.

Work short rows for Tail Tip:
Short row 1: K11, W+Tk.
Short row 2: P7, W+Tp.
Short row 3: K6, W+Tk.
Short row 4: P5, W+Tp.
Short row 5: K4, W+Tk.
Short row 6: P3, W+Tp.
Short row 7: K2, W+Tk.
Short row 8: P1, W+Tp.
Short row 9: K8 to end of row.

Cut yarn AB, join yarn DF, continue with the underside of the tail as follows:
Row 4: Purl.
Row 5 (dec): K2tog, knit to last 2 sts, k2tog. – 13sts
Row 6: Purl.
Row 7 (dec): [K2tog, k1] four times, k1. – 9sts
Row 8 (dec): [P3tog] three times. – 3sts
Cut yarn, thread end through all 3 sts for Underside Tail Point.

Join Tail Seam
Follow the instructions for Peter Rabbit: Join Tail Seam.

FORELEGS
The Left and Right Forelegs are knitted independently of the rabbit's body and joined after stuffing onto the Back as directed with the pattern, using the Foreleg Placement Marker as a guide.
The details are embroidered on once the foreleg is completed.

Left Foreleg
With yarn AB cast on 7 sts.
Row 1: Purl.
Row 2 (inc): Kfb, knit to last st, kfb. – 9sts
Row 3: Purl.
Row 4: Knit.
Row 5: Purl, PM on first and last stitch of row for Shoulder Markers.
Row 6 (inc): Cast on 3 sts for Left Under-Foreleg Side 1, knit across all 12 sts.
Row 7 (inc): Cast on 3 sts for Left Under-Foreleg Side 2, purl across all 15 sts.

Rows 8-11: Beginning with a knit row, work four rows stocking stitch.

Work short rows for Left Knee Joint:
Short row 1: K11, W+Tk.
Short row 2: P5, W+Tp.
Short row 3: K4, W+Tk.
Short row 4: P3, W+Tp.
Short row 5: K2, W+Tk.
Short row 6: P1, W+Tp.
Short row 7: K7 to end of row.

Rows 12-18: Beginning with a purl row, work seven rows stocking stitch.

Work short rows for Left Paw Front:
Short row 1: K5, W+Tk.
Short row 2: P3, W+Tp.
Short row 3: K2, W+Tk.
Short row 4: P1, W+Tp.
Short row 5: K12 to end of row.

Row 19: Purl all 15 sts.
Row 20 (dec): [K2tog, k1] five times. – 10sts
Row 21 (dec): P2tog, purl to last 2 sts, p2tog. – 8sts
Row 22 (dec): K2tog, k1, k2tog, k1, k2tog. – 5sts
Cast off all 5 Paw Edge sts purl-wise.

"Benjamin tried on the tam-o'-shanter, but it was too big for him."

Right Foreleg
With yarn AB cast on 7 sts.
Row 1: Knit.
Row 2 (inc): Pfb, purl to last st, pfb. – 9sts
Row 3: Knit.
Row 4: Purl.
Row 5: Knit, PM on first and last stitch of row for Shoulder Markers.
Row 6 (inc): Cast on 3 sts for Right Under-Foreleg Side 1, purl across all 12 sts.
Row 7 (inc): Cast on 3 sts for Right Under-Foreleg Side 2, knit across all 15 sts.
Rows 8-11: Beginning with a purl row, work four rows stocking stitch.

Work short rows for Right Knee Joint:
Short row 1: P11, W+Tp.
Short row 2: K5, W+Tk.
Short row 3: P4, W+Tp.
Short row 4: K3, W+Tk.
Short row 5: P2, W+Tp.
Short row 6: K1, W+Tk.
Short row 7: P7 to end of row.

Rows 12-18: Beginning with a knit row, work seven rows stocking stitch.

Work short rows for Right Paw Front:
Short row 1: P5, W+Tp.
Short row 2: K3, W+Tk.
Short row 3: P2, W+Tp.

Short row 4: K1, W+Tk.
Short row 5: P12 to end of row.

Row 19: Knit all 15 sts.
Row 20 (dec): [P2tog, p1] five times. – 10sts
Row 21 (dec): K2tog, knit to last 2 sts, k2tog. – 8sts
Row 22 (dec): P2tog, p1, p2tog, p1, p2tog. – 5sts
Cast off all 5 Paw Edge sts.

Join Foreleg Seam
Follow the instructions for Peter Rabbit: Join Foreleg Seam.

Join Forelegs to the Back
Follow the instructions for Peter Rabbit: Join Forelegs to the Back.

FACE DETAIL
Refer to Body A, **Fig. 20** in Making Up.

With a doubled length of yarn C, using embroidered straight stitches work a 'Y' either side of the Nose and along the Nose Seam.
With the same threaded up yarn then embroider two straight lines along a small section of the Chin to Muzzle Seam to create a mouth.
Then with yarn E work smaller straight stitches to fill in the nose a little adding a little yarn G as a highlight.

BENJAMIN BUNNY'S CLOTHES

TAM'O'SHANTER YARN
You will need no more than one ball of each of:
A: DROPS Alpaca shade 2917 Turquoise
B: DROPS Alpaca shade 9021 Fog
C: DROPS Alpaca shade 9026 Blush
D: DROPS Kid-Silk shade 33 Rust
Unless otherwise stated, double strands of yarn are used together throughout this pattern. The exact combinations of yarn to be used are indicated by multiple letters (see How to Use This Book).

TENSION
13 stitches and 16 rows over 5cm (2in) with garter stitch

NEEDLES
4mm (US 6) knitting needles

PATTERN NOTES
• Use cable cast-on unless otherwise stated
• General knitting abbreviations can be found in How to Use This Book

OTHER TOOLS AND MATERIALS
• Sharp hand sewing needle, embroidery needle, pins, scissors

Coat and Slippers
• 20 x 20cm (8 x 8in) olive-green wool felt, 1.5mm (¹⁄₁₆in) thick, and sewing thread to match
• 4 x 10mm (½in) horn-coloured, 4-hole buttons and sewing thread to match

Onion
• Small piece of beige wool felt, approx. 1mm (¹⁄₃₂in) thick, and sewing thread to match
• Small piece of green wool felt, approx. 1mm (¹⁄₃₂in) thick, and sewing thread to match
• Toy stuffing or yarn/fabric scraps
• Embroidery threads to add detail

Handkerchief
• Small piece of red wool felt, 1.5mm (¹⁄₁₆in) thick
• White stranded embroidery threads to add detail

TAM'O'SHANTER
Work in garter stitch (all knit) throughout.
With yarn AB cast on 30 sts.

1st rounding section
*Rounding short row 1: K24, W+Tk.
Rounding short row 2: K24.
Rounding short row 3: K18, W+Tk.
Rounding short row 4: K18.
Rounding short row 5: K12, W+Tk.
Rounding short row 6: K12.
Rounding short row 7: K6, W+Tk.
Rounding short row 8: K6.**

Rows 1-2: Work two rows garter stitch.

2nd Rounding section
Repeat as Rounding short row 1 to Rounding short row 8 from * to **.
Rows 3-4: Work two rows garter stitch.

3rd Rounding section
Repeat as Rounding short row 1 to Rounding short row 8 from * to **.
Rows 5-6: Work two rows garter stitch.

4th Rounding section
Repeat as Rounding short row 1 to Rounding short row 8 from * to **.

Divide for Ears
Row 7 (dec): K9, cast off next 4 sts, knit next 3 sts, cast off next 4 sts, knit 8 to end. – 22sts
Row 8 (inc): K9, cast on 4 sts, k4, cast on 4 sts, knit 9 to end. – 30sts

5th Rounding section
Repeat as Rounding short row 1 to Rounding short row 8 from * to **.
Rows 9-10: Work two rows garter stitch.

6th Rounding section
Repeat as Rounding short row 1 to Rounding short row 8 from * to **.
Rows 11-12: Work two rows garter stitch.

7th Rounding section
Repeat as Rounding short row 1 to Rounding short row 8 from * to **.
Rows 13-14: Work two rows garter stitch.
Cast off all 30 sts.

Join Seam
Working on one side of the hat at a time, match the two straight edges together and mattress stitch to join the hat into an oval/'eye' shape.
Fold a rim (about 4 rows of knitting) under to create the hat's brim and carefully over-sew to hold in place all around.

Pompom
1. Wrap yarns C and D not too tightly around and around two of your ring and middle fingers until you've amounted a small bundle.
2. With the bundle still over your fingers cut a length of yarn C, slip it in-between your fingers and tie it securely over the centre of the bundle.
3. Slip the bundle off your fingers and snip the folded ends to create a pompom. Trim to neaten.
4. Sew the pompom securely onto the centre of the tam'o'shanter.

COAT
Trace Benjamin's Coat (see Templates) and cut one Front/Back on the fold, two Sleeves and a one Pocket, all from olive-green felt.
1. Working on one sleeve at a time, fold and match the long Underarm Seam ends together.
2. Either hand- or machine-sew along the underarm seam to join the long ends together.
3. Turn out to the RS.

4. Push the sleeve into the armhole. The underarm seam should lie at the bottom of the armhole.

5. Carefully hand work small back stitches to join the edges of the sleeve to the armhole allowing for roughly a 3mm (1/8in) seam. Repeat for the other sleeve.

6. Sew the buttons on securely in positions shown on the template.

7. Fold the pocket flap over as shown by the grey line on the template. Work small running stitches to sew down the flap then sew the pocket onto the coat front, working small running stitches all around the side and bottom of the pocket, leaving the folded top open.

SLIPPERS

Trace the Slippers (see Templates) and cut two Uppers and two Soles, all from olive-green felt.

1. Working on one slipper at a time, fold and match the Heel Seam ends together.

2. Either hand- or machine-sew along the heel seam to join the short ends together.

3. Place a pin in the centre of the heel of the sole and match it with the heel seam. Work a stitch to hold in place, remove the pin.

4. Place a pin in the centre of the toe of the sole and match it with the centre of the toe of the upper. Work a stitch to hold in place, remove the pin.

5. Carefully hand work small back stitches to join the edges of the upper to the sole allowing for roughly a 3mm (1/8in) seam.

6. Turn out to RS.

ONION

Trace the Onion and Shoot (see Templates) and cut one onion from beige felt and one shoot from green felt.

1. Work back stitch approx. 5mm (1/4in) in from the edge. Pull up to gather and at the same time add some yarn snippings or a small amount of toy stuffing before completely gathering up the top and securing the thread.

2. Mould the shape a little with your fingers to shape the ball into more of an onion shape.

3. Wrap the straight edge of the green shoot around the gathered-up bundle and work stitches to hold the shoot in place at the top of the onion.

4. Work in a few white/off-white strands of embroidery thread to emerge at the bottom of the onion as roots.

5. Work a few embroidered straight stitches as lines all around the onion to add extra detail.

6. Sew the onion onto Benjamin's hand.

HANDKERCHIEF

Trace the Handkerchief (see Templates) and cut one from red felt.

1. With 2 strands of white embroidery thread work a running stitch all around all four edges, approx. 5mm (1/4in) in from the edge, then another 5mm (1/4in) in from that to create a tramline effect.

2. Work white straight stitches or large French knots as a design feature, as the template shows.

3. Sew the handkerchief onto Benjamin's hand.

FLOPSY BUNNY™

WHEN the cupboard is bare at the Flopsy Bunnies
burrow, the family all have to go in search of food.
They soon find some old lettuces on Mr. McGregor's rubbish
heap, but who can imagine the horrors that await them as
they enjoy a nap after lunch!

FINISHED SIZE
Approx. 24cm (9½in) tall from feet to tip of ears

YARN
You will need no more than one ball of each of:
A: DROPS Alpaca shade 0100 Off White
B: DROPS Kid-Silk shade 29 Vanilla
C: DROPS Alpaca shade 0302 Camel
D: DROPS Kid-Silk shade 42 Almond
E: DROPS Kid-Silk shade 01 Off White
F: DROPS Kid-Silk shade 40 Pink Pearl
PLUS For the claws and facial features a few doubled-up lengths of DROPS Kid-Silk shade 15 Dark Brown

Unless otherwise stated, double or triple strands of yarn are used together throughout this pattern. The exact combinations of yarn to be used are indicated by multiple letters (see How to Use This Book).

TENSION
13 stitches and 16 rows over 5cm (2in)

NEEDLES
3.5mm (US 4) knitting needles

OTHER TOOLS AND MATERIALS
- 3 large safety pins or stitch holders
- 24 coloured locking stitch markers (see How to Use This Book: Stitch Markers)
- 2 x 15mm (⅝in) light-brown toy safety eyes
- Toy stuffing or yarn/fabric scraps
- Tapestry or darning needle

PATTERN NOTES
- Use cable cast-on unless otherwise stated
- General knitting abbreviations can be found in How to Use This Book

HEAD
Beginning at the Nose.
With yarn AB cast on 10 sts for Nose Seam.
Row 1: Purl.
Row 2 (inc): Kfb, k4, turn (flip work over so purl-side faces) to work on Left Muzzle as follows:

Left Muzzle
Row 3: P6.
Row 4 (inc): Kfb, k4, kfb, pick up and knit 2 sts into the purl row from Row 1 for Nose, k4 sts across Right Muzzle, kfb. – 16sts
Row 5: P6, turn (flip work over so knit-side faces) to work on Right Muzzle as follows:

Right Muzzle
Row 6 (inc): Kfb, k4, kfb. – 18 sts
Row 7: Purl across all 18 sts (i.e. Right Muzzle, Nose and Left Muzzle).
Row 8 (inc): Kfb, k6, [kfb] 4 times, k6, kfb. – 24sts
Row 9: Purl.
Row 10 (inc): Kfb, knit to last st, kfb. – 26sts
Row 11: Purl.
Cut yarn A, join yarn C, continue with yarn BC as follows:
Row 12 (inc): K10, kfb, k4, kfb, k10 to end. – 28sts
Row 13: Purl.
Row 14 (inc): Kfb, knit to last st, kfb. – 30sts

Row 15: Purl, PM on first and last stitch of row for Left and Right Neck Markers.

Divide the Nose from the Cheeks
Row 16: K20, PM on last stitch (20th stitch) for Right Nose Marker, turn.
Row 17: P10, PM on last stitch (10th stitch) for Left Nose Marker, turn to knit-side to work on Top of Nose and Forehead only (leave the two sets of 10 Cheek sts on the needle as you work in between them).

Top of Nose and Forehead
Row 18 (inc): K2, kfb, k4, kfb, k2, turn. – 12sts
Row 19: P12, turn.
Row 20 (inc): K3, kfb, k4, kfb, k3, turn. – 14sts
Row 21: P14, turn.
Row 22 (inc): K4, kfb, k4, kfb, k4, turn. – 16sts
Rows 23-26: Beginning with a purl row, work four rows stocking stitch on all 16 Forehead sts.
Row 27 (dec): P2tog, p12, p2tog. – 14sts

Cut yarn and place all 14 sts for Forehead onto a safety pin.

Right Cheek

RS facing rejoin yarn BC to 10 sts on LH needle for Right Cheek, continue as follows:
Row 1: Knit.
Row 2 (dec): P2tog, p6, p2tog. – 8sts
Rows 3-6: Beginning with a knit row, work four rows stocking stitch.
Row 7 (inc): Cast on 2 sts, knit all 10 sts. – 10sts
Row 8: P10, PM on last stitch for Right Eye Corner Marker.
Cut yarn and place all 10 Right Cheek sts onto a safety pin.

Left Cheek

WS facing rejoin yarn BC to 10 sts on LH needle for Left Cheek, continue as follows:
Row 1 (dec): P2tog, p6, p2tog. – 8sts
Rows 2-6: Beginning with a knit row, work five rows stocking stitch.
Row 7 (inc): Cast on 2 sts, PM on first stitch for Left Eye Corner Marker, purl all 10 sts.
Do not cut yarn.

Join Left Cheek, Nose and Right Cheek

Row 1 (dec): Knit across all 10 Left Cheek sts; slip all 14 Forehead sts off the safety pin and onto a knitting needle, work across these 14 sts as follows, k1, skpo, k8, k2tog, k1; slip all 10 Right Cheek sts off the safety pin and onto a knitting needle, knit all 10 sts. – 32sts
Rows 2-4: Beginning with a purl row, work three rows stocking stitch.
Row 5 (inc): Kfb, k9, kfb, k10, kfb, knit to last st, kfb. – 36sts
Row 6: Purl.
Row 7: K14, PM on last stitch (14th stitch) for Left Ear Front Marker, knit next 9 sts, PM on last stitch (9th stitch) for Right Ear Front Marker, k13 to end of row.
Row 8: Purl.
Row 9 (dec): K12, skpo, k8, k2tog, k12 to end of row. – 34sts
Row 10: Purl.
Row 11 (dec): K12, skpo, k6, k2tog, k12 to end of row. – 32sts
Row 12: Purl.
Row 13 (dec): K10, skpo, k1, PM on last stitch for Left Ear Back Marker, knit next 7 sts, PM on last stitch (7th stitch) for Right Ear Back Marker, k2tog, k10 to end of row. – 30sts
Row 14: Purl.

Divide the Head Back to Create Head Back Seam

Row 15 (dec): Cast off 9 sts for Head Back Seam, Left-Side, knit next 11 sts, cast off last 9 sts for Head Back Seam, Right-Side. – 12sts

Head Back

WS facing rejoin yarn BC to 12 sts for Head Back, continue as follows:
Rows 16-24: Beginning with a purl row, work nine rows stocking stitch.
Cut yarn, place all 12 Head Back sts onto a large safety pin for now.

Join Head Seams

Refer to Body A, **Fig. 1** in Making Up.

RS together fold the Nose Cast-On Edge from the beginning of the pattern in half and join both halves together with back stitch – join dotted line A to B.
Turn out to RS.

NECK AND BACK

Refer to Body A, **Fig. 2** in Making Up.

Join Left Side of Head

With yarn BC, begin at rabbit's Left Neck Marker, RS facing pick up and knit 8 sts evenly along row ends to the left-side corner of Head Back Seam Cast-Off Edge; slip all 12 Head Back sts from the safety pin onto a knitting needle then from corner of Head Back Cast-Off Edge knit across all 12 Head Back sts.

Join Right Side of Head

Continue to pick up across the right side of the head, all onto the same needle as follows:
Pick up and knit 8 sts evenly along row ends from right corner of Head Back Seam Cast-Off Edge to Right Neck Marker – 28sts – pick up and knit from A to B; knit across from C to D; pick up and knit from E to F.

Row 1: Purl all 28 sts.

BODY

Back

Row 2 (dec): K10, skpo, k4, k2tog, k10 to end of row. – 26sts
Row 3: Purl.
Row 4 (dec): K10, skpo, k2, k2tog, k10 to end of row. – 24sts
Row 5: Purl.

Short row 1 (inc): Cast on 8 sts, k9, W+Tk.
Short row 2: P2, W+Tp.
Short row 3: K3, W+Tk.
Short row 4: P4, W+Tp.
Short row 5: K5, W+Tk.
Short row 6: P6, W+Tp.
Short row 7: K7, W+Tk.
Short row 8: P8, W+Tp.
Short row 9: K9, W+Tk.
Short row 10: P10, W+Tp.
Short row 11: K11, W+Tk.
Short row 12: P12, W+Tp.
Short row 13: K13, W+Tk.
Short row 14: P14, W+Tp.
Short row 15 (dec): K14, skpo, k33 to end of row. – 49sts

Work short rows for Right Hind Leg:
Short row 1 (inc): Cast on 8 sts, p9, W+Tp.
Short row 2: K2, W+Tk.
Short row 3: P3, W+Tp.
Short row 4: K4, W+Tk.
Short row 5: P5, W+Tp.
Short row 6: K6, W+Tk.
Short row 7: P7, W+Tp.
Short row 8: K8, W+Tk.
Short row 9: P9, W+Tp.
Short row 10: K10, W+Tk.
Short row 11: P11, W+Tp.
Short row 12: K12, W+Tk.
Short row 13: P13, W+Tp.
Short row 14: K14, W+Tk.
Short row 15 (dec): P14, p2tog, p40 to end of row. – 56sts

"When Benjamin Bunny grew up, he married his Cousin Flopsy. They had a large family, and they were very improvident and cheerful."

Row 6 (dec): K10, skpo, k2tog, k10 to end of row. – 22sts
Row 7: Purl.
Row 8 (inc): Kfb, k6, kfb, k6, kfb, k6, kfb. – 26sts
Row 9: Purl.
Row 10 (inc): Kfb, k5, PM on last knitted stitch for Left Foreleg Placement, knit next 15 sts, PM on last knitted stitch for Right Foreleg Placement, k4, kfb. – 28sts
Row 11: Purl.
Row 12 (inc): Kfb, k9, kfb, k6, kfb, k9, kfb. – 32sts

Row 13: Purl.
Row 14 (inc): Kfb, knit to last st, kfb. – 34sts
Row 15: Purl.
Row 16 (inc): K13, kfb, k6, kfb, k13 to end of row. – 36sts
Rows 17-23: Beginning with a purl row, work seven rows stocking stitch.
Row 24 (inc): K14, kfb, k6, kfb, k14 to end of row. – 38sts
Rows 25-29: Beginning with a purl row, work five rows stocking stitch.
Row 30 (inc): Kfb, k1, kfb, knit to last 3 sts, kfb, k1, kfb. – 42sts
Row 31: Purl, PM on first and last stitch of row for Left and Right Thigh Markers.
Join yarn D, continue with yarn BCD as follows:

Hind Legs
Work short rows (see Techniques) for Left Hind Leg:

Row 32 (dec): K2tog, k12, k2tog, k7, skpo, k6, k2tog, k7, k2tog, k12, k2tog. – 50sts
Row 33: Purl.
Row 34 (dec): K11, k2tog, k7, skpo, k6, k2tog, k7, k2tog, k11 to end of row. – 46sts
Row 35: Purl.
Row 36 (dec): K10, k2tog, k6, skpo, k6, k2tog, k6, k2tog, k10 to end of row. – 42sts
Row 37: Purl.
Row 38 (dec): K9, k2tog, k20, k2tog, k9 to end of row. – 40sts
Row 39: Purl.
Row 40 (dec): K8, k2tog, k20, k2tog, k8 to end of row. – 38sts
Row 41: Purl.

Lower Back

Work short rows for Lower Back:

Short row 1: K31, W+Tk.
Short row 2: P24, W+Tp.
Short row 3: K23, W+Tk.
Short row 4: P22, W+Tp.
Short row 5: K21, W+Tk.
Short row 6: P20, W+Tp.
Short row 7 (dec): K6, cast off next 8 sts for Tail Space, knit next 4 sts, W+Tk.
Short row 8 (inc): P5, cast on 6 sts for Under Tail Space, purl next 5 sts, W+Tp.
Short row 9: K15, W+Tk.
Short row 10: P14, W+Tp.
Short row 11: K13, W+Tk.
Short row 12: P12, W+Tp.
Short row 13: K24 to end of row. – 36sts

Row 42: Purl all 36 sts.
Row 43 (dec): K13, skpo, k6, k2tog, k13 to end of row. – 34sts
Row 44: Purl.
Row 45 (dec): K2tog, k7, k2tog, k2, skpo, k4, k2tog, k2, k2tog, k7, k2tog. – 28sts
Row 46: Purl, PM on first and last stitch of row for Left and Right Belly Markers.
Row 47 (dec): Cast off 10 sts for Left Paw Edge, knit next 7 sts, cast off last 10 sts for Right Paw Edge. – 8sts

Belly

WS facing, rejoin yarn ABE to 8 sts on knitting needle.

Row 1: Purl across all 8 Belly sts.
Rows 2-9: Beginning with a knit row, work eight rows stocking stitch, PM on first and last stitch of last row for Left and Right Inner Belly Markers.
Rows 10-15: Beginning with a knit row, work six rows stocking stitch.
Row 16 (inc): K1, kfb, k4, kfb, k1. – 10sts
Rows 17-19: Beginning with a purl row, work three rows stocking stitch.
Row 20 (inc): K2, kfb, k4, kfb, k2. – 12sts
Rows 21-23: Beginning with a purl row, work three rows stocking stitch.
Row 24 (inc): K3, kfb, k4, kfb, k3. – 14sts
Rows 25-33: Beginning with a purl row, work nine rows stocking stitch,

PM on first and last stitch of last row for Left and Right Inner Thigh Markers.

Cut yarn B, continue with yarn AE as follows:
Rows 34-39: Beginning with a knit row, work six rows stocking stitch.
Row 40 (dec): K1, skpo, knit to last 3 sts, k2tog, k1. – 12sts
Rows 41-47: Beginning with a purl row, work five rows stocking stitch.

Breast

Work short rows for Breast:
Short row 1: K11, W+Tk.
Short row 2: P10, W+Tp.
Short row 3: K9, W+Tk.
Short row 4: P8, W+Tp.
Short row 5: K7, W+Tk.
Short row 6: P6, W+Tp.
Short row 7: K5, W+Tk.
Short row 8: P4, W+Tp.
Short row 9: K8 to end of row.

Row 48: Purl.
Row 49 (inc): Kfb, knit to last st, kfb. – 14sts
Rows 50-52: Beginning with a purl row, work three rows stocking stitch. Cast off all 14 sts for Neck Edge, PM on first and last cast-off stitch

for Left and Right Inner Neck Markers.

Join Thigh Front Seam

Follow the instructions for Peter Rabbit: Join Thigh Front Seam.

Join Belly to Back Seam

Follow the instructions for Peter Rabbit: Join Belly to Back Seam.

CHIN

Return to the Neck Cast-Off Edge. RS and Belly facing, with yarn AE, starting at Left Neck Marker (on your right), pick up and knit 14 sts across row ends and cast-off edge from Left Neck Marker to Right Neck Marker. Remove both Neck Markers.
Row 1: Purl.
Row 2 (inc): Kfb, knit to last st, kfb. – 16sts
Row 3: Purl.
Row 4 (dec): K4, skpo, k4, k2tog, k4. – 14sts
Row 5 (dec): P2tog, purl to last 2 sts, p2tog. – 12sts
Row 6 (dec): K3, skpo, k2, k2tog, k3. – 10sts

Row 7 (dec): P2tog, purl to last 2 sts, p2tog. – 8sts
Row 8 (dec): K1, skpo, k2, k2tog, k1. – 6sts

Work short rows for Chin:
Short row 1: P5, W+Tp.
Short row 2: K4, W+Tk.
Short row 3 (dec): P1, p2tog, p2 to end of row. – 5sts

Cut yarn, thread end through all 5 sts, pull up to gather and fasten end to secure for Chin Point.

Join Chin to Muzzle Seam
Follow the instructions for Peter Rabbit: Join Chin to Muzzle Seam.

EYES
With yarn D, follow the instructions for Peter Rabbit: Eyes.

EARS
With yarn AB for Outer Ears and yarn E for Inner Ears, follow the instructions for Peter Rabbit: Ears.

Join Head Back Seam
Follow the instructions for Peter Rabbit: Join Head Back Seam.

HIND PAWS
Refer to Body A, **Fig. 14** in Making Up.

The Left and Right Hind Paws are picked up and knitted along the Hind Paw Cast-Off Edge, knitted into a paw shape, the seam is sewn all along the paw's heel, upper and sole, stuffing at the same time.
The details are embroidered on once the paw is completed.

Left Hind Paw
RS and rabbit's Left Thigh facing, begin at Left Belly Marker, with yarn BC pick up and knit 9 sts along Left Paw Cast-Off Edge from Left Belly Marker to the other corner of the cast-off edge near the rabbit's Back – pick up as dotted line from A to B. Remove Left Belly Marker.
Row 1: Purl.
Row 2 (inc): Cast on 8 sts for Left Paw Upper, knit across all 17 sts.
Rows 3-7: Beginning with a purl row work, five rows stocking stitch.

Work short rows for Left Paw Front Outer Edge:
Short row 1: K8, W+Tk.
Short row 2: P6, W+Tp.
Short row 3: K5, W+Tk.
Short row 4: P4, W+Tp.
Short row 5: K3, W+Tk.
Short row 6: P2, W+Tp.
Short row 7: K13 to end of row.

Row 8: Purl.

Work short rows for Left Paw Front Inside Edge:
Short row 1: K8, W+Tk.
Short row 2: P6, W+Tp.
Short row 3: K5, W+Tk.
Short row 4: P4, W+Tp.
Short row 5: K3, W+Tk.
Short row 6: P2, W+Tp.
Short row 7: K13 to end of row.

Rows 9-13: Beginning with a purl row, work five rows stocking stitch.
Row 14 (dec): Cast off 8 sts for Paw Upper Inside Edge, knit to end of row. – 9sts
Row 15: Purl.
Cast off all 9 sts for Paw Inside Edge.

Right Hind Paw
RS and rabbit's Right Thigh facing, begin at the opposite corner to Right Belly Marker, with yarn BC pick up and knit 9 sts along Right Paw Cast-Off Edge to Right Belly Marker. Remove Right Belly Marker.
Row 1 (inc): Cast on 8 sts for Right Paw Upper, purl across all 17 sts.
Rows 2-6: Beginning with a knit row, work five rows stocking stitch.

Work short rows for Right Paw Front Outer Edge:
Short row 1: P8, W+Tp.
Short row 2: K6, W+Tk.
Short row 3: P5, W+Tp.

Short row 4: K4, W+Tk.
Short row 5: P3, W+Tp.
Short row 6: K2, W+Tk.
Short row 7: P13 to end of row.

Row 7: Knit.

Work short rows for Right Paw Front Inside Edge:
Short row 1: P8, W+Tp.
Short row 2: K6, W+Tk.
Short row 3: P5, W+Tp.
Short row 4: K4, W+Tk.
Short row 5: P3, W+Tp.
Short row 6: K2, W+Tk.
Short row 7: P13 to end of row.

Rows 8-12: Beginning with a knit row, work five rows stocking stitch.
Row 13 (dec): Cast off 8 sts purl-wise for Paw Upper Inside Edge, purl to end of row. – 9sts
Row 14: Knit.
Cast off all 9 sts purl-wise for Paw Inside Edge.

Join Hind Paw Seam
Refer to Body A, **Fig. 15** in Making Up.

Working on one paw at a time, WS together fold paw in half across the row ends at the heel. Mattress stitch

the Paw Inside Cast-Off Edge to the row ends at the Belly.
Work mattress stitch to join the cast-on and cast-off edges of the paw upper and the row ends that will become the paw front.
Stuff the paw through the last seam at the heel before closing that seam with mattress stitch.
Flatten the front of the paw with your thumb and forefinger then with a doubled length of yarn C work four lots of straight stitches to create toe sections, pulling the straight stitches as you sew them to make the paw indent a little.

TAIL
Refer to Body A, **Fig. 16** in Making Up.

The Tail is picked up and knitted along the Tail Cast-Off Edge, the under-tail edges are cast-on either side of the picked-up and knitted stitches then the Tail is knitted in its entirety. The seam is sewn all along the tail from tip to cast-on edges. The cast-on edges are then joined to the Tail Cast-On Edge.
Add any more stuffing (also stuff your yarn snippings) through the tail opening.
RS and rabbit's Back facing, return to the Tail Cast-Off Edge. With yarn BC, begin at rabbit's left side (your right side) of the cast-off edge, pick up and knit 9 sts into the cast-off edge, all along from your right to your left – Tail already picked up and knitted as dotted line from A to B.
Row 1 (inc): Cast on 3 sts for Tail Underside 1, purl all 12 sts.
Row 2 (inc): Cast on 3 sts for Tail Underside 2, knit all 15 sts.
Row 3: Purl.

Work short rows for Tail Tip:
Short row 1: K11, W+Tk.
Short row 2: P7, W+Tp.
Short row 3: K6, W+Tk.
Short row 4: P5, W+Tp.
Short row 5: K4, W+Tk.
Short row 6: P3, W+Tp.
Short row 7: K2, W+Tk.
Short row 8: P1, W+Tp.
Short row 9: K8 to end of row.

> *It is said that the effect of eating too much lettuce is "soporific." They certainly had a very soporific effect upon the Flopsy Bunnies!*

Cut yarn BC, join yarn AE, continue with the underside of the tail as follows:
Row 4: Purl.
Row 5 (dec): K2tog, knit to last 2 sts, k2tog. – 13sts
Row 6: Purl.
Row 7 (dec): K1, [K2tog, k1] four times. – 9sts
Row 8 (dec): [P3tog] three times. – 3sts
Cut yarn, thread end through all 3 sts for Underside Tail Point.

Join Tail Seam
Follow the instructions for Peter Rabbit: Join Tail Seam.

FORELEGS
The Left and Right Forelegs are knitted independently of the rabbit's body and joined after stuffing onto the Back as directed with the pattern, using the Foreleg Placement Marker as a guide. The details are embroidered on once the foreleg is completed.

Left Foreleg
With yarn BC cast on 7 sts.
Row 1: Purl.
Row 2 (inc): Kfb, knit to last st, kfb.
– 9sts
Row 3: Purl.
Row 4: Knit.
Row 5: Purl, PM on first and last stitch of row for Shoulder Markers.
Row 6 (inc): Cast on 3 sts for Left Under-Foreleg Side 1, knit across all 12 sts.
Row 7 (inc): Cast on 3 sts for Left Under-Foreleg Side 2, purl across all 15 sts.
Rows 8-11: Beginning with a knit row, work four rows stocking stitch.

Work short rows for Left Knee Joint:
Short row 1: K11, W+Tk.
Short row 2: P5, W+Tp.
Short row 3: K4, W+Tk.
Short row 4: P3, W+Tp.
Short row 5: K2, W+Tk.
Short row 6: P1, W+Tp.

Short row 7: K7 to end of row.

Rows 12-18: Beginning with a purl row, work seven rows stocking stitch.

Cut yarn C, join yarn A, continue with yarn AB as follows:

Work short rows for Left Paw Front:
Short row 1: K5, W+Tk.
Short row 2: P3, W+Tp.
Short row 3: K2, W+Tk.
Short row 4: P1, W+Tp.
Short row 5: K12 to end of row.

Row 19: Purl all 15 sts.
Row 20 (dec): [K2tog, k1] five times. – 10sts
Row 21 (dec): P2tog, purl to last 2 sts, p2tog. – 8sts
Row 22 (dec): K2tog, k1, k2tog, k1, k2tog. – 5sts
Cast off all 5 sts for Paw Edge purl-wise.

Right Foreleg
With yarn BC cast on 7 sts.
Row 1: Knit.
Row 2 (inc): Pfb, purl to last st, pfb.
– 9sts
Row 3: Knit.
Row 4: Purl.
Row 5: Knit, PM on first and last stitch of row for Shoulder Markers.
Row 6 (inc): Cast on 3 sts for Right Under-Foreleg Side 1, purl across all 12 sts.
Row 7 (inc): Cast on 3 sts for Right Under-Foreleg Side 2, knit across all 15 sts.
Rows 8-11: Beginning with a purl row, work four rows stocking stitch.

Work short rows for Right Knee Joint:
Short row 1: P11, W+Tp.
Short row 2: K5, W+Tk.
Short row 3: P4, W+Tp.
Short row 4: K3, W+Tk.
Short row 5: P2, W+Tp.
Short row 6: K1, W+Tk.
Short row 7: P7 to end of row.

Rows 12-18: Beginning with a knit row, work seven rows stocking stitch.
Cut yarn C, join yarn A, continue with yarn AB as follows:

Work short rows for Right Paw Front:
Short row 1: P5, W+Tp.
Short row 2: K3, W+Tk.
Short row 3: P2, W+Tp.
Short row 4: K1, W+Tk.
Short row 5: P12 to end of row.

Row 19: Knit all 15 sts.
Row 20 (dec): [P2tog, p1] five times. – 10sts
Row 21 (dec): K2tog, knit to last 2 sts, k2tog. – 8sts
Row 22 (dec): P2tog, p1, p2tog, p1, p2tog. – 5sts
Cast off all 5 sts for Paw Edge.

Join Foreleg Seam
Follow the instructions for Peter Rabbit: Join Foreleg Seam.

Join Forelegs to the Back
Follow the instructions for Peter Rabbit: Join Forelegs to the Back.

" The Flopsy Bunnies followed at a safe distance.
They watched him go into his house.
And then they crept up to the window to listen. "

FACE DETAIL
Refer to Body A, **Fig. 20** in Making Up.

With a doubled length of yarn C, with embroidered straight stitches work a 'Y' either side of the Nose and along the Nose Seam.
With the same threaded up yarn then embroider two straight lines along a small section of the Chin to Muzzle Seam to create a mouth.
Then with yarn E work smaller straight stitches to fill in the nose a little adding a little yarn G as a highlight.

NOTE: To make Flopsy's feet sit under her abdomen more (and you can also do this for Peter and Benjamin) join, with a few discreet stitches, the top of each foot to the lower part of the belly, placing the feet quite close together.

FLOPSY BUNNY'S CLOTHES

OTHER TOOLS AND MATERIALS

Cape
- 20 x 40cm (8 x 15¾in) red wool felt, 1–1.5mm (¹⁄₁₆in) thick, and sewing thread to match

- 1 x 10mm (½in) gold bead-type/round buttons and sewing thread to match
- Sharp hand sewing needle
- Scissors

CAPE
Trace Flopsy's Cape (see Templates) and cut one on the fold from red felt.

1. Sew the button on securely in position shown on the template.
2. Carefully cut the buttonhole slit to match the button.
3. Fold down the collar and either press down with an iron or work a few discreet slip stitches to hold the collar in place.

43

MRS. TIGGY-WINKLE™

A LITTLE girl called Lucie discovers a hidden home high in the hills. She knocks on the door, and meets Mrs. Tiggy-Winkle who does all the washing and ironing for the neighbouring animals. Lucie spends a lovely day helping her, but it's only later that she realises Mrs. Tiggy-Winkle is a hedgehog!

FINISHED SIZE
Approx. 13cm (5¼in) tall from feet to top of head

YARN
You will need no more than one ball of each of:
A: DROPS Alpaca shade 0618 Light Beige Mix
B: DROPS Kid-Silk shade 15 Dark Brown
C: DROPS Kid-Silk shade 42 Almond
D: King Cole Luxury Fur shade 4212 Foxy
And small amounts of these:
E: DROPS Alpaca shade 1101 White
F: DROPS Kid-Silk shade 04 Old Pink
G: DROPS Kid-Silk shade 31 Mauve
H: DROPS Kid-Silk shade 29 Vanilla
I: DROPS Kid-Silk shade 47 Pistachio Ice Cream

Unless otherwise stated, double and triple strands of yarn are used together throughout this pattern. The exact combinations of yarn to be used are indicated by multiple letters (see How to Use This Book).

TENSION
13 stitches and 16 rows over 5cm (2in)

NEEDLES
3.5mm (US 4) knitting needles

OTHER TOOLS AND MATERIALS
• 1 small safety pin
• 16 coloured locking stitch markers (see How to Use This Book: Stitch Markers)
• 2 x 4mm or 5mm (³⁄₁₆in) black toy safety eyes
• Toy stuffing or yarn/fabric scraps
• Tapestry or darning needle

PATTERN NOTES
• Use cable cast-on unless otherwise stated
• General knitting abbreviations can be found in How to Use This Book

HEAD
Beginning at the Nose.
With yarn A cast on 7 sts for Nose Seam.
Row 1: Purl.
Row 2 (inc): [Kfb, k1] three times, kfb. – 11sts
Row 3: Purl.
Row 4 (inc): Kfb, knit to last st, kfb. – 13sts
Row 5: Purl.
Join yarn B, continue with yarn AB as follows:
Row 6 (inc): [Kfb, k3] three times, kfb. – 17sts
Row 7: Purl, PM on first and last stitch of row for Left and Right Neck Markers.

Row 8 (inc): Kfb, k2, kfb, k9, kfb, k2, kfb. – 21sts
Row 9: Purl.
Row 10 (inc): Kfb, k5, [kfb] twice, k5, [kfb] twice, k5, kfb. – 27sts
Row 11: Purl.
Cut yarn B, join yarn C continue with yarn AC as follows:
Rows 12-15: Beginning with a knit row, work four rows stocking stitch.
Row 16: K8, PM on last stitch (8th stitch) for Left Ear Position Marker, knit next 12 sts, PM on last stitch (12th stitch) for Right Ear Position Marker, k7 to end of row.
Cut yarn AC, join yarn D (as this is faux fur yarn, work as noted below) and continue with yarn D as follows:

NOTE: Faux fur yarn knits up much fluffier when the purl-side is RS so for the next few rows you'll work reverse stocking stitch, so purling on RS/knitting on WS.

Row 17 (WS): Knit.
Row 18 (dec, RS): P2tog, p8, p2tog, p3, p2tog, p8, p2tog. – 23sts

Row 19 (WS): Knit.
Row 20 (RS): Purl.
Row 21 (WS): Knit.
Row 22 (RS): Purl.

Divide the Head Back to Create Head Back Seam
Row 23 (dec, WS): Cast off 5 sts for Head Back Seam, Right-Side, knit next 12sts, cast off last 5 sts for Head Back Seam, Left-Side. – 13sts

Head Back
RS (knit-side) facing, rejoin yarn D to 13 sts for Head Back, continue as follows:
Rows 24-29: Beginning with a purl row, work five rows reverse stocking stitch.
Cut yarn, leave all 13 sts for Head Back on the knitting needle for now.

NECK AND BACK
Refer to Body A, **Fig. 2** in Making Up.

Joining Right Side of Head
With yarn D begin at hedgehog's Right Neck Marker, WS facing (still

46

working in reverse stocking stitch)
pick up and knit 6 sts evenly along
row ends to the right-side corner
of Head Back Seam Cast-Off Edge;
knit across all 13 Head Back sts.
Do not turn.

Joining Left Side of Head

Continue to pick up across the left
side of the head, all onto the same
needle as follows:
Pick up and knit 6 sts evenly along
row ends from right corner of Head
Back Seam Cast-Off Edge to Left
Neck Marker – 25sts – pick up and
knit from A to B; knit across from
C to D; pick up and knit from E to
F, although for Hedgehog you'll be
picking up in reverse, from right-side
to left-side.
Row 1 (RS): Purl all 25 sts.
Row 2 (inc, WS): K10, kfb, k3, kfb, k10
to end of row. – 27sts
Row 3 (RS): Purl all 27 sts.
Row 4 (WS): Knit all 27 sts, PM on
first and last stitch of row for Left and
Right Mob Cap Markers.
Cut yarn D, join yarn EFG, continue
as follows:

BODY
Back

Work short rows (see Techniques) for
Blouse/Body Back:
Short row 1 (RS): K26, W+Tk.
Short row 2: P25, W+Tp.
Short row 3: K5, PM on last stitch (5th
stitch) for Left Foreleg Placement, knit
next 16 sts, PM on last stitch (16th
stitch) for Right Foreleg Placement, k3,
W+Tk.
Short row 4: P23, W+Tp.
Short row 5: K22, W+Tk.
Short row 6: P21, W+Tp.
Short row 7: K20, W+Tk.
Short row 8: P19, W+Tp.
Short row 9: K18, W+Tk.
Short row 10: P17, W+Tp.
Short row 11: K16, W+Tk.
Short row 12: P15, W+Tp.
Short row 13: K14, W+Tk.
Short row 14: P13, W+Tp.
Short row 15: K20 to end of row.

Row 5: Purl.
Row 6: Knit.

Row 7: Purl.
Row 8 (inc): Kfb, knit to last st, kfb.
– 29sts
Row 9: Purl, PM on first and last
stitch of row for Left and Right
Thigh Markers.
Cut yarn EFG, join yarn HHI (use the
other end of yarn ball H), continue
with yarn HHI (three lace-weight
mohair yarn) as follows:

Work short rows for Skirt/Left
Hind Leg:
Short row 1 (inc): Cast on 5 sts, k6,
W+Tk.
Short row 2: P2, W+Tp.
Short row 3: K3, W+Tk.
Short row 4: P4, W+Tp.
Short row 5: K5, W+Tk.
Short row 6: P6, W+Tp.
Short row 7: K7, W+Tk.
Short row 8: P8, W+Tp.
Short row 9: K33 to end of row.
– 34sts

Work short rows for Skirt/Right
Hind Leg:
Short row 1 (inc): Cast on 5 sts, p6,
W+Tp.

Short row 2: K2, W+Tk.
Short row 3: P3, W+Tp.
Short row 4: K4, W+Tk.
Short row 5: P5, W+Tp.
Short row 6: K6, W+Tk.
Short row 7: P7, W+Tp.
Short row 8: K8, W+Tk.
Short row 9: P38 to end of row.
– 39sts

Work short rows for Skirt Bustle:
Short row 1: K29, W+Tk.
Short row 2: P19, W+Tp.
Short row 3: K18, W+Tk.
Short row 4: P17, W+Tp.
Short row 5: K16, W+Tk.
Short row 6: P15, W+Tp.
Short row 7: K27 to end of row.

Row 10: Purl.
Row 11 (dec): K2tog, k6, k2tog, k6,
skpo, k3, k2tog, k6, k2tog, k6, k2tog.
– 33sts
Row 12: Purl.
Row 13 (dec): K5, k2tog, k6, skpo, k3,
k2tog, k6, k2tog, k5 to end of row.
– 29sts
Row 14: Purl.

Row 15 (dec): K4, k2tog, k5, skpo, k3, k2tog, k5, k2tog, k4 to end of row. – 25sts

Rows 16-20: Beginning with a purl row, work five rows stocking stitch.

Row 21 (dec): K3, k2tog, k15, k2tog, k3 to end of row. – 23sts

Rows 22-24: Beginning with a purl row, work three rows stocking stitch. PM on first and last stitch of last row for Left and Right Skirt Edge/ Belly Markers.

Row 25 (dec): Cast off 4 sts for Left Shoe/Paw Edge, knit next 14 sts, cast off last 4 sts for Right Shoe/Paw Edge. – 15sts

Skirt Front/Belly

WS facing, rejoin yarn HHI to 15 sts on knitting needle.

Row 1: Purl across all 15 Belly sts.

Rows 2-7: Beginning with a knit row, work six rows stocking stitch. PM on first and last stitch of last row for Left and Right Skirt Front/Inner Belly Markers.

Rows 8-13: Beginning with a knit row, work six rows stocking stitch.

Row 14 (inc): K1, kfb, k11, kfb, k1. – 17sts

Rows 15-17: Beginning with a purl row, work three rows stocking stitch.

Row 18 (inc): K2, kfb, k11, kfb, k2. – 19sts

Rows 19-21: Beginning with a purl row, work three rows stocking stitch.

Row 22 (inc): K3, kfb, k11, kfb, k3. – 21sts

Rows 23-27: Beginning with a purl row, work five rows stocking stitch. PM on first and last stitch of last row for Left and Right Skirt Front/Inner Thigh Markers.

Cut yarn HHI, join yarn DEF, continue as follows:

Blouse Front

Row 28 (inc): [K3, kfb] five times, k1. – 26sts

Row 29: Purl.

Work short rows for Blouse Front:

Short row 1: K25, W+Tk.

Short row 2: P24, W+Tp.

Short row 3 (dec): K11, k2tog, k10, W+Tk.

Short row 4: P21, W+Tp.

Short row 5: K20, W+Tk.

Short row 6: P19, W+Tp.

Short row 7: K18, W+Tk.

Short row 8: P17, W+Tp.

Short row 9: K21 to end of row. – 25sts

Row 30: Purl all 25 sts.

Cut yarn DEF, join yarn AB continue with Chin as follows:

Row 31 (dec): [K2tog, k2] six times, k1. – 19sts

Rows 32: Purl.

Row 33 (dec): [K2tog, k1] six times, k1. – 13sts

Row 34: Purl.

Row 35 (dec): [K2tog] six times, k1. – 7sts

Row 36: Purl.

Row 37 (dec): K2, k3tog, k2. – 5sts

Row 38 (dec): P2tog, p1, p2tog. – 3sts

Row 39 (dec): K3tog, fasten off for Chin Point.

MOB CAP

The Mob Cap is picked up and knitted into knitted stitches at the back of the head, just after last row of the faux fur yarn. When completed the Mob Cap will fold back over the faux fur head and is sewn down just behind the ear markers.

With RS and the Blouse/Body Back towards you, begin at hedgehog's Right Mob Cap Marker (on your right), with yarn E pick up and knit 27 sts into the first row of Blouse Back stitches, just in front of the last row

> *Her print gown was tucked up, and she was wearing a large apron over her striped petticoat. Her little black nose went sniffle, sniffle, snuffle, and her eyes went twinkle, twinkle*

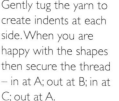

knitted in faux fur yarn, from Right Mob Cap Marker across to Left Mob Cap Marker.
Remove both Mob Cap Markers.
Row 1 (WS): Purl.
Row 2 (inc): K1, [k4, kfb] five times, k1. – 32sts
Row 3: Purl.
Row 4 (inc): K1, [k4, kfb] six times, k1. – 37sts
Row 5: Purl.
Row 6 (inc): Kfb, knit to last st, kfb. – 39sts
Row 7: Purl.

Work short rows for Mob Cap Top:
Short row 1 (RS): K38, W+Tk.
Short row 2: P37, W+Tp.
Short row 3: K36, W+Tk.
Short row 4: P35, W+Tp.
Short row 5: K34, W+Tk.
Short row 6: P33, W+Tp.
Short row 7: K32, W+Tk.
Short row 8: P31, W+Tp.
Short row 9: K35 to end of row.

Row 8 (WS): Purl.
Row 9 (dec): *K2tog, cast off 1 st**, repeat from * to ** all along, fasten off last stitch.

Join Skirt Front Seam/Thigh Front Seam
Refer to Body A, **Fig. 3** in Making Up.

Working on one side at a time, WS together match Inner Thigh to Thigh Markers, match Inner Belly to Belly Markers, work mattress stitch to join Thigh Front Seam so joining Thigh to Belly from Inner Thigh/Thigh Markers to Inner Belly/Belly Markers – join as dotted line A to B.
Remove Inner Belly and Inner Thigh Markers.

Join Blouse Front to Blouse Back/ Belly to Back Seam
Refer to Body A, **Fig. 4** in Making Up.

Working on one side at a time, WS together match colour change for Blouse at the neck (near the beginning and end of the Mob Cap picked-up stitches), ease seam together and work mattress stitch to join Belly

and Breast Seam so joining Belly and Breast to Back from colour change at the blouse to Thigh Markers – join as dotted line A to B.
Remove Thigh Markers.
At this stage you can add stuffing into the head and body.
Add a little at a time using the stuffing and yarn endings to pad out the shaping at the head and body.

HEAD DETAILS
Thread up some yarn C and secure one end.
Pass the tip of the sewing needle into one side of the head just to the side of the eye.

NOTE: If you're planning to embroider the eyes then insert the sewing needle where you want the eyes to be, work this shaping technique then, with black yarn or thread, work French Knots inside the indents.

Pass the thread through the head to emerge to the side of the other eye on the other side of the head. Pass the thread back in, near where you have you have just pulled through to emerge back where you started.

Gently tug the yarn to create indents at each side. When you are happy with the shapes then secure the thread – in at A; out at B; in at C; out at A.

Join Nose and Chin Seam
Refer to Body C, **Fig. 23** in Making Up.

1. RS together fold the Nose Cast-On Edge from the beginning of the pattern in half and join both halves together with back stitch – join dotted line A to B.
2. Turn out to RS.
3. WS together match both Neck Markers together, work mattress stitch to join seam under the nose from markers to the Nose Seam you've just sewn. Remove the Neck Markers.
4. Match the fastened-off Chin Point from belly stitches to the seam at the neck and mattress stitch to join both sides of the triangle that created at the chin.

Add Eyes
Push the toy eyes into the knitting from front/knit-side to back/ purl-side at the place where the eyes

 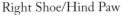

are to be (refer to the photographs for placement) and secure them in place firmly with the plastic or metal backing.

Create Indents for Head Shaping
Refer to Body D, **Fig. 27** in Making Up.

Join Mob Cap to the Head
1. Pull the Mob Cap over the fur/spiny head.
2. Join the corners of the cast-off edge to just-behind the backs of the ears, just beneath the out edges of the ears.
3. Working on one side at a time, join the mob cap sides to the side of the head with whip stitch.
4. Join the cast-off edge to the top of the head with whip stitch leaving three of four rows of the faux fur visible.
5. As an added little detail, with a yarn sewing needle or very fine crochet hook tease some of the strands of fur through the knitted stitches of the mob cap to look like the spines are pushing through the cap.
6. Brush the faux fur and trim a little to neaten and so that all strands of 'fur' are roughly the same length.

SHOES/HIND PAWS
Refer to Body A, **Fig. 14** in Making Up.

The Left and Right Shoes/Hind Paws are picked up and knitted along the Hind Paw Cast-Off Edge, knitted into a shoe shape, the seam is sewn all along the shoe's heel, upper and sole, stuffing at the same time.

Left Shoe/Hind Paw
RS and hedgehog's Left Thigh facing, begin at Left Belly Marker, with yarn BB pick up and knit 4 sts along Left Paw Cast-Off Edge from left belly marker to the other corner of the cast-off edge near the hedgehog's Back – pick up as dotted line from A to B.
Remove Left Belly Marker.
Row 1: Purl.
Row 2 (inc): Cast on 3 sts for Left Shoe/Paw Upper, knit across all 7 sts.
Rows 3-8: Beginning with a purl row, work six rows stocking stitch.
Cast off all 7 sts purl-wise for Left Shoe/Paw Upper Inside Edge.

Right Shoe/Hind Paw
RS and hedgehog's Right Thigh facing, begin at the opposite corner to Right Belly Marker, with yarn BB pick up and knit 4 sts along Right Paw Cast-Off Edge to Right Belly Marker.
Remove Right Belly Marker.
Row 1 (inc): Cast on 3 sts for Right Paw/Shoe Upper, purl across all 7 sts.
Rows 2-8: Beginning with a knit row, work seven rows stocking stitch.
Cast off all 7 sts purl-wise for Right Shoe/Paw Upper Inside Edge.

Join Shoe Seam/Hind Paw Seam
Refer to Body A, **Fig. 15** in Making Up.

Working on one paw at a time, WS together fold paw in half across the row ends at the heel.
Mattress stitch the Paw Inside Cast-Off Edge to the row ends at the Belly.
Work mattress stitch to join the cast-on and cast-off edges of the paw upper and the row ends that will become the paw front.
Stuff the paw through the last seam at the heel with a small amount of yarn B snippings before closing that seam with mattress stitch.

Flatten the front of the paw with your thumb and forefinger then with a doubled length of yarn C work four lots of straight stitches to create toe sections, pulling the straight stitches as you sew them to make the paw indent a little.

FORELEGS
The Left and Right Forelegs are knitted independently of the hedgehog's body and joined, after stuffing, onto the Back as directed with the pattern, using the Foreleg Placement Marker as a guide.
The details are embroidered on once the foreleg is completed.

Left Sleeve and Paw/Foreleg
With yarn DEF cast on 5 sts.
Row 1: Purl.
Row 2 (inc): Kfb, knit to last st, kfb. – 7sts
Row 3: Purl, PM on first and last stitch of row for Shoulder Markers.

Row 4 (inc): Cast on 3 sts for Left Under-Foreleg Side 1, knit across all 10 sts.
Row 5 (inc): Cast on 3 sts for Left Under-Foreleg Side 2, purl across all 13 sts.
Rows 6-7: Beginning with a knit row, work two rows stocking stitch.

Work short rows for the 'Elbow':
Short row 1: K10, W+Tk.
Short row 2: P3, W+Tp.
Short row 3: K2, W+Tk.
Short row 4: P1, W+Tp.
Short row 5: K5 to end of row.

Rows 8-14: Beginning with a purl row, work seven rows stocking stitch.

Cut yarn DEF, join yarn BC, continue to work with yarn BC as follows:
Row 15 (dec): K2tog, knit to last 2 sts, k2tog. – 11sts
Row 16: Purl.
Row 17: Knit.
Row 18: Purl.

Work short rows for Left Paw:
Short row 1: K9, W+Tk.
Short row 2: P7, W+Tp.
Short row 3: K6, W+Tk.
Short row 4: P5, W+Tp.
Short row 5: K8 to end of row.

Row 19 (dec): P2tog, cast off 7 sts, p2tog, cast off last 2 sts.

Right Sleeve and Paw/Foreleg

With yarn DEF cast on 5 sts.
Row 1: Purl.
Row 2 (inc): Kfb, knit to last st, kfb. – 7sts
Row 3: Purl, PM on first and last stitch of row for Shoulder Markers.
Row 4 (inc): Cast on 3 sts for Right Under-Foreleg Side 1, knit across all 10 sts.
Row 5 (inc): Cast on 3 sts for Right Under-Foreleg Side 2, purl across all 13 sts.
Rows 6-7: Beginning with a knit row, work two rows stocking stitch.

Work short rows for the 'Elbow':
Short row 1: K6, W+Tk.
Short row 2: P3, W+Tp.

Lucie's pocket-handkerchiefs were folded up inside her clean pinny, and fastened with a silver safety-pin. And then they made up the fire with turf, and came out and locked the door, and hid the key under the door-sill

Short row 3: K2, W+Tk.
Short row 4: P1, W+Tp.
Short row 5: K9 to end of row.

Rows 8-14: Beginning with a purl row, work seven rows stocking stitch.
Cut yarn DEF, join yarn BC, continue to work with yarn BC as follows:
Row 15 (dec): K2tog, knit to last 2 sts, k2tog. – 11sts
Row 16: Purl.
Row 17: Knit.
Row 18: Purl.

Work short rows for Right Paw:
Short row 1: K9, W+Tk.
Short row 2: P7, W+Tp.
Short row 3: K6, W+Tk.
Short row 4: P5, W+Tp.
Short row 5: K8 to end of row.

Row 19 (dec): P2tog, cast off 7 sts, p2tog, cast off last 2 sts.

Join Sleeve and Paw/Foreleg Seam
Refer to Body A, **Fig. 18** in Making Up.

Working on one foreleg at a time, WS together fold Paw Cast-Off Edge in half and mattress stitch to join the two halves.
Mattress stitch the row ends to join the Foreleg Seam up to the Shoulder Markers (matching the colour change at the edge of the sleeve), so leaving the first five shoulder rows free to join onto the body – join dotted line A to B.

Stuff the sleeve/foreleg through the opening at the shoulder, the paws are not stuffed.

Remove the Shoulder Markers. With a doubled length of yarn H work four lots of straight stitches to create claw sections.

Join Forelegs to the Back
Refer to Body A, **Fig. 19** in Making Up.

Find the centre of the Shoulder Cast-On Edge and mark with a pin. Working on one foreleg at a time, and making sure you have the correct foreleg for the side of the body, match the pin to the Foreleg Placement

Marker and hold in place with a stitch or two.
Remove the placement marker. Mattress stitch each side of the cast-on edge, working either side of the centre of the shoulder – you're wanting to create a round shoulder shape. Then mattress stitch the few shoulder row ends joining the shoulder to the side of the body/onto the Back.
Complete the seam by joining, with mattress stitch, the Under-Foreleg Cast-On Edge to the body.

EARS
The Left and Right Ears are knitted independently of the hedgehog's body and joined, after stuffing, onto the Head as directed with the pattern, using the Ear Position Marker as a guide.

Left and Right Ears – Make 2 alike
With yarn A cast on 10 sts.
Join yarn B, continue with yarn AB as follows:
Rows 1-5: Beginning with a purl row work five rows stocking stitch.

Cut yarn, thread end through all 10 sts, pull up tightly and secure the gathered up sts.

Refer to Body C, **Fig. 24** in Making Up.

Join Ears to Head
1. Use the tail ends to join each ear onto each side of the head – the backs of the ears are the RS/knit-side which lie against the head.
2. Working on one ear at a time, pinch the corners of the cast-on edge together, hold in place with a stitch or two then and sit the ear over the Ear Position Marker. Remove the marker as you carefully over-sew to join the base of the ear onto the head.

FACE DETAIL
With a single length of yarn F, with embroidered straight stitches work a few vertical straight stitches over the tip of the nose, similar to Satin Stitch, almost creating a solid rectangle of stitches.

NOTE: Mrs. Tiggy-Winkle sits better if you apply pressure to the top of her head and gently squash her downwards as if her chin is nestling into her chest.

POSE
To pose her so that she looks like one of Beatrix's illustrations have her arms crossed a little at the front and join with a few discreet stitches to hold them in place.

MRS. TIGGY-WINKLE'S CLOTHES

OTHER TOOLS AND MATERIALS

Apron

- Front: 21 x 9cm (8¼ x 3½in) white felt, 5–10mm (¹⁄₁₆in) thick, and sewing thread to match

- Tie: 21cm x 6mm (8¼ x ¼in) white felt, 5–10mm (¹⁄₁₆in) thick
- Sharp hand sewing needle
- Scissors

APRON

Trace Mrs. Tiggy-Winkle's Apron (see Templates) and cut one Front on the fold and one Tie on the fold, both from white felt.

1. Working on the apron, fold over at the Waistband Channel (on the template fold over from A to B). Pin down and work a sewn running stitch either by machine or by hand all along the waistband channel, approx. 1cm (³⁄₈in) from the folded edge.

2. Thread the tie through the channel and gather the apron so that its width becomes approx. 14cm (5½in) wide.
3. Tie around the waist.
4. You can pull the felt a little to give the impression of flowing fabric as an added detail.

TOM KITTEN™

THE *Tale of Tom Kitten* is set in the cottage garden
Beatrix created herself at Hill Top, the farm she
owned near the village of Sawrey. Tom and his sisters
look so smart in their new clothes. When their mother
sends them outside while she waits for her visitors, she
couldn't possibly guess what kind of mess they
are going to get themselves into!

FINISHED SIZE
Approx. 22cm (8½in) tall from feet to tip of ears

YARN
You will need no more than one ball of each of:
A: DROPS Alpaca, shade 0100 Off White
B: DROPS Kid-Silk, shade 01 Off White
C: DROPS Alpaca, shade 0302 Camel
D: DROPS Kid-Silk, shade 35 Chocolate
E: DROPS Kid-Silk, shade 15 Dark Brown
F: For the Nose a length of DROPS Alpaca, shade 9026 Blush
Unless otherwise stated, double strands of yarn are used together throughout this pattern. The exact combinations of yarn to be used are indicated by multiple letters (see How to Use This Book).

TENSION
13 stitches and 16 rows over 5cm (2in) in stocking stitch

NEEDLES
3.5mm (US 4) knitting needles

OTHER TOOLS AND MATERIALS
- 3 large safety pins or stitch holders
- 22 coloured locking stitch markers (see How to Use This Book: Stitch Markers)
- 2 x 15mm (⅝in) green cat (with oval pupils) toy safety eyes
- Toy stuffing or yarn/fabric scraps
- Tapestry or darning needle

PATTERN NOTES
- Use cable cast-on unless otherwise stated
- General knitting abbreviations can be found in How to Use This Book

HEAD
With yarn AB, cast on 8 sts for Nose Seam.
Row 1 (inc): Kfb, k2, [kfb] twice, k2, kfb. – 12sts
Row 2: Purl.

Left Muzzle
Work short rows (see Techniques) for Left Muzzle:
Short row 1: K4, W+Tk.
Short row 2: P4.
Short row 3 (inc): Kfb, k2, W+Tk.
Short row 4: P4.
Short row 5: K3, W+Tk.
Short row 6: P3.

Row 3: K6, turn (flip work over so purl-side faces), continue to work on kitten's Left Cheek only.
Cut yarn A, join yarn C, continue with yarn BC as follows:

Left Cheek
Row 4: Purl.

Row 5: Kfb, k3, k2tog, PM on last stitch for Left Eye Corner Marker, turn
Row 6: P6.
Row 7 (inc): Kfb, k5, turn. – 7sts
Row 8: P7.
Row 9: Kfb, k4, k2tog, turn.
Row 10: P7.
Cut yarn and slip all 7 sts for Left Cheek onto a safety pin.

Right Muzzle
Rejoin yarn AB to 7 sts on LH needle.
Row 3: K7.

Work short rows for Right Muzzle:
Short row 1: P4, W+Tp.
Short row 2: K4.
Short row 3 (inc): Pfb, p2, W+Tp.
Short row 4: K4.
Short row 5: P3, W+Tp.
Short row 6: K3.

Row 4: P6, turn (flip work over so purl-side faces) continue to work on kitten's Right Cheek only.
Cut yarn A, join yarn C, continue with yarn BC as follows:

Right Cheek
Row 5: K2tog, k3, kfb, PM on first

stitch for Right Eye Corner Marker.
Row 6: P6, turn (flip work over so knit-side faces).
Row 7 (inc): K5, kfb. – 7sts
Row 8: P7, turn.
Row 9: K2tog, k4, kfb.
Row 10: P7.
Cut yarn and slip all 7 sts for Right Cheek onto a safety pin.

Nose
WS facing, rejoin yarn BC to 2 sts on LH needle.
Row 4 (inc): [Pfb] twice. – 4sts
Row 5 (inc): Kfb, k2, kfb, PM on first and last stitch of row for Left and Right Nose Markers. – 6sts
Row 6: Purl.
Row 7 (inc): K1, kfb, k2, kfb, k1. – 8sts
Row 8: Purl.
Row 9: Knit.
Row 10: Purl.
Cut yarn and slip all 8 sts for Nose onto a small safety pin.

Join Left Cheek, Nose and Right Cheek
Row 1 (inc): Slip all 7 sts for Left Cheek off the safety pin and onto a knitting needle, rejoin yarn CD, kfb, k6;

slip all 8 sts for Nose off the safety pin and onto a knitting needle, cast on 3 sts for Left Eye Brow, knit across all 11 sts; slip all 7 sts for Right Cheek off the safety pin and onto a knitting needle, cast on 3 sts for Right Eye Brow, knit 9, kfb. – 30sts

Row 2: Purl all 30 sts.

Cut yarn D, join yarn B, continue with yarn BC as follows:

Row 3: Kfb, knit to last st, kfb. – 32sts

Row 4: Purl, PM on first and last stitch for Left and Right Neck Markers.

Row 5: K11, kfb, k8, kfb, k11 to end of row. – 34sts

Row 6: Purl.

Row 7: K11, kfb, k10, kfb, k11 to end of row. – 36sts

Row 8: Purl.

Row 9: K13, PM on last stitch for Left Ear Front Marker, knit next 11 sts, PM on last stitch for Right Ear Front Marker, knit 12 to end of row.

Cut yarn B, join yarn D, continue with yarn CD as follows:

Row 10: Purl.

Row 11 (dec): K12, skpo, k8, k2tog, k12 to end of row. – 34sts

Row 12: Purl.

Row 13: Knit.

Row 14: Purl.

Row 15 (dec): K10, skpo, PM on last stitch for Left Ear Back Marker, knit next 10 sts, k2tog, PM on last stitch for Right Ear Back Marker, k10 to end of row. – 32sts

Row 16: Purl.

Row 17 (dec): K9, skpo, k10, k2tog, k9 to end of row. – 30sts

Row 18: Purl.

Divide the Head Back to Create Head Back Seam

Row 19 (dec): Cast off 9 sts for Head Back Seam, Left-Side, knit next 11 sts, cast off last 9 sts for Head Back Seam, Right-Side. – 12sts

Head Back

WS facing rejoin yarn CD to 12 sts for Head Back, continue as follows:

Rows 20-28: Beginning with a purl row, work nine rows stocking stitch. Cut yarn, place all 12 sts for Head Back onto a large safety pin for now.

Join Head Seams

Refer to Body B, **Fig. 21** in Making Up.

1. WS together fold the Nose Cast-On Edge from the beginning of the pattern in half and join both halves together with mattress stitch – seam already-sewn shown as dotted line A to B.

2. Then match Left Eye Corner Marker to Left Nose Markers and work mattress stitch to join the small seam to join Left Muzzle to Nose Left-Side, from markers to the split – join dotted line C to D.

3. Join Right Muzzle to Nose Right-Side similarly.

Remove Left and Right Nose Markers.

NECK AND BACK

Refer to Body A, **Fig. 2** in Making Up.

Join Left Side of Head

With yarn CE, begin at kitten's Left Neck Marker, RS facing pick up and knit 6 sts evenly along row ends to the left-side corner of Head Back Seam Cast-Off Edge; slip all 12 sts for Head Back from the safety pin onto a knitting needle then from corner of Head Back Cast-Off Edge knit across all 12 sts for Head Back.

Join Right Side of Head

Continue to pick up across the right side of the head, all onto the same needle as follows:

Pick up and knit 6 sts evenly along row ends from right corner of Head Back Seam Cast-Off Edge to Right Neck Marker – 24sts – pick up and knit from A to B; knit across from C to D; pick up and knit from E to F.

Row 1: Purl all 24 sts.

NOTE: As you work the Back you will occasionally switch yarn to add the characteristic 'tabby fur' effect – when you see CE to CD switch yarn E to D and when you see CD to CE switch yarn D to E.

BODY
Back

Row 2 (inc): Kfb, knit to last st, kfb. – 26sts

Row 3: Purl.

Row 4 (dec): CE to CD, k10, skpo, k2, k2tog, k10 to end of row. – 24sts

Row 5: Purl.

Row 6 (dec): K10, skpo, k2tog, k10 to end of row. – 22sts

Row 7: CD to CE, purl.

Row 8 (inc): Kfb, k6, kfb, k6, kfb, k6, kfb. – 26sts

Row 9: P7, CE to CD, p19 to end of row.

Row 10 (inc): Kfb, k5, PM on last stitch for Left Foreleg Placement, knit next 15 sts, PM on last stitch for Right Foreleg Placement, k4, kfb. – 28sts

Row 11: Purl.

Row 12 (inc): Kfb, k9, kfb, k6, kfb, k9, kfb. – 32sts

Row 13: Purl.

Row 14 (inc): Kfb, knit to last st, kfb. – 34sts

Row 15: Purl.

Row 16 (inc): CD to CE, k13, kfb, k6, kfb, k13 to end of row. – 36sts

Rows 17-18: Beginning with a purl row, work two rows stocking stitch.

Row 19: P11, CE to CD, p25 to end of row.

Rows 20-21: Beginning with a knit row, work two rows stocking stitch.
Row 22 (inc): K14, kfb, k6, kfb, k14 to end of row. – 38sts
Rows 23-25: Beginning with a purl row, work three rows stocking stitch.
Row 26 (inc): Kfb, k1, kfb, k5, CD to CE, knit to last 3 sts, kfb, k1, kfb. – 42sts
Row 27: Purl.
Row 28 (inc): Kfb, k1, kfb, k22, CE to CD, knit to last 3 sts, kfb, k1, kfb. – 46sts
Row 29: Purl, PM on first and last stitch of row for Left and Right Thigh Markers.

Hind Legs
Work short rows for Left Hind Leg:
Short row 1 (inc): Cast on 8 sts, k9, W+Tk.
Short row 2: P2, W+Tp.
Short row 3: K3, W+Tk.
Short row 4: P4, W+Tp.
Short row 5: K5, W+Tk.
Short row 6: P6, W+Tp.
Short row 7: K7, W+Tk.
Short row 8: P8, W+Tp.
Short row 9: K9, W+Tk.
Short row 10: P10, W+Tp.

Short row 11: K11, W+Tk.
Short row 12: P12, W+Tp.
Short row 13: K13, W+Tk.
Short row 14: P14, W+Tp.
Short row 15 (dec): K14, skpo, k37 to end of row.

Work short rows for Right Hind Leg:
Short row 1 (inc): Cast on 8 sts, p9, W+Tp.
Short row 2: K2, W+Tk.
Short row 3: P3, W+Tp.
Short row 4: K4, W+Tk.
Short row 5: P5, W+Tp.
Short row 6: K6, W+Tk.
Short row 7: P7, W+Tp.
Short row 8: K8, W+Tk.
Short row 9: P9, W+Tp.
Short row 10: K10, W+Tk.
Short row 11: P11, W+Tp.
Short row 12: K12, W+Tk .
Short row 13: P13, W+Tp.
Short row 14: K14, W+Tk.
Short row 15 (dec): P14, p2tog, p44 to end of row.

Row 30 (dec): CD to CE, k2tog, k12, k2tog, k9, skpo, k6, k2tog, k9, k2tog, k12, k2tog. – 54sts
Row 31: Purl.

Row 32 (dec): K11, k2tog, k9, skpo, k6, k2tog, k9, k2tog, k11 to end of row. – 50sts
Row 33: Purl.
Row 34 (dec): CE to CD, k10, k2tog, k8, skpo, k6, k2tog, k8, k2tog, k10 to end of row. – 46sts
Row 35: Purl.
Row 36 (dec): K9, k2tog, k7, skpo, k6, k2tog, k7, k2tog, k9 to end of row. – 42sts
Row 37: Purl.
Row 38 (dec): CD to CE, K8, k2tog, k6, skpo, k6, k2tog, k6, k2tog, k8 to end of row. – 38sts
Row 39: Purl.

Lower Back
Work short rows for Lower Back:
Short row 1: K31, W+Tk.
Short row 2: P24, W+Tp.
Short row 3: K23, W+Tk.
Short row 4: P3, CE to CD, p19, W+Tp.
Short row 5: K21, W+Tk.
Short row 6: P20, W+Tp.
Short row 7 (dec): K6, cast off next 8 sts for Tail Space, knit next 4 sts, W+Tk.
Short row 8 (inc): P5, cast on 6 sts for Under Tail Space, purl next 5 sts, W+Tp.
Short row 9: K15, W+Tk.
Short row 10: P14, W+Tp.
Short row 11: K25 to end of row.

Row 40: Purl all 36 sts.
Row 41 (dec): CD to CE, k13, skpo, k6, k2tog, k13 to end of row. – 34sts
Row 42: Purl.
Row 43 (dec): CE to CD, k2tog, k7, k2tog, k2, skpo, k4, k2tog, k2, k2tog, k7, k2tog. – 28sts
Row 44: Purl, PM on first and last stitch of last row for Left and Right Belly Markers.
Row 45 (dec): Cast off 10 sts for Left Paw Edge, knit next 7 sts, cast off last 10 sts for Right Paw Edge. – 8sts

Belly
WS facing, rejoin yarn BC to 8 sts on knitting needle.
Row 1: Purl across all 8 Belly sts.
Rows 2-9: Beginning with a knit row, work eight rows stocking stitch, PM

on first and last stitch of last row for Left and Right Inner Belly Markers.
Rows 10-15: Beginning with a knit row, work six rows stocking stitch.
Row 16 (inc): K1, kfb, k4, kfb, k1. – 10sts
Rows 17-19: Beginning with a purl row, work three rows stocking stitch.
Row 20 (inc): K2, kfb, k4, kfb, k2. – 12sts
Rows 21-23: Beginning with a purl row, work three rows stocking stitch.
Row 24 (inc): K3, kfb, k4, kfb, k3. – 14sts
Rows 25-35: Beginning with a purl row, work 11 rows stocking stitch. PM on first and last stitch of last row for Left and Right Inner Thigh Markers.
Rows 36-39: Beginning with a knit row, work four rows stocking stitch.
Row 40 (dec): K1, skpo, knit to last 3 sts, k2tog, k1. – 12sts
Rows 41-45: Beginning with a purl row, work five rows stocking stitch.

Breast
Work short rows for Breast:
Short row 1: K11, W+Tk.
Short row 2: P10, W+Tp.
Short row 3: K9, W+Tk.
Short row 4: P8, W+Tp.
Short row 5: K7, W+Tk.
Short row 6: P6, W+Tp.
Short row 7: K9 to end of row.

Row 46: Purl.
Row 47 (inc): Kfb, knit to last st, kfb. – 14sts
Row 48: Purl.
Cast off all 14 sts for Neck Edge, PM on first and last cast-off stitch for Left and Right Inner Neck Markers.

Join Thigh Front Seam
Refer to Body A, **Fig. 3** in Making Up.

Working on one side at a time, WS together match Inner Thigh to Thigh Markers, match Inner Belly to Belly Markers, work mattress stitch for Thigh Front Seam so joining Thigh to Belly from Inner Thigh/Thigh Markers to Inner Belly/Belly Markers – join as dotted line A to B.
Remove Inner Belly and Inner Thigh Markers.

Once upon a time there were three little kittens, and their names were Mittens, Tom Kitten, and Moppet. They had dear little fur coats of their own; and they tumbled about the doorstep and played in the dust.

Join Belly to Back Seam
Refer to Body A, **Fig. 4** in Making Up.

Working on one side at a time, WS together match Inner Neck to Neck Markers, ease seam together and work mattress stitch to join Belly and Breast Seam so joining Belly and Breast to Back from Inner Neck/Neck Markers to Thigh markers – join as dotted line A to B.
Remove Inner Neck and Thigh Markers.
At this stage you can add stuffing into the body.
Add a little at a time using the stuffing to pad out the shaping at the thighs, breast, belly and back.

CHIN
Return to the Neck Cast-Off Edge. RS and Belly facing, with yarn AB, starting at Left Neck Marker (on your right), pick up and knit 10 sts across row ends and cast-off edge from Left Neck Marker to Right Neck Marker. Remove both Neck Markers.
Row 1: Purl.
Row 2 (inc): Kfb, knit to last st, kfb. – 12sts
Row 3: Purl.
Row 4 (inc): Kfb, knit to last st, kfb. – 14sts
Row 5: Purl.
Row 6 (dec): K3, skpo, k4, k2tog, k3. – 12sts
Row 7: Purl.
Row 8 (dec): K3, skpo, k2, k2tog, k3. – 10sts

"Now keep your frocks clean, children! You must walk on your hind legs. Keep away from the dirty ash-pit, and from Sally Henny Penny, and from the pigsty and the Puddle-ducks."

Work short rows for Chin:
Short row 1: P7, W+Tp.
Short row 2: K4, W+Tk.
Short row 3: P3, W+Tp.
Short row 4: K2, W+Tk.
Short row 5: P6 to end of row.

Row 9 (dec): K1, [k2tog, cast off 1 st] four times, cast off last 2 sts.

Join Chin to Muzzle Seam
Refer to Body A, **Fig. 5** in Making Up.

Stuff the head a little to make it easier to join the seams.
Find the centre of the Chin Cast-Off Edge and mark with a pin.
WS together, match the pin to the Nose Seam, hold with a stitch or two. Remove the pin.

Working on one side at a time join the muzzle to the chin with mattress stitch, easing the seam together as you do so.

EYES
The eyes are picked up and knitted into the cast-on edge above the cheeks, knitted into an eye shape that matches the eye socket, pushed into the eye socket and then carefully joined by over-sewing into the socket space before adding the toy safety eyes.

Left Eye
Refer to Body A, **Fig. 6** in Making Up.

RS and kitten's Left Eye Socket facing, with yarn A pick up and knit 6 sts along the edge at the top of the left cheek (this is also the lower edge of the eye socket) from your right to your left at Left Eye Corner Marker– pick up as dotted line from A to B. Remove Left Eye Corner Marker.
*****Rows 1-3**: Beginning with a purl row, work three rows stocking stitch.
Row 4 (dec): K2tog, k2, k2tog. – 4sts
Row 5: Purl.
Row 6 (dec): [K2tog] twice. – 2sts
Row 7 (dec): P2tog.**

Right Eye
RS and kitten's Right Eye Socket facing, with yarn A pick up and knit 6 sts along the edge at the top of the right cheek (this is also the lower edge of the eye socket) from the Right Eye Corner Marker (on your right) to the left.
Remove Right Eye Corner Marker.
Continue as Left Eye from * to **.

Join Eye to Eye Socket Seam
Refer to Body A, **Fig. 7** in Making Up.

Working on one eye at a time, WS together push the knitted eye into the eye socket. Matching the eye to the socket carefully over-sew all around the eye joining it slightly inside the socket.
Push the toy eye into the centre of the knitted eye, from front/knit-side to back/purl-side and secure it in place firmly with the plastic or metal backing.

EARS
Left Outer Ear
Refer to Body A, **Fig. 8** in Making Up.

RS and with the top of the head facing, begin near kitten's Left Ear Front Marker and with yarn CD pick up and knit 7 sts into the knitted stitches at the top of the head in a straight line across to Left Ear Back Marker– pick up and knit as dotted line from A to B.
Remove both Left Ear Markers.
Row 1 (inc): Cast on 7 sts, purl across all 14 sts.
Row 2 (inc): Kfb, knit to last st, kfb. – 16sts

Row 3: Purl.
Row 4 (dec): K5, skpo, k2, k2tog, k5.
– 14sts
Row 5: Purl.
Row 6 (dec): K4, skpo, k2, k2tog, k4.
– 12sts
Row 7 (dec): P2tog, purl to last 2 sts,
p2tog. – 10sts
Row 8 (dec): K2, skpo, k2, k2tog, k2.
– 8sts
Row 9 (dec): P2tog, purl to last 2 sts,
p2tog. – 6sts
Row 10 (dec): Skpo, k2, k2tog. – 4sts
Row 11 (dec): P2tog twice. – 2 sts
Cut yarn, thread end through both sts
for Ear Point, pull up then weave the
tail end in and out along ear edge.

Right Outer Ear
RS and with the top of the head
facing, begin near kitten's Right Ear
Back Marker and with yarn CD pick
up and knit 7 sts into the knitted
stitches at the top of the head in a
straight line across to Right Ear Front
Marker – stitches shown picked up
and knitted as dotted line from A to B.
Remove both Right Ear Markers.
Row 1: Purl.
Row 2 (inc): Cast on 7 sts, knit across
all 14 sts.
Row 3 (inc): Pfb, purl to last st, pfb.
– 16sts
Row 4 (dec): K5, skpo, k2, k2tog, k5.
– 14sts
Row 5: Purl.
Row 6 (dec): K4, skpo, k2, k2tog, k4.
– 12sts
Row 7 (dec): P2tog, purl to last 2 sts,
p2tog. – 10sts
Row 8 (dec): K2, skpo, k2, k2tog, k2.
– 8sts
Row 9 (dec): P2tog, purl to last 2 sts,
p2tog. – 6sts
Row 10 (dec): Skpo, k2, k2tog. – 4sts
Row 11 (dec): [P2tog] twice. – 2 sts
Cut yarn, thread end through both sts
for Ear Point, pull up then weave the
tail end in and out along ear edge.

Left Inner Ear Side 1
Refer to Body A, **Fig. 9** in Making Up.

RS facing, with yarn B starting at the
corner of Left Ear Outer Edge pick up

and knit 9 sts evenly along row ends
up to Left Ear Point – stitches shown
picked up and knitted as dotted line
from A to B.
Row 1: Purl.
Row 2 (dec): Knit to last 2 sts, k2tog
– 8sts
Rows 3-6 (dec): Repeat last 2 rows
twice more. – 6sts
Row 7: Purl.
Cast off all 6 sts of Left Inner Ear
Centre Side 1.

Left Inner Ear Side 2
RS facing, with yarn B starting at Left
Ear Point pick up and knit 9 sts evenly
along row ends to the corner of
Left Ear Inner Edge – stitches shown
picked up and knitted as dotted line
from C to D.
Row 1: Purl.
Row 2 (dec): K2tog, knit to end. – 8sts
Rows 3-6 (dec): Repeat last 2 rows
twice more. – 6sts
Row 7: Purl.
Cast off all 6 sts of Left Inner Ear
Centre Side 2.

Right Inner Ear Side 1
RS facing, with yarn B starting at the
corner of Right Ear Inner Edge pick up
and knit 9 sts evenly along row ends
up to Right Ear Point.
Row 1: Purl.
Row 2 (dec): Knit to last 2 sts, k2tog.
– 8sts
Rows 3-6 (dec): Repeat last 2 rows
twice more. – 6sts
Row 7: Purl.
Cast off all 6 sts of Right Inner Ear
Centre Side 1.

Right Inner Ear Side 2
RS facing, with yarn B starting at Right
Ear Point pick up and knit 9 sts evenly
along row ends to the corner of Right
Ear Outer Edge.
Row 1: Purl.
Row 2 (dec): K2tog, knit to end. – 8sts
Rows 3-6 (dec): Repeat last 2 rows
twice more. – 6sts
Row 7: Purl.
Cast off all 6 sts of Right Inner Ear
Centre Side 2.

Join Inner Ear Seam
Refer to Body A, **Fig. 10** in Making Up.

Working on one Inner Ear at a time,
with RS together, match Inner Ear
Centre Side 1 to Inner Ear Centre
Side 2 and work back stitch to join
along both cast-off edges, continue to
join the seam along the diagonal row
ends up to the Ear Point. Leave the
straight edges at the base of the ear
inner open for turning through – join
dotted lines A to B.
Turn out to RS and trim the tail ends
(it's best not to have any stuffing for
inside the ears).

Refer to Body B, **Fig. 22** in Making Up.

Then, WS facing, carefully over-sew to
join the straight edges from the Inner
Ears to the base of the outer ear/the
picked-up edge and the cast-on edge
from outer ear.

Join Ears to the Head
Refer to Body A, **Fig. 12** in Making Up.

Complete the Ear by joining the Ear Back onto the head by curving it around in a kind of arc, the corner of the Ear Back should almost join with the corner at the front of the ear creating a 'petal' shape. Pin in place and when you are happy with your placement, make a stitch or two to hold the corner of the ear in place and then securely sew down the ear back onto the head, either with mattress stitch or by over-sewing – join as shown.

Join Head Back Seam
Refer to Body A, **Fig. 13** in Making Up.

WS together, working on one side at a time, work mattress stitch to join the Head Back Seam Cast-Off Edge

to the row ends at the back of the head, at the same time adding a little stuffing to pad out the head back. You can also add little bits of stuffing into the muzzle and nose to pad out those too.

HIND PAWS
Refer to Body A, **Fig. 14** in Making Up.

The Left and Right Hind Paws are picked up and knitted along the Hind Paw Cast-Off Edge, knitted into a paw shape, the seam is sewn all along the paw's heel, upper and sole, stuffing at the same time.
The details are embroidered on once the paw is completed.

Left Hind Paw
RS and kitten's Left Thigh facing, begin at Left Belly Marker, with yarn CD pick up and knit 9 sts along Left Paw Cast-Off Edge – pick up as dotted line from A to B.
Remove Left Belly Marker.
Row 1: Purl.
Row 2 (inc): Cast on 6 sts for Left Paw Upper, knit across all 15 sts.
Rows 3-7: Beginning with a purl row, work five rows stocking stitch.

Work short rows for Left Paw Front Outer Edge:
Short row 1: K6, W+Tk.
Short row 2: P6.
Short row 3: K5, W+Tk.
Short row 4: P5.
Short row 5: K4, W+Tk.
Short row 6: P4.
Short row 7: K3, W+Tk.
Short row 8: P3.

Rows 8-9: Beginning with a knit row, work two rows stocking stitch.

Work short rows for Left Paw Front Inside Edge:
Short row 1: K6, W+Tk.
Short row 2: P6.
Short row 3: K5, W+Tk.
Short row 4: P5.
Short row 5: K4, W+Tk.
Short row 6: P4.
Short row 7: K3, W+Tk.
Short row 8: P3.

Rows 10-13: Beginning with a knit row, work four rows stocking stitch.
Row 14 (dec): Cast off 6 sts for Paw Upper Inside Edge, knit to end of row. – 9sts
Row 15: Purl.
Cast off all 9 sts for Paw Inside Edge.

Right Hind Paw
RS and kitten's Right Thigh facing, begin at the opposite corner to Right Belly Marker, with yarn AB pick up and knit 9 sts along Right Paw Cast-Off Edge to Right Belly Marker.
Remove Right Belly Marker.
Row 1 (inc): Cast on 6 sts for Right Paw Upper, purl across all 15 sts.
Rows 2-6: Beginning with a knit row, work five rows stocking stitch.

Work short rows for Right Paw Front Outer Edge:
Short row 1: P6, W+Tp.
Short row 2: K6.
Short row 3: P5, W+Tp.
Short row 4: K5.
Short row 5: P4, W+Tp.
Short row 6: K4.
Short row 7: P3, W+Tp.
Short row 8: K3.

Rows 7-8: Beginning with a purl row, work two rows stocking stitch.

Work short rows for Right Paw Front Inside Edge:
Short row 1: P6, W+Tp.
Short row 2: K6.
Short row 3: P5, W+Tp.
Short row 4: K5.
Short row 5: P4, W+Tp.
Short row 6: K4.
Short row 7: P3, W+Tp.
Short row 8: K3.

Rows 9-12: Beginning with a purl row, work four rows stocking stitch.
Row 13 (dec): Cast off 6 sts purl-wise for Paw Upper Inside Edge, purl to end of row. – 9sts
Row 14: Knit.
Cast off all 9 sts purl-wise for Paw Inside Edge.

Join Hind Paw Seam
Refer to Body A, **Fig. 15** in Making Up.

Working on one paw at a time, WS together fold paw in half across the row ends at the heel.

Mattress stitch the Paw Inside Cast-Off Edge to the row ends at the Belly.

Work mattress stitch to join the cast-on and cast-off edges of the paw upper and the row ends that will become the paw front.

Stuff the paw through the last seam at the heel before closing that seam with mattress stitch.

Flatten the front of the paw with your thumb and forefinger then, with a doubled length of yarn E, work four lots of straight stitches to create toe sections, pulling the straight stitches as you sew them to make the paw indent a little.

TAIL
Refer to Body A, **Fig. 16** in Making Up.

The Tail is picked up and knitted along the Tail Cast-Off Edge, the under-tail edges are cast on either side of the picked-up and knitted stitches then the Tail is knitted in its entirety. The seam is sewn all along the tail from tip to cast-on edges. The cast-on edges are then joined to the Tail Cast-On Edge.
Add any more stuffing (also stuff your yarn snippings) through the tail opening.

NOTE: As you work the Tail you will occasionally switch yarn to add the characteristic 'tabby fur' effect – when you see CE to CD switch yarn E to D and when you see CD to CE switch yarn D to E.

RS and kitten's Back facing, return to the Tail Cast-Off Edge. With yarn CE, begin at kitten's left side (your right side) of the cast-off edge, pick up and knit 10 sts into the cast-off edge, all along from your right to your left – Tail already picked up and knitted as dotted line from A to B.
Row 1 (inc): Cast on 5 sts for Tail Underside 1, purl all 15 sts.
Row 2 (inc). Cast on 5 sts for Tail Underside 2, knit all 20 sts.
Rows 3-5: Beginning with a purl row, work three rows stocking stitch.
Rows 6-9: CE to CD, beginning with a

knit row, work four rows stocking stitch.
Rows 10-13: CD to CE, beginning with a knit row, work four rows stocking stitch.

Work short rows for Tail Tip:
Short row 1: CE to CD, k19, W+Tk.
Short row 2: P18, W+Tp.
Short row 3: K17, W+Tk.
Short row 4: P16, W+Tp.
Short row 5: K15, W+Tk.
Short row 6: P14, W+Tp.
Short row 7: CD to CE, k13, W+Tk.
Short row 8: P12, W+Tp.
Short row 9: 11, W+Tk.
Short row 10: P10, W+Tp.
Short row 11: K9, W+Tk.
Short row 12: P8, W+Tp.
Short row 13: K7, W+Tk.
Short row 14: P6, W+Tp.
Short row 15: K5, W+Tk.
Short row 16: P4, W+Tp.
Short row 17: K3, W+Tk.
Short row 18: P2, W+Tp.
Short row 19: K11 to end of row.

Row 14: K1, [p2tog, cast off 1 st] nine times, cast off last 2 sts.

Join Tail Seam
Refer to Body A, **Fig. 17** in Making Up.

WS together, fold tail at cast-off edge and mattress stitch both halves together. Continue to work mattress stitch all along the tail row ends stopping the seam at the Tail Underside Cast-On Edges.
Stuff the tail fairly firmly.
Just before closing the seam completely you can also add more stuffing, if needs be, to the body and head.
Complete the seam by joining, with mattress stitch, the Under-Tail Cast-On Edges to Tail Cast-on Edge at the Back.

FORELEGS
The Left and Right Forelegs are knitted independently of the kitten's body and joined after stuffing onto the Back as directed with the pattern, using the Foreleg Placement Marker as a guide. The details are embroidered on once the foreleg is completed.

NOTE: As you work the Forelegs you will occasionally switch yarn to add the

characteristic 'tabby fur' effect – when you see CE to CD switch yarn E to D and when you see CD to CE switch yarn D to E.

Left Foreleg
With yarn CE cast on 7 sts.
Row 1: Purl.
Row 2 (inc): Kfb, knit to last st, kfb. – 9sts
Row 3: Purl.
Row 4: Knit.
Row 5: Purl, PM on first and last stitch for Shoulder Markers.
Row 6 (inc): Cast on 3 sts for Left Under-Foreleg Side 1, knit across all 12 sts.
Row 7 (inc): Cast on 3 sts for Left Under-Foreleg Side 2, purl across all 15 sts.
Rows 8-11: CE to CD, beginning with a knit row, work four rows stocking stitch.

Work short rows for Left Knee Joint:
Short row 1: CD to CE, k11, W+Tk.
Short row 2: P5, W+Tp.
Short row 3: K4, W+Tk.
Short row 4: P3, W+Tp.
Short row 5: K2, W+Tk.
Short row 6: P1, W+Tp.
Short row 7: K7 to end of row.

Row 12: Purl.
Rows 13-18: CE to CD, beginning with a knit row, work six rows stocking stitch.
Rows 19-20: CD to CE, beginning with a knit row, work two rows stocking stitch.
Cut yarn E, join yarn B, continue with yarn BC as follows:

Work short rows for Left Paw Front:
Short row 1: K7, W+Tk.
Short row 2: P6, W+Tp.
Short row 3: K5, W+Tk.
Short row 4: P4, W+Tp.
Short row 5: K13 to end of row.

Row 21: Purl all 15 sts.
Row 22 (dec): [K2tog, k1] five times. – 10sts
Row 23 (dec): P2tog, purl to last 2 sts, p2tog. – 8sts
Row 24 (dec): K2tog, k1, k2tog, k1, k2tog. – 5sts
Cast off all 5 Paw Edge sts purl-wise.

Right Foreleg
With yarn CE, cast on 7 sts.
Row 1: Knit.
Row 2 (inc): Pfb, purl to last st, pfb. – 9sts
Row 3: Knit.
Row 4: Purl.
Row 5: Knit, PM on first and last stitch for Shoulder Markers.
Row 6 (inc): Cast on 3 sts for Right Under-Foreleg Side 1, purl across all 12 sts.
Row 7 (inc): Cast on 3 sts for Right Under-Foreleg Side 2, knit across all 15 sts.
Rows 8-11: CE to CD, beginning with purl row, work four rows stocking stitch.

Work short rows for Right Knee Joint:
Short row 1: CD to CE, p11, W+Tp.
Short row 2: K5, W+Tk.
Short row 3: P4, W+Tp.
Short row 4: K3, W+Tk.
Short row 5: P2, W+Tp.
Short row 6: K1, W+Tk.
Short row 7: P7 to end of row.

Row 12: Knit.
Rows 13-18: CE to CD, beginning with purl row, work six rows stocking stitch.
Rows 19-20: CD to CE, beginning with purl row, work two rows stocking stitch.
Cut yarn E, join yarn B, continue with yarn BC as follows:

Work short rows for Right Paw Front:
Short row 1: P7, W+Tp.

Short row 2: K6, W+Tk.
Short row 3: P5, W+Tp.
Short row 4: K4, W+Tk.
Short row 5: P13 to end of row.

Row 21: Knit all 15 sts.
Row 22 (dec): [P2tog, p1] five times. – 10sts
Row 23 (dec): K2tog, knit to last 2 sts, k2tog. – 8sts
Row 24 (dec): P2tog, p1, p2tog, p1, p2tog. – 5sts
Cast off all 5 Paw Edge sts.

Join Foreleg Seam
Refer to Body A, **Fig. 18** in Making Up.

Working on one foreleg at a time, WS together fold Paw Cast-Off Edge in half and mattress stitch to join the two halves.
Mattress stitch the row ends to join the Foreleg Seam up to the Shoulder Markers, so leaving the first five shoulder rows free to join onto the body – join dotted line A to B.
Stuff the paw through the opening at the shoulder.
Remove the Shoulder Markers.
Flatten the front of the paw with your thumb and forefinger then, with a doubled length of yarn C, work four lots of straight stitches to create toe sections, pulling the straight stitches as you sew them to make the paw indent a little.

Join Forelegs to the Back
Refer to Body A, **Fig.19** in Making Up.

Find the centre of the Shoulder Cast-On Edge and mark with a pin.
Working on one foreleg at a time and, making sure you have the correct foreleg for the side of the body, match the pin to the Foreleg Placement Marker and hold in place with a stitch or two.
Remove the Foreleg Placement Marker.
Mattress stitch each side of the cast-on edge, working either side of the centre of the shoulder – you're

wanting to create a round shoulder shape.
Then mattress stitch the few shoulder row ends joining the shoulder to the side of the body/onto the Back.
Complete the seam by joining, with mattress stitch, the Under-Foreleg Cast-On Edge to the body.

FACE DETAIL
Refer to Body A, **Fig. 20** in Making Up.

With a doubled length of yarn E, with embroidered straight stitches work a 'Y' either side of the Nose and along the Nose Seam.
With the same threaded up yarn, then embroider two straight lines along a small section of the Chin to Muzzle Seam to create a mouth.
Then with yarn F work two horizontal straight stitches across the tip of the nose with two vertical stitches working over the centre of them
To add a finishing detail to the head, refer to the illustration and work several duplicate stitches with a single strand of yarn E.

TOM KITTEN'S CLOTHES

OTHER TOOLS AND MATERIALS

Breeches and Coat
- 20 x 40cm (8 x 15¾in) light-blue wool felt, 1mm (¹⁄₃₂in) thick, and sewing thread to match
- 6 x 8mm (⁵⁄₁₆in) ivory, 4-hole buttons and thread to match
- Sharp hand sewing needle
- Scissors

BREECHES

Trace Tom's Breeches (see Templates) and cut one on the fold from light-blue felt.

1. Match the Centre Back Seam edges together and either hand- or machine-sew along the centre back seam, allowing for a 4mm (³⁄₁₆in) seam allowance, leaving open the space for the tail.

2. Open out the seam and match Inside Leg A to Inside Leg B and either hand- or machine-sew along the curved inside leg seam, allowing for a 4mm (³⁄₁₆in) seam allowance.

3. Either hand- or machine-sew along the other curved inside leg seam, allowing for a 4mm (³⁄₁₆in) seam allowance for the other leg.

4. Turn out to the RS.

NOTE: You may find the next step easier to join with the breeches fitted onto the kitten first.

5. Turn in a 10mm (³⁄₈in) waist band to WS at the Waist Edge. Either by hand or machine, work a running stitch approx. 5mm (³⁄₈in) in from the folded edge all around the waistband, pulling to gather very slightly at the back of the breeches.

6. Make the pleat by folding line A onto line B. Secure in place with a couple of stitches and sew a button onto the front of the pleat. Make the other pleat by folding in the opposite direction.

7. Turn in a 6mm (¼in) hem to WS at the Leg Edge for each trouser leg. Either by hand or machine, work a running stitch approx. 4mm (³⁄₁₆in) in from the folded edge, all around each leg edge.

8. Turn in a 6mm (¼in) hem to WS at either side of the opening for the tail. Either by hand or machine, work a running stitch approx. 4mm (³⁄₁₆in) in from the folded edge all around each tail opening edge.

COAT

Trace Tom's Coat (see Templates) and cut one Front/Back on the fold and two Sleeves, all from light-blue felt.

1. Working on one sleeve at a time, fold and match the long Underarm Seam ends together.

2. Either hand- or machine-sew along the underarm seam, join the long ends together.

3. Turn out to the RS.

4. Push the sleeve into the armhole. The underarm seam should lie at the bottom of the armhole.

5. Carefully hand work small back stitches to join the edges of the sleeve to the armhole allowing for roughly a 3mm (⅛in) seam. Repeat for the other sleeve.

6. Sew the buttons on securely in positions shown on the template.

Squirrel Nutkin™

BEATRIX Potter's famous tale of a naughty squirrel
who loses his tail. Nutkin, his brother Twinkleberry
and all his cousins make their way over to Owl Island to
gather nuts, but Old Brown, the terrifying owl guardian of
the island has decided he has had enough of silly
Nutkin's cheekiness!

FINISHED SIZE
Approx. 16cm (6¼in) tall from feet to top of head

YARN
You will need no more than one ball of each of:
A: DROPS Fabel shade 110 Rust
B: DROPS Kid-Silk shade 42 Almond
C: DROPS Alpaca shade 0100 Off White
D: DROPS Kid-Silk shade 01 Off White
E: For the claws and facial features a few doubled-up
lengths of DROPS Kid-Silk shade 15 Dark Brown
F: King Cole Luxury Fur shade 4212 Foxy
G: DROPS Kid-Silk shade 30 Curry

Unless otherwise stated, double and triple strands of
yarn are used together throughout this pattern. The
exact combinations of yarn to be used are indicated by
multiple letters (see How to Use This Book).

TENSION
13 stitches and 16 rows over 5cm (2in)

NEEDLES
• 3.5mm (US 4) knitting needles for the head
• 3.75mm (US 5) knitting needles for the body

OTHER TOOLS AND MATERIALS
• 3 large safety pins or stitch holders
• 20 coloured locking stitch markers (see How to Use
  This Book: Stitch Markers)
• 2 x 10mm (½in) light-brown toy safety eyes
• Toy stuffing or yarn/fabric scraps
• Tapestry or darning needle

PATTERN NOTES
• Use cable cast-on unless otherwise stated
• General knitting abbreviations can be found How
  to Use This Book

HEAD
Beginning at the Nose.
With yarn AB and smaller 3.5mm
needles, cast on 9 sts for Nose Seam.
Work short rows (see Techniques) for
Left Muzzle:
Short row 1: K3, W+Tk.
Short row 2: P3.
Short row 3: K2, W+Tk.
Short row 4: P2.
Short row 5: K1, W+Tk.
Short row 6: P1.

Row 1: Knit across all 9 sts.

Work short rows to create the
squirrel's Left Muzzle:
Short row 1: P3, W+Tp.
Short row 2: K3.
Short row 3: P2, W+Tp.
Short row 4: K2.
Short row 5: P1, W+Tp.
Short row 6: K1.

Row 2: Purl across all 9 sts.
Row 3 (inc): [Kfb, k1] four times, kfb.
– 14sts
Row 4: Purl.

Forehead
Row 5 (inc): [K4, kfb] twice, turn (flip
work over so purl-side faces) to work
on Forehead as follows:
Row 6: P8, turn (flip work over so
knit-side faces) continue to work
on just 8 Forehead sts as follows
(the two sets 4 Cheek sts you
leave on the needle as you work in
between them):
Row 7 (inc): Kfb, k6, kfb, turn so purl-
side faces. – 10sts for Forehead
Row 8: Purl 10 sts, turn so
knit-side faces.

Row 9 (inc): Kfb, k8, kfb, turn so purl-
side faces. – 12sts for Forehead
Rows 10-12: Beginning with a purl
row, work three rows stocking stitch
on just these 12 forehead sts.
Cut yarn and place all 12 Forehead sts
onto a safety pin.

Right Cheek
With RS facing, return to squirrel's
right muzzle stitches (on your left),
with yarn AB and smaller 3.5mm
needles continue as follows:
Row 1: Knit across all 4 sts.
Row 2 (inc): P3, pfb, PM on first stitch
of row for Right Neck Marker. – 5sts
for Right Cheek
Rows 3-4: Beginning with a knit row,
work two rows stocking stitch.
Cut yarn and place all 5 Right Cheek
sts onto a safety pin.

Left Cheek
With WS facing, rejoin yarn AB and
with smaller 3.5mm needles to 4 sts
for Left Cheek, continue as follows:
Row 1 (inc): Pfb, purl to end, PM
on last stitch of row, for Left Neck

Marker. – 5sts for Left Cheek
Rows 2-3: Beginning with a knit row, work two rows stocking stitch.
Do not cut yarn.

Join Left Cheek, Forehead and Right Cheek
Row 1 (inc, RS): Knit across all 5 Left Cheek sts; slip all 12 Forehead sts off the safety pin and onto a knitting needle, k12; slip all 5 Right Cheek sts off the safety pin and onto a knitting needle, k5. – 22sts for Head Back
Row 2: Purl.

Work short rows for Head Back:
Short row 1: K15, W+Tk.
Short row 2: P8, W+Tp.
Short row 3: K7, W+Tk.
Short row 4: P6, W+Tp.
Short row 5: K5, W+Tk.
Short row 6: P4, W+Tp.
Short row 7: K13 sts across to the end of the row.

Row 3: Purl.
Row 4: K7, PM on last stitch (7th stitch) for Left Ear Front Marker, knit next 9 sts, PM on last stitch (9th stitch) for Right Ear Front Marker, k6 to end of row.
Row 5: Purl.
Row 6 (dec): K7, skpo, k4, k2tog, k7. – 20sts
Row 7: Purl.
Row 8: K7, PM on last stitch for Left Ear Back Marker, knit next 7 sts, PM on last stitch for Right Ear Back Marker, k6 to end of row.
Row 9: Purl.
Divide the Head Back to create Head Back Seam as follows:
Row 10 (dec): Cast off 5 sts for Head Back Seam, Left-Side, knit next 9 sts, cast off last 5 sts for Head Back Seam, Right-Side. – 10sts

Head Back
WS facing rejoin yarn AB and smaller 3.5mm needles to 10 sts for Head Back, continue as follows:
Rows 11-13: Beginning with a purl row, work three rows stocking stitch.
Row 14 (dec): K1, skpo, k4, k2tog, k1 to end of row. – 8sts
Row 15: Purl.

Cut yarn, place all 8 Head Back sts onto a safety pin for now.

JOIN HEAD SEAMS
Refer to Body A, **Fig. 1** in Making Up.

RS together, fold the Nose Cast-On Edge from the beginning of the pattern in half and join both halves together with back stitch – join dotted line A to B.
Turn out to RS.

NECK AND BACK
Refer to Body A, **Fig. 2** in Making Up.

Join Left Side of Head
With yarn AB and smaller 3.5mm needles, begin at squirrel's Left Neck Marker, RS facing pick up and knit 5 sts evenly along row ends to the left-side corner of Head Back Seam Cast-Off Edge; slip all 8 Head Back sts from the safety pin onto a knitting needle then from corner of Head Back Cast-Off Edge knit across all 8 Head Back sts.

Join Right Side of Head
Continue to pick up across the right side of the head, all onto the same needle as follows:
Pick up and knit 5 sts evenly along row ends from right corner of Head Back Seam Cast-Off Edge to Right Neck Marker – 18sts – pick up and knit from A to B; knit across from C to D; pick up and knit from E to F.
Row 1: Purl all 18 sts.
Join yarn B to work with ABB (use the other end of the yarn B ball) continue as follows:

> *This is a Tale about a tail—a tail that belonged to a little red squirrel, and his name was Nutkin*

BODY
Back
Row 2: Kfb, k5, skpo, k2, k2tog, k5, kfb.
Row 3: Purl.
Row 4 (dec): K6, skpo, k2, k2tog, k6 to end of row. – 16sts
Row 5: Purl.
Row 6 (inc): [Kfb, k4] three times, kfb. – 20sts
Row 7: Purl.
Row 8 (inc): Kfb, k4, PM on last stitch for Left Foreleg Placement, knit next 11 sts, PM on last stitch for Right Foreleg Placement, k3, kfb. – 22sts
Row 9: Purl.
Row 10 (inc): [Kfb, k6] three times, kfb. – 26sts
Row 11: Purl.
Row 12 (inc): Kfb, knit to last st, kfb. – 28sts
Row 13: Purl.
Row 14 (inc): K10, kfb, k6, kfb, k10 to end of row. – 30sts
Rows 15-17: Beginning with a purl row, work three rows stocking stitch.
Row 18 (inc): Kfb, k1, kfb, knit to last 3 sts, kfb, k1, kfb. – 34sts
Switch to larger 3.75mm needles,

continue as follows:
Row 19: Purl, PM on first and last stitch of row for Left and Right Thigh Markers.

Hind Legs
Work short rows for Left Hind Leg:
Short row 1 (inc): Cast on 8 sts, k9, W+Tk.
Short row 2: P2, W+Tp.
Short row 3: K3, W+Tk.
Short row 4: P4, W+Tp.
Short row 5: K5, W+Tk.
Short row 6: P6, W+Tp.
Short row 7: K7, W+Tk.
Short row 8: P8, W+Tp.
Short row 9: K9, W+Tk.
Short row 10: P10, W+Tp.
Short row 11: K11, W+Tk.
Short row 12: P12, W+Tp.
Short row 13: K13, W+Tk.
Short row 14: P14, W+Tp.
Short row 15 (dec): K14, skpo, k17 to end of row. – 41sts

Work short rows for Right Hind Leg:
Short row 1 (inc): Cast on 8 sts, p9, W+Tp.

Short row 2: K2, W+Tk.
Short row 3: P3, W+Tp.
Short row 4: K4, W+Tk.
Short row 5: P5, W+Tp.
Short row 6: K6, W+Tk.
Short row 7: P7, W+Tp.
Short row 8: K8, W+Tk.
Short row 9: P9, W+Tp.
Short row 10: K10, W+Tk.
Short row 11: P11, W+Tp.
Short row 12: K12, W+Tk.
Short row 13: P13, W+Tp.
Short row 14: K14, W+Tk.
Short row 15 (dec): P14, p2tog, p32 to end of row. – 48sts

Row 20 (dec): K2tog, k12, k2tog, k3, skpo, k6, k2tog, k3, k2tog, k12, k2tog. – 42sts
Row 21: Purl.
Row 22 (dec): K11, k2tog, k3, skpo, k6, k2tog, k3, k2tog, k11 to end of row. – 38sts
Row 23: Purl.
Row 24 (dec): K10, k2tog, k2, skpo, k6, k2tog, k2, k2tog, k10 to end of row. – 34sts
Row 25: Purl.
Row 26 (dec): K5, k2tog, k20, k2tog, k5 to end of row. – 32sts
Row 27: Purl.

Lower Back
Work short rows for Lower Back:
Short row 1: K22, W+Tk.
Short row 2: P12, W+Tp.
Short row 3: K11, W+Tk.
Short row 4: P10, W+Tp.
Short row 5: K9, W+Tk.
Short row 6: P8, W+Tp.
Short row 7 (dec): K1, cast off next 6 sts for Tail Space, knit next 12 to end of row. – 26sts

Row 28 (inc): P13, cast on 4 sts for Under Tail Space, p13 to end of row. – 30sts
Row 29 (dec): K10, skpo, k6, k2tog, k10 to end of row. – 28sts
Row 30: Purl.
Row 31 (dec): K2tog, k4, k2tog, k2, skpo, k4, k2tog, k2, k2tog, k4, k2tog. – 22sts
Row 32: Purl, PM on first and last stitch of row for Left and Right Belly Markers.

Row 33 (dec): Cast off 7 sts for Left Paw Edge, knit next 7 sts, cast off last 7 sts for Right Paw Edge. – 8sts

Belly
WS facing, rejoin yarn BBC to 8 sts on knitting needle.
Row 1: Purl across all 8 Belly sts.
Rows 2-7: Beginning with a knit row, work six rows stocking stitch, PM on first and last stitch of last row for Left and Right Inner Belly Markers.
Cut yarn B, join yarn D, continue with yarn BCD as follows:
Rows 8-13: Beginning with a knit row, work six rows stocking stitch.
Row 14 (inc): K1, kfb, k4, kfb, k1. – 10sts
Rows 15-17: Beginning with a purl row, work three rows stocking stitch.
Row 18 (inc): K2, kfb, k4, kfb, k2. – 12sts
Rows 19-21: Beginning with a purl row, work three rows stocking stitch.
Row 22 (inc): K3, kfb, k4, kfb, k3. – 14sts
Rows 23-29: Beginning with a purl row, work seven rows stocking stitch, PM on first and last stitch of last row for Left and Right Inner Thigh Markers. Switch to smaller 3.5mm needles.

Cut yarn B, join yarn D (use both ends of yarn D ball), continue with yarn CDD as follows:
Rows 30-33: Beginning with a knit row, work four rows stocking stitch.
Row 34 (dec): K1, skpo, knit to last 3 sts, k2tog, k1. – 12sts
Rows 35-37: Beginning with a purl row, work three rows stocking stitch.

Breast
Work short rows for Breast:
Short row 1: K11, W+Tk.
Short row 2: P10, W+Tp.
Short row 3: K9, W+Tk.
Short row 4: P8, W+Tp.
Short row 5: K10 to end of row.

Row 38: Purl.
Row 39 (dec): K2tog, knit to last 2 sts, k2tog. – 10sts
Row 40: Purl.
Row 41 (dec): K2tog, knit to last 2 sts, k2tog. – 8sts
Row 42: Purl.
Cast off all 8 sts for Neck Edge PM on first and last cast-off stitch for Left and Right Inner Neck Markers.

Join Thigh Front Seam
Refer to Body A, **Fig. 3** in Making Up.

Working on one side at a time, WS together match Inner Thigh to Thigh Markers, match Inner Belly to Belly Markers, work mattress stitch to join Thigh Front Seam so joining Thigh to Belly from inner thigh/thigh markers to inner belly/belly markers – join as dotted line A to B.
Remove Inner Belly and Inner Thigh Markers.

Join Belly to Back Seam
Refer to Body A, **Fig. 4** in Making Up.

Working on one side at a time, WS together match Inner Neck to Neck Markers, ease seam together and work mattress stitch to join Belly and Breast Seam so joining Belly and Breast to Back from inner neck/neck markers to thigh markers – join as dotted line A to B.
Remove Inner Neck and Thigh Markers.
At this stage you can add stuffing into the body.
Add a little at a time using the stuffing to pad out the shaping at the thighs, breast, belly and back.

CHIN
Return to the Neck Cast-Off Edge. RS and Belly facing, with yarn CDD and smaller 3.5mm needles, starting at Left Neck Marker (on your right), pick up and knit 6 sts across row ends and cast-off edge from Left neck marker to Right Neck Marker.
Remove both Neck Markers.
Row 1: Purl.
Row 2 (inc): Kfb, knit to last st, kfb. – 8sts
Row 3: Purl.

Work short rows for Chin:
Short row 1: K6, W+Tk.
Short row 2: P4, W+Tp.
Short row 3: K3, W+Tk.
Short row 4: P2, W+Tp.
Short row 5: K5 to end of row.

Row 4 (dec): P3tog, p2, p3tog. – 4sts
Cut yarn, thread end through all 4

Chin Point sts, pull up tightly and secure end.

Join Chin to Muzzle Seam
Refer to Body A, **Fig. 5** in Making Up.

Stuff the head a little to make it easier to join the seams.
Find the centre of the Chin Cast-Off Edge and mark with a pin.
WS together, match the pin to the Nose Seam, hold with a stitch or two. Remove the pin.
Working on one side at a time join the muzzle to the chin with mattress stitch, easing the seam together as you do so.
The chin is not stuffed, instead, when you've completed the head stuffing, with your thumb push the chin under the muzzle and nose. You can leave it like that; or you can secure the chin inwards by working a few discreet stitches.

EYES
The eyes are picked up and knitted into the cast-on edge above the cheeks, knitted into an eye shape that matches the eye socket, pushed into the eye socket and then carefully joined by over-sewing into the socket space before adding toy safety eyes.

Left Eye
Refer to Body A, **Fig. 6** in Making Up.

RS and squirrel's Left Eye Socket facing, with yarn B and smaller 3.5mm needles pick up and knit 6 sts along the edge at the top of the left cheek (this is also the lower edge of the eye socket) beginning at the split on your right and ending at the split on your left – pick up as dotted line from A to B.
*Row 1: Purl.

Work short rows for Eye:
Short row 1: K5, W+Tk.

Short row 2: P4, W+Tp.
Short row 3: K3, W+Tk.
Short row 4: P2, W+Tp.
Short row 5: K4 to end of row.

Cast off all 6 sts for Upper Eye Edge purl-wise.**

Right Eye
RS and squirrel's Right Eye Socket facing, with yarn B and smaller 3.5mm needles pick up and knit 6 sts along the edge at the top of the right cheek (this is also the lower edge of the eye socket) beginning at the split on your right and ending at the split on your left – stitches shown picked up and knitted as dotted line from A to B.
Continue as Left Eye from * to **.

Join Eye to Eye Socket Seam
Refer to Body A, **Fig. 7** in Making Up.

Working on one eye at a time, WS together push the knitted eye into the eye socket. Matching the Upper Eye Cast-Off Edge to the top of the Eye Socket carefully over-sew the two edges together with a single length yarn C, the row end edges of the knitted eye are naturally bunched up as they squeeze into the eye socket space, work a stitch or two to close any small gaps.
Push the toy eye into the centre of the knitted eye, from front/knit-side to back/purl-side and secure it in place firmly with the plastic or metal backing.

EARS
Left Outer Ear
Refer to Body A, **Fig. 8** in Making Up.

RS and with the top of the head facing, begin near squirrel's Left Ear Front Marker and with yarn AB and smaller 3.5mm knitting needles, pick up and knit 5 sts into the knitted stitches at the top of the head in a straight line across to Left Ear Back Marker – pick up and knit as dotted line from A to B.
Remove Left Ear Back Marker.
Row 1 (inc): Cast on 5 sts, purl across all 10 sts.

> *But Nutkin, who had no respect, began to dance up and down, tickling old Mr. Brown with a nettle*

Row 10: Knit.
Row 11 (dec): [P2tog] three times. – 3sts
Row 12 (dec): K3tog, fasten off for Ear Point.
Weave the tail end in and out along ear edge.

Join Ears then join the Ears to the Head
Refer to Body A, **Fig. 12** in Making Up.

1. WS together, working on one side at a time, pinch the corner of the cast-on edge together with the stitch at the Inner Ear Marker and join with a stitch or two to hold in place.
2. Remove Inner Ear Marker.
3. The Ear should lie back towards squirrel's Back so push it back with your fingers then work mattress stitch to join the cast-on edge to the head, securing the ear in this backwards position.
4. For a little detailing inside the ear, thread up yarn BB and work horizontal straight lines, similar to Satin Stitch, just inside the ear making sure the stitches aren't seen on the backs of the ear nor the ear edges, I then gently brushed the inner ears towards the tops of the ears with a soft, clean, nail brush to make them extra fluffy!

Join Head Back Seam
Refer to Body A, **Fig. 13** in Making Up.

WS together, working on one side at a time, work mattress stitch to join the Head Back Seam Cast-Off Edge to the row ends at the back of the head, at the same time adding a little stuffing to pad out the head back.

Row 2 (inc): Kfb, knit to last st, kfb. – 12sts
Row 3: Purl.
Row 4 (dec): K3, skpo, k2, k2tog, k3. – 10sts
Row 5: Purl.
Row 6 (dec): K2, skpo, k2, k2tog, k2. – 8sts
Row 7: Purl.
Row 8 (dec): K1, skpo, k2, k2tog, k1. – 6sts
Row 9: Purl.
Row 10 (dec): [K2tog] three times. – 3sts
Row 11 (dec): P3tog, fasten off for Ear Point.
Weave the tail end in and out along ear edge.

Right Outer Ear
RS and with the top of the head facing, begin near squirrel's Right Ear Back Marker and with yarn AB and smaller 3.5mm knitting needles, pick up and knit 5 sts into the knitted stitches at the top of the head in a straight line across to Right Ear Front Marker – stitches shown picked up and knitted as dotted line from A to B. Remove Right Ear Back Marker.
Row 1: Purl.
Row 2 (inc): Cast on 5 sts, knit across all 10 sts.
Row 3 (inc): Pfb, purl to last st, pfb. – 12sts
Row 4: Knit.
Row 5 (dec): P3, p2tog, p2, p2tog, p3. – 10sts
Row 6: Knit.
Row 7 (dec): P2, p2tog, p2, p2tog, p2. – 8sts
Row 8: Knit.
Row 9 (dec): P1, p2tog, p2, p2tog, p1. – 6sts

You can also add little bits of stuffing into the muzzle and nose to pad out those too.

HIND PAWS
Refer to Body A, **Fig. 14** in Making Up.

The Left and Right Hind Paws are picked up and knitted along the Hind Paw Cast-Off Edge, knitted into a paw shape, the seam is sewn all along the paw's heel, upper and sole, stuffing at the same time.
The details are embroidered on once the paw is completed.

Left Hind Paw
RS and squirrel's Left Thigh facing, begin at Left Belly Marker, with yarn AB and smaller 3.5mm knitting needles, pick up and knit 7 sts along

Left Paw Cast-Off Edge from left belly marker to the other corner of the cast-off edge near the squirrel's Back – pick up as dotted line from A to B. Remove Left Belly Marker.
Row 1: Purl.
Row 2 (inc): Cast on 5 sts for Left Paw Upper, knit across all 12 sts.
Rows 3-7: Beginning with a purl row, work five rows stocking stitch.

Work short rows for Left Paw Front Outer Edge:
Short row 1: K4, W+Tk.
Short row 2: P4.
Short row 3: K3, W+Tk.
Short row 4: P3.
Short row 5: K2, W+Tk.
Short row 6: P2.
Short row 7: K1, W+Tk.
Short row 8: P1.

Row 8: Knit.
Row 9: Purl.

Work short rows for Left Paw Front Inside Edge:
Short row 1: K4, W+Tk.
Short row 2: P4.
Short row 3: K3, W+Tk.
Short row 4: P3.
Short row 5: K2, W+Tk.
Short row 6: P2.
Short row 7: K1, W+Tk.
Short row 8: P1.

Rows 10-15: Beginning with a knit row, work six rows stocking stitch.
Row 16 (dec): Cast off 5 sts for Paw Upper Inside Edge, knit to end of row. – 7sts
Row 17: Purl.
Cast off all 7 sts for Paw Inside Edge.

Right Hind Paw
RS and squirrel's Right Thigh facing, begin at the opposite corner to Right Belly Marker, with yarn AB and smaller 3.5mm knitting needles, pick up and knit 7 sts along Right Paw Cast-Off Edge to Right Belly Marker. Remove Right Belly Marker.
Row 1 (inc): Cast on 5 sts for Right Paw Upper, purl across all 12 sts.
Rows 2-6: Beginning with a knit row, work five rows stocking stitch.

Work short rows for Right Paw Front Outer Edge:
Short row 1: P4, W+Tp.
Short row 2: K4.
Short row 3: P3, W+Tp.
Short row 4: K3.
Short row 5: P2, W+Tp.
Short row 6: K2.
Short row 7: P1, W+Tp.
Short row 8: K1.

Row 7: Purl.
Row 8: Knit.

Work short rows for Right Paw Front Inside Edge:
Short row 1: P4, W+Tp.
Short row 2: K4.
Short row 3: P3, W+Tp.
Short row 4: K3.
Short row 5: P2, W+Tp.

One autumn when the nuts were ripe, and the leaves on the hazel bushes were golden and green—Nutkin and Twinkleberry and all the other little squirrels came out of the wood, and down to the edge of the lake

Short row 6: K2.
Short row 7: P1, W+Tp.
Short row 8: K1.

Rows 9-14: Beginning with a purl row, work six rows stocking stitch.
Row 15 (dec): Cast off 5 sts purl-wise for Paw Upper Inside Edge, purl to end of row. – 7sts
Row 16: Knit.
Cast off all 7 sts purl-wise for Paw Inside Edge.

Join Hind Paw Seam
Refer to Body A, **Fig. 15** in Making Up.

Working on one paw at a time, WS together fold paw in half across the row ends at the heel.
Mattress stitch the Paw Inside Cast-Off Edge to the row ends at the Belly. Work mattress stitch to join the cast-on and cast-off edges of the paw upper and the row ends that will become the paw front.

Stuff the paw through the last seam at the heel before closing that seam with mattress stitch.
Flatten the front of the paw with your thumb and forefinger then with a doubled length of yarn F work four lots of straight stitches to create toe sections, pulling the straight stitches as you sew them to make the paw indent a little.

TAIL
Refer to Body A, **Fig. 16** in Making Up.

The Tail is picked up and knitted along the Tail Cast-Off Edge, the tail edges are cast on either side of the picked-up and knitted stitches then the Tail is knitted in its entirety. The tail is folded and the seam is sewn all along the tail sides back down to where it was picked up.

NOTE: Faux fur yarn knits up much fluffier when the purl-side is RS so for this tail work reverse stocking stitch, so purling on RS/knitting on WS.

RS and squirrel's Back facing, return to the Tail Cast-Off Edge. With yarn FG (as this is faux fur yarn, work as noted above) and larger 3.75mm knitting needles begin at squirrel's left side (your right side) of the cast-off edge, pick up and knit 7 sts into the cast-off edge, all along from your right to your left – Tail already picked up and knitted as dotted line from A to B.
Row 1 (WS): Knit.
Row 2 (RS): Purl.
Row 3 (inc): Kfb, knit to last st, kfb. – 9sts
Rows 4-6: Beginning with a purl row, work three rows reverse stocking stitch.
Row 7 (inc): Kfb, knit to last st, kfb. – 11sts
Rows 8-12: Beginning with a purl row, work five rows reverse stocking stitch.
Row 13 (inc): Kfb, knit to last st, kfb. – 13sts
Rows 14-16: Beginning with a purl row, work three rows reverse stocking stitch.

Row 17 (dec): K2tog, knit to last 2 sts, k2tog. – 11sts
Rows 18-20: Beginning with a purl row, work three rows reverse stocking stitch.
Row 21 (dec): K2tog, knit to last 2 sts, k2tog. – 9sts
Rows 22-24: Beginning with a purl row, work three rows reverse stocking stitch.
Row 25 (dec): K2tog, knit to last 2 sts, k2tog. – 7sts
Rows 26-28: Beginning with a purl row, work seven rows reverse stocking stitch.
Row 29 (inc): Kfb, knit to last st, kfb. – 9sts
Rows 30-32: Beginning with a purl row, work three rows reverse stocking stitch.
Row 33 (inc): Kfb, knit to last st, kfb. – 11sts
Rows 34-36: Beginning with a purl row, work three rows reverse stocking stitch.

Row 37 (inc): Kfb, knit to last st, kfb. – 13sts

Rows 38-42: Beginning with a purl row, work five rows reverse stocking stitch.

Row 43 (dec): K2tog, knit to last 2 sts, k2tog. – 11sts

Rows 44-46: Beginning with a purl row, work three rows reverse stocking stitch.

Row 47 (dec): K2tog, knit to last 2 sts, k2tog. – 9sts

Rows 48-50: Beginning with a purl row, work three rows reverse stocking stitch.

Row 51 (dec): K2tog, knit to last 2 sts, k2tog. – 7sts

Rows 52-53: Beginning with a purl row, work two rows reverse stocking stitch.

Cast off all 7 sts purl-wise for Tail Base.

Join Tail Seam

Fold the tail with WS together and match the Tail Base Cast-Off Edge to the Tail Underside Cast-on Edge. Join the two edges together with mattress stitch.

With row ends matching, join as best you can (fur is a little tricky to sew together) all along so joining tail row end edges on both sides of the tail, at the same time stuffing the tail a little – but not too much!

Extra Tail Detail: As an added extra I joined in doubled strands of yarn G in amongst the fluffy-fur to give an yellow-orange glow to the tail.

FORELEGS

The Left and Right Forelegs are knitted independently of the squirrel's body and joined, after stuffing, onto the Back as directed with the pattern, using the Foreleg Placement Marker as a guide.

The details are embroidered on once the foreleg is completed.

Left Foreleg

With yarn AB and smaller 3.5mm needles cast on 5 sts.

Row 1 (WS): Purl.

Row 2: Kfb, knit to last st, kfb. – 7sts

Row 3: Purl.

Row 4: Knit.

Row 5: Purl, PM on first and last stitch of row for Left- and Right-Side Shoulder Markers.

Row 6 (inc): Cast on 3 sts for Left Under-Foreleg Side 1, knit across all 10 sts.

Row 7 (inc): Cast on 3 sts for Left Under-Foreleg Side 2, purl across all 13 sts.

Rows 8-11: Beginning with a knit row, work four rows stocking stitch.

Work short rows for Left 'Elbow' Joint:

Short row 1: K8, W+Tk.

Short row 2: P3, W+Tp.

Short row 3: K2, W+Tk.

Short row 4: P1, W+Tp.

Short row 5: K7 to end of row.

Rows 12-18: Beginning with a purl row, work seven rows stocking stitch.

Work short rows for Left Paw:

Short row 1 (dec): K1, k2tog, k7, k2tog, W+Tk.

Short row 2: P9, W+Tp.

Short row 3 (dec): K1, k2tog, k3, k2tog, W+Tk.

Short row 4: P5, W+Tp.

Short row 5: K4, W+Tk.

Short row 6: P3, W+Tp.

Short row 7: K2, W+Tk.

Short row 8: P1, W+Tp.

Short row 9: K5 to end of row. – 9sts

Row 19 (dec): [P2tog, cast off 1 st purl-wise] four times, cast off last st for Left Paw Edge purl-wise.

Right Foreleg

With yarn AB and smaller 3.5mm needles cast on 5 sts.

Row 1 (RS): Knit.

Row 2 (inc): Pfb, purl to last st, pfb. – 7sts

Row 3: Knit.

Row 4: Purl.

Row 5: Knit, PM on first and last stitch of row for Left- and Right-Side Shoulder Markers.

Row 6 (inc): Cast on 3 sts for Right Under-Foreleg Side 1, purl across all 10 sts.

Row 7 (inc): Cast on 3 sts for Right Under-Foreleg Side 2, knit across all 13 sts.

Rows 8-11: Beginning with a purl row, work four rows stocking stitch.

Work short rows for Right 'Elbow' Joint:

Short row 1: P8, W+Tp.

Short row 2: K3, W+Tk.

Short row 3: P2, W+Tp.

Short row 4: K1, W+Tk.

Short row 5: P7 to end of row.

Rows 12-18: Beginning with a knit row, work seven rows stocking stitch.

Work short rows for Right Paw:

Short row 1 (dec): P1, p2tog, p7, p2tog, W+Tp.

Short row 2: K9, W+Tk.

Short row 3 (dec): P1, p2tog, p3, p2tog, W+Tp.

Short row 4: K5, W+Tk.

Short row 5: P4, W+Tp.

Short row 6: K3, W+Tk.

Short row 7: P2, W+Tp.

Short row 8: K1, W+Tk.

Short row 9: P5 to end of row. – 9sts

Row 19 (dec): [K2tog, cast off 1 st] four times, cast off last st for Right Paw Edge.

Join Foreleg Seam

Refer to Body A, **Fig. 18** in Making Up.

Working on one foreleg at a time, WS together fold Paw Cast-Off Edge in half and mattress stitch to join the two halves.

Mattress stitch the row ends to join the Foreleg Seam up to the Shoulder Markers, so leaving the first five shoulder rows free to join onto the body – join dotted line A to B. Stuff the paw through the opening at the shoulder.

Remove the Shoulder Markers.

Flatten the front of the paw with your thumb and forefinger then with a doubled length of yarn F work four lots of straight stitches to create toe sections, pulling the straight stitches as you sew them to make the paw indent a little.

Join Forelegs to the Back

Refer to Body A, **Fig. 19** in Making Up.

Find the centre of the Shoulder Cast-On Edge and mark with a pin. Working on one foreleg at a time – and making sure you have the correct foreleg for the side of the body – match the pin to the Foreleg Placement Marker and hold in place with a stitch or two.

Remove the placement marker. Mattress stitch each side of the cast-on edge, working either side of the centre of the shoulder – you're wanting to create a round shoulder shape. Then mattress stitch the few shoulder row ends joining the shoulder to the side of the body/onto the Back.

Complete the seam by joining, with mattress stitch, the Under-Foreleg Cast-On Edge to the body.

FACE DETAIL

Refer to Body A, **Fig. 20** in Making Up.

With a single length of yarn F, with embroidered straight stitches work a 'Y' either side of the Nose and along the Nose Seam.

With the same threaded up yarn then embroider two straight lines along a small section of the Chin to Muzzle Seam to create a mouth.

Then with yarn B work smaller straight stitches to fill in the nose a little.

POSE

To pose him so that he looks like one of Beatrix's illustrations, have his arms crossed a little at the front and join with a few discreet stitches to hold them in place.

Also – in the story you may recall that poor Squirrel Nutkin actually lost his tail! So, if you want to be more authentic, you can omit the fur tail completely – just either omit the part in the pattern where you cast-off and cast-on for the tail or simply join that seam together at the end!

MR. JEREMY FISHER™

THE *Tale of Mr. Jeremy Fisher* endures as one of Beatrix Potter's most popular and well-loved tales. It tells of an optimistic and slightly accident-prone frog, who sets off on a fishing expedition across the pond, only to find himself bitten on the toe by a water beetle, fighting with a stickleback, and eventually nearly being eaten by a trout!

FINISHED SIZE
Approx. 18cm (7in) tall from feet to top of head

YARN
You will need no more than one ball of each of:
A: DROPS Alpaca, shade 9029 Wheat Field
B: DROPS Kid-Silk, shade 33 Rust
C: DROPS Alpaca, shade 0100 Off White
D: DROPS Kid-Silk, shade 46 Cherry Sorbet
E: DROPS Alpaca, shade 9026 Blush
Unless otherwise stated, double strands of yarn are used together throughout this pattern. The exact combinations of yarn to be used are indicated by multiple letters (see How to Use This Book).

TENSION
13 stitches and 16 rows over 5cm (2in)

NEEDLES
3.5mm (US 4) knitting needles

OTHER TOOLS AND MATERIALS
• 4 coloured locking stitch markers (see How to Use This Book: Stitch Markers)
• 2 x 12mm (½in) gold coloured cat (oval pupil) toy safety eyes
• Toy stuffing or yarn/fabric scraps, plus, if you want to add wire to the legs you'll need two approx. 15cm (6in) lengths of fine, flexible wire
• Tapestry or darning needle

PATTERN NOTES
• Use cable cast-on unless otherwise stated
• General knitting abbreviations can be found in How to Use This Book

BODY
Beginning at the Rear end of the Back. With yarn AB, cast on 3 sts.
Row 1 (RS, inc): Kfb, k1, kfb. – 5sts
Row 2: Purl.
Row 3 (inc): [Kfb, k1] twice, kfb. – 8sts
Row 4: Purl.
Row 5 (inc): Kfb, k1, kfb, k2, kfb, k1, kfb. – 12sts
Row 6: Purl.

Row 7 (inc): Kfb, k1, kfb, k6, kfb, k1, kfb. – 16sts
Row 8: Purl.

Work short rows (see Techniques) for the Back Ridge Side 1:
Short row 1: K5, W+Tk.
Short row 2: P3, W+Tp.
Short row 3: K2, W+Tk.
Short row 4: P1, W+Tp.
Short row 5: K13 to end of row.

Work short rows for the Back Ridge Side 2:
Short row 1: P5, W+Tp.
Short row 2: K3, W+Tk.
Short row 3: P2, W+Tp.
Short row 4: K1, W+Tk.
Short row 5: P13 to end of row.

Row 9: Kfb, k3, skpo, k4, k2tog, k3, kfb.
Row 10: Purl.
Row 11 (inc): K3, kfb, k8, kfb, k3. – 18sts
Row 12: Purl, PM on first and last stitch for left and right Back Markers.
Row 13 (dec): K3, skpo, k8, k2tog, k3. – 16sts
Row 14: Purl.

Row 15 (dec): K2tog, knit to last 2 sts, k2tog. – 14sts
Rows 16-17: Repeat last two rows once more. – 12sts
Row 18: Purl.
Row 19 (inc): K1, kfb, knit to last 2 sts, kfb, k1. – 14sts
Row 20: Purl.
Row 21 (inc): K2, kfb, k1, kfb, k4, kfb, k1, kfb, k2. – 18sts

Work short rows for Left Eye:
Short row 1: P8, W+Tp.
Short row 2: K6, W+Tk.
Short row 3: P5, W+Tp.
Short row 4: K4, W+Tk.
Short row 5: P3, W+Tp.
Short row 6: K2, W+Tk.
Short row 7: P14 to end.

Work short rows for Right Eye:
Short row 1: K8, W+Tk.
Short row 2: P6, W+Tp.
Short row 3: K5, W+Tk.
Short row 4: P4, W+Tp.
Short row 5: K3, W+Tk.
Short row 6: P2, W+Tp.
Short row 7 (dec): K4, k2tog, k8 to end of row. – 17sts

Row 22 (dec): P2tog, purl to last 2 sts, p2tog. – 15sts
Row 23 (dec): K3, skpo, k5, k2tog, k3 to end of row. – 13sts
Row 24: Purl.
Row 25 (dec): K3, skpo, k3, k2tog, k3 to end of row. – 11sts
Row 26 (dec): P2tog, purl to last 2 sts, p2tog. – 9sts
Row 27 (dec): K2, skpo, k1, k2tog, k2 to end of row. – 7sts
Row 28 (dec): P1, p2tog, p1, p2tog, p1. – 5sts

Work short rows for the Nose Front:
Short row 1: K4, W+Tk.
Short row 2.: P3, W+Tp.
Short row 3 (dec): K3tog, k1 to end of row. – 3sts

Row 29: Purl.
Row 30 (inc): Kfb, knit to last st, kfb. – 5sts
Rows 31-34 (inc): Repeat last two rows twice more. – 9sts
Row 35 (dec): P2, p2tog, p1, p2tog, p2. – 7sts
Row 36: Knit.
Row 37 (inc): Pfb, purl to last st, pfb. – 9sts
Row 38 (inc): K3, kfb, k1, kfb, k3. – 11sts
Row 39: Purl.
Row 40 (inc): K3, kfb, k1, kfb, k1, kfb, k3. – 14sts
Cut yarn AB, join yarn CD, continue as follows:
Row 41: Purl.

Work short rows for the Waistcoat:
Short row 1: K13, W+Tk.
Short row 2: P12, W+Tp.
Short row 3: K11, W+Tk.
Short row 4: P10, W+Tp.
Short row 5: K9, W+Tk.
Short row 6: P8, W+Tp.
Short row 7: K7, W+Tk.
Short row 8: P6, W+Tp.
Short row 9: K10 to end of the row.

Row 42: Purl.
Row 43: Kfb, k2, skpo, k4, k2tog, k2, kfb, PM on first and last stitch for left and right Belly Markers.
Rows 44-46: Beginning with a purl row, work three rows stocking stitch.

Row 47: Kfb, k1, skpo, k6, k2tog, k1, kfb.
Row 48 (dec): P2tog, purl to last 2 sts, p2tog. – 12sts
Row 49 (dec): Skpo, k8, k2tog. – 10sts
Row 50 (dec): P2tog, p6, p2tog. – 8sts
Cut yarn CD, join yarn AB, continue as follows:
Row 51 (dec): Skpo, k4, k2tog. – 6sts
Row 52 (dec): P2tog, p2, p2tog. – 4sts
Cast off all 4 sts for Belly Rear End.

Join Body Seams
Refer to Body E, **Fig. 30** in Making Up.

WS together, ease together and mattress stitch to join Rear End Cast-On Edge to Belly Rear End Cast-Off Edge.
Working on one side at a time, match the Belly Marker to Back Marker, pinning together if necessary, and mattress stitch from the rear end seam to markers to join Back to Belly; then from the markers, mattress stitch to join the remaining seam up

to the natural fold at the nose front/chin, at the same time stuffing the frog and inserting the eyes in place and securing the backs – join lines A to B & join lines C to D.
Remove Back and Belly Markers.

MOUTH
Refer to Body E, **Fig. 31** in Making Up.

Beginning at the frog's Right-Side Head, with yarn A, pick up and knit 5 sts into knitted stitches at the head seam that runs along the side of the right side of the head; pick up and knit 3 sts into knitted sts all around the nose at the seam; pick up and knit 5 sts into knitted stitches all along the seam that runs at the Left-Side Head – pick up and knit from A to B; B to C; C to D.

Cast off all 13 picked up sts for Mouth knit-wise.

LEFT HIND LEG
Refer to Body E, **Fig. 32** in Making Up.

Left Side of frog facing, starting about five rows before the seam at the cast-on/cast-off edge of the rear end, with yarn AB, pick up and knit 4 sts into knitted stitches near the body to belly seam from five rows towards the rear end seam, pick up and knit from A to B.

NOTE: As you work the Hind Legs you will occasionally switch yarn to add the characteristic 'stripy legs' effect – when you see AB to BE switch yarn A to E and when you see BE to AB switch yarn E to A.

Row 1: Purl.
Row 2 (inc): Cast on 4 sts for Inside/Under Hind Leg, k4, k2tog, k2 to end. – 7sts
You'll now work 'i-cord' on these 7 Left Hind Leg sts, as follows:

NOTE: Have RS/knit-side facing at all times.

‡ **i-cord row 1**: AB to BE, *RS facing, with the 7 sts on the needle in your right hand, slip the 7 sts off the RH needle onto the LH needle – keeping RS/knit-side facing and the working yarn pulled taut behind the work, knit the 7 sts**.
Then, without turning the work (so RS facing) continue as follows:
i-cord row 2: Repeat as i-cord row 1 from * to **.
i-cord rows 3-5: BE to AB, repeat as i-cord row 1 from * to ** three more times.

NOTE: What you are essentially achieving here is an i-cord tube – the working yarn is pulled across the back to the tube so creating a knitted leg that doesn't need seaming, if you are happy working with double-pointed needles (dpns) then you may find this section quicker!

i-cord row 6 (dec): AB to BE, RS facing, with the 7 sts on the needle in your right hand, slip the 7 sts off the RH needle onto the LH needle – keeping RS/knit-side facing and the working yarn behind the work, k3, skpo, k2. – 6sts
i-cord row 7: *RS facing, with the 6 sts on the needle in your right hand, slip the 6 sts off the RH needle onto the LH needle – keeping RS/knit-side facing and the working yarn behind the work, knit the 6 sts**.
i-cord rows 8-10: BE to AB, repeat as i-cord row 7 from * to ** three more times.

First Leg Joint
i-cord row 11 (dec): AB to BE, RS facing, with the 6 sts on the needle in your right hand, slip the 6 sts off the RH needle onto the LH needle – keeping RS/knit-side facing and the working yarn behind the work, k2tog, three times. – 3sts
i-cord row 12: RS facing, with the 3 sts on the needle in your right hand, slip the 3 sts off the RH needle onto the LH needle – keeping RS/knit-side facing and the working yarn behind the work, knit the 3 sts.
i-cord row 13 (inc): RS facing, with the 3 sts on the needle in your right hand, slip the 3 sts off the RH needle onto the LH needle – keeping RS/knit-side facing and the working yarn behind the work, kfb, k1, kfb. – 5sts
i-cord row 14: BE to AB, *RS facing, with the 5 sts on the needle in your right hand, slip the 5 sts off the RH

" *Once upon a time there was a frog called Mr. Jeremy Fisher; he lived in a little damp house amongst the buttercups at the edge of a pond.* "

needle onto the LH needle – keeping RS/knit-side facing and the working yarn behind the work, knit the 5 sts**.
i-cord rows 15-20: Repeat as i-cord row 14 from * to ** six more times.

Second Leg Joint
i-cord row 21 (dec): RS facing, with the 5 sts on the needle in your right hand, slip the 5 sts off the RH needle onto the LH needle – keeping RS/knit-side facing and the working yarn behind the work, k2tog, k1, k2tog. – 3sts

Add Spat Detail
Cut yarn AB, join yarn C, continue with the spats as follows:
i-cord row 22: *RS facing, with the 3 sts on the needle in your right hand, slip the 3 sts off the RH needle onto the LH needle – keeping RS/knit-side facing and the working yarn behind the work, knit the 3 sts**.
i-cord rows 23-26: Repeat as i-cord row 22 from * to ** four more times. Cut yarn, thread end through all 3 Spat sts, pull up to gather and secure the end. Thread end back through into the i-cord.
Weave in all toe yarn ends and thread them into the i-cord = perfect stuffing!! ‡ ‡

RIGHT HIND LEG
RS of frog facing, beginning near the rear end cast-on/cast-off seam, with yarn AB, pick up and knit 4 sts into knitted stitches, near the back to belly seam and about five rows away from the seam – pick up and knit from C to D.
Row 1 (inc): Cast on 4 sts for Inside/Under Hind Leg, p4, p2tog, p2 to end. – 7sts
Row 2: Knit.
You'll now work 'i-cord' on these 7 Right Hind Leg sts, keeping RS/knit-side facing, continue as for Left Hind Leg from ‡ to ‡ ‡.

JOIN THE HIND LEG SEAM
Refer to Body E, **Fig. 33** in Making Up.

Working on one leg at a time, place the Hind Leg Inside Cast-On Edge against the belly to back seam

and mattress stitch (or over-sew, whichever is easiest) to join the hind leg to the Back.

Flip the leg up and if there is a slight gap where you made your first i-cord row then work a stitch or two to join the gap (sometimes there can be a small ladder appearing after one or two i-cord rows, which is easily neatened with a couple of discreet stitches!).

LEFT FORELEG
Refer to Body E, **Fig. 34** in Making Up.

Left Side of frog facing, begin near the mouth, with yarn AB pick up and knit 3 sts into knitted stitches near the back to belly seam from near the mouth and along three rows away near the colour change at the waistcoat – pick up and knit from A to B.
Row 1: Purl.
Row 2 (inc): Cast on 3 sts for Inside/Under-Foreleg, k3, k2tog, k1 to end. – 5sts
You'll now work 'i-cord' on these 5 Left Foreleg sts, working i-cord similar to Hind Legs as follows:

NOTE: Have RS/knit-side facing at all time.

‡ **i-cord row 1 (inc)**: RS facing, with the 5 sts on the needle in your right hand, slip the 5 sts off the RH needle onto the LH needle – keeping RS/knit-side facing and the working yarn pulled behind the work, k2, kfb, k2. – 6sts

Then, without turning the work so RS facing continue as follows:
i-cord row 2 (dec): Slip the 6 sts off the RH needle onto the LH needle, k2tog, k2, k2tog. – 4sts
i-cord row 3 (inc): Slip the 4 sts off the RH needle onto the LH needle, k1, [kfb] twice, k1. – 6sts
i-cord row 4 (dec): Slip the 6 sts off the RH needle onto the LH needle, k2tog, k2, k2tog. – 4sts

First Leg Joint
i-cord row 5 (dec): Slip the 4 sts off

the RH needle onto the LH needle, k1, k2tog, k1. – 3sts
i-cord row 6: Slip the 3 sts off the RH needle onto the LH needle, knit the 3 sts.
i-cord row 7 (inc): Slip the 3 sts off the RH needle onto the LH needle, kfb, k1, kfb. – 5sts
i-cord row 8: *Slip the 5 sts off the RH needle onto the LH needle, knit the 5 sts**.
i-cord rows 9-13: Repeat as i-cord row 8 from * to ** five more times.
i-cord row 14 (dec): Slip the 5 sts off the RH needle onto the LH needle, k1, k3tog, k1. – 3sts
i-cord row 15: Slip the 3 sts off the RH needle onto the LH needle, knit the 3 sts.
Cut yarn B, continue with yarn A as follows:
Turn the work so that purl-side faces, continue with Webbed Foot as follows:
Row 3 (inc): Pfb, p1, pfb. – 5sts
Row 4 (inc): [K1, kfb] twice, k1. – 7sts

First 'Toe'
P2, turn; k2, turn; p2tog; fasten off. WS facing rejoin yarn A to 5 sts on knitting needle:

Middle 'Toe'
P3, turn; k3, turn; p2tog, p1, turn; k2tog; fasten off.

WS facing rejoin yarn A to 2 sts on knitting needle:

Last 'Toe'
P2, turn; k2, turn; p2tog; fasten off. Weave in all toe yarn ends and thread them into the i-cord. ‡ ‡

RIGHT FORELEG
RS of frog facing, pin a point near the mouth, begin about three rows away from the pin, near the colour change at the waistcoat, with yarn AB pick up and knit 3 sts into knitted stitches, near the back to belly seam along to the pin.

Row 1 (inc): Cast on 3 sts for Inside/Under Foreleg, p3, p2tog, p1 to end. – 5sts

Row 2: Knit.
You'll now work 'i-cord' on these 5 Right Foreleg sts, keeping RS/knit-side facing, continue as for Left Foreleg from ‡ to ‡ ‡.

Join the Foreleg Seam
Working on one leg at a time, place the Foreleg Back Cast-On Edge against the belly to back seam and mattress stitch (or over-sew, whichever is easier) to join the foreleg to the body.

Flip the leg up and if there is a slight gap where you made your first i-cord row then work a stitch or two to join the gap (sometimes there can be a small ladder appearing after one or two i-cord rows, easily neatened with a couple of discreet sts!).

Add Wire (Optional)
Working on one leg at a time, thread a yarn sewing needle with one end of the wire and pass the wire carefully through the i-cord limb. Bend the sharp end of the wire over and using yarn work a few stitches over the end to make it secure – this is not suitable for young children.

LITTLE ADDITION
You may know that in the story of Jeremy Fisher, Jeremy had his fingers bitten by a big fish and hence, tied them in a bandage – If you want the same, simply tie some white yarn around a finger!

MR. JEREMY FISHER'S CLOTHES

OTHER TOOLS AND MATERIALS
- Sharp hand sewing needle and scissors

Coat
- 20 x 20cm (8 x 8in) burgundy or deep-red wool felt, 1mm (¹⁄₃₂in) thick, and sewing thread to match

Neck-Tie & Spats
- Small piece of white wool felt, 1mm (¹⁄₃₂in) thick, for the Neck-Tie at the top of the waistcoat, and sewing thread to match
- Small piece of black wool felt, 1mm (¹⁄₃₂in) thick for the spat soles, and thread to match

Hamper
- Small pieces of beige wool felt, 1mm (¹⁄₃₂in) thick, for the handle and straps, and sewing thread to match

- Small pieces of wool felt, 1mm (¹⁄₃₂in) thick in pink and green for the fish, and sewing thread to match
- Small amount yarn A: DROPS Flora, shade 07 Beige
- Embroidery thread for fish details and yellow buckles
- Stitch markers or pins

TENSION
13 stitches and 16 rows over 5cm (2in) in stocking stitch

NEEDLES
3.5mm (US 4) knitting needles

COAT

Trace Jeremy's Coat (see Templates) and cut one Front/Back on the fold and two Sleeves, all from burgundy or deep-red felt.

1. Working on one sleeve at a time, fold and match the Underarm Seam edges together.
2. Either hand- or machine-sew along the underarm seam to join the long ends together.
3. Turn out to the RS.
4. Push the sleeve into the armhole. The underarm seam should lie at the bottom of the armhole.
5. Carefully hand work small back stitches to join the edges of the sleeve to the armhole allowing for roughly a 3mm (⅛in) seam. Repeat for the other sleeve.
6. Turn the coat collar down.

NECK-TIE

Trace Jeremy's Neck-Tie (see Templates) and cut one from white felt.

1. Fit the cut shape around the frog's neck and work small, neat over-sew stitches joining it to the top of the knitted waistcoat and behind the neck.
2. Work a few straight stitches over the front of the bow tie to create the effect of the knot.

SPATS

Trace Jeremy's Spats (see Templates) and cut two Spat Soles from black felt.

1. Join the each spat heel with a stitch. Turn out to RS.
2. Working on one hind leg at a time, fit the cut spat sole shape around the knitted spat/white of the frog's hind legs and work small, neat over-sew stitches, joining around the edge of the white knitted spat. Then join along the bottom at the sole, so that the heel seam lies at the back.

HAMPER

Trace Jeremy's Fishing Hamper (see Templates) and cut two Straps and one Handle from beige felt, and four or six Fish Halves (for two or three fish) from pink and green felt.

To create the knitted part

With yarn A, cast on 12 sts.
Work moss stitch as follows:
Row 1: *K1, p1**, repeat from * to ** across.
Row 2: *P1, k1**, repeat from * to ** across.
Repeat last 2 rows until the knitting measures 8cm (3in) long.
Cast off.

Join the Hamper Seam

1. Measure 2cm (¾in) down from the cast-off edge, and mark each end with a pair of markers or pins.

2. Fold the cast-on edge up to the markers/pins and, working on one side at a time, work mattress stitch to join the seam from the fold to the markers/pins.
3. Remove the markers/pins.

Assemble the Hamper

1. Fold the flap over the hamper and sew the straps on (refer to the photographs for placement). Add a couple of stitches in yellow thread for buckles.
2. Join the handle to the tops of the seam at either side of the hamper.
3. Join the two sides of the fish, stuff with a little stuffing or yarn snippings before closing the seam. Embroider small details onto the fish with single strands of embroidery thread.
4. Sew the little felt fish to the hamper, over-hanging at one side of the hamper.

JEMIMA PUDDLE-DUCK™

JEMIMA was a real duck belonging to Beatrix Potter. All Jemima wants to do is lay her eggs in peace. At last she flies off and finds the perfect place. Little does the silly duck realise that the charming gentleman who has lent her his woodshed is busily planning a delicious meal of . . . roast duck!

FINISHED SIZE
Approx. 27cm (10½in) tall from feet to top of head

YARN
You will need no more than one ball of each of:
A: Small amount DROPS Alpaca shade 2923
Goldenrod for Bill and Feet
B: DROPS Alpaca shade 1101 White
C: DROPS Kid-Silk shade 01 Off White
D: For the facial features a few doubled-up lengths of
DROPS Kid-Silk shade 15 Dark Brown
Unless otherwise stated, double or triple strands of
yarn are used together throughout this pattern. The
exact combinations of yarn to be used are indicated by
multiple letters (see How to Use This Book).

TENSION
11 stitches and 15 rows over 5cm (2in)

NEEDLES
• 3.75mm (US 5) knitting needles for head and body
• 3.5mm (US 4) knitting needles for the bill and feet

OTHER TOOLS AND MATERIALS
• 1 large safety pin
• 24 coloured locking stitch markers (see How to Use
  This Book: Stitch Markers)
• 2 x 9mm (⅜in) light-brown toy safety eyes
• Toy stuffing or yarn/fabric scraps
• Tapestry or darning needle

PATTERN NOTES
• Use cable cast-on unless otherwise stated
• General knitting abbreviations can be found in
  How to Use This Book

BILL
Beginning at the Front of the Bill with
yarn AA (use other end of yarn ball
A) and smaller 3.5mm needles cast
on 8 sts.
Rows 1-3: Beginning with a purl row,
work three rows stocking stitch.
Row 4 (inc): Kfb, k6, kfb. – 10sts
Row 5: Purl.
Row 6 (inc): K4, [kfb] twice, k4.
– 12sts
Row 7: Purl.
Row 8 (inc): K5, [kfb] twice, k5.
– 14sts
Row 9: Purl.

Work short rows (see Techniques) for
Beak Edge Side 1:
Short row 1: K5, W+Tk.
Short row 2: P5.

Row 10: Knit all 14 Beak sts.

Work short rows for Beak Edge
Side 2:
Short row 1: P5, W+Tp.
Short row 2: K5.

Cut yarn AA, join on yarn BCC (use
other end of yarn ball C), switching
to larger 3.75mm needles continue
as follows:

HEAD
Row 1: Purl, PM on first and last stitch
for Left and Right Neck Markers.
Row 2 (inc): K4, kfb, k4, kfb, k4. – 16sts
Row 3: Purl.
Row 4 (inc): K5, kfb, k4, kfb, k5. – 18sts
Row 5: Purl.
Row 6 (inc): K6, kfb, k4, kfb, k6. – 20sts
Row 7: Purl.
Row 8 (inc): K7, kfb, k4, kfb, k7. – 22sts
Row 9 Purl.

Row 10 (inc): K8, kfb, k4, kfb, k8.
– 24sts
Row 11: Purl.
Row 12 (inc): K9, kfb, k4, kfb, k9.
– 26sts
Row 13: Purl.
Row 14 (dec): K9, skpo, k4, k2tog, k9.
– 24sts
Row 15 (dec): P2tog, purl to last 2 sts,
p2tog. – 22sts
Row 16 (dec): K7, skpo, k4, k2tog, k7.
– 20sts
Row 17 (dec): P2tog, purl to last 2 sts,
p2tog. – 18sts

Divide the Head Back to Create
Head Back Seam
Row 18 (dec): Cast off 6 sts for Head
Back Seam, Left-Side, knit next 5 sts,
cast off last 6 sts for Head Back Seam,
Right-Side. – 6sts

Head Back
WS facing rejoin yarn BCC to 6 sts
for Head Back, continue with larger
3.75mm needles as follows:
Row 19: Purl.
Row 20 (inc): Kfb, k4, kfb. – 8sts

Rows 21-23: Beginning with a purl row, work three rows stocking stitch.
Row 24 (inc): Kfb, k6, kfb. – 10sts
Rows 25-27: Beginning with a purl row, work three rows stocking stitch. Cut yarn, place all 10 Head Back sts onto a large safety pin for now.

NECK AND BACK
Refer to Body A, **Fig. 2** in Making Up.

Join Left Side of Head
With yarn BCC and larger 3.75mm needles, begin at duck's Left Neck Marker, RS facing pick up and knit 6 sts evenly along row ends to the left-side corner of Head Back Seam Cast-Off Edge; slip all 10 Head Back sts from the safety pin onto a knitting needle then from corner of Head Back Cast-Off Edge knit across all 10 Head Back sts.

Join Right Side of Head
Continue to pick up across the right side of the head, all onto the same needle as follows:
Pick up and knit 6 sts evenly along row ends from right corner of Head Back Seam Cast-Off Edge to Right Neck Marker – 22sts – pick up and knit from A to B; knit across from C to D; pick up and knit from E to F.
Row 1: Purl all 22 sts.

BODY
Neck
Row 2 (inc): K6, kfb, k8, kfb, k6 to end of row. – 24sts
Row 3: Purl.
Row 4 (dec): K4, skpo, k12, k2tog, k4 to end of row. – 22sts
Row 5: Purl.
Row 6: Kfb, k3, skpo, k10, k2tog, k3, kfb.
Row 7: Purl.
Row 8: Kfb, k4, skpo, k8, k2tog, k4, kfb.
Row 9: Purl.
Row 10: Kfb, k5, skpo, k6, k2tog, k5, kfb.
Row 11: Purl.
Row 12: Kfb, k6, skpo, k4, k2tog, k6, kfb.
Rows 13-15: Beginning with a purl row, work three rows stocking stitch.
Row 16 (inc): K8, kfb, k4, kfb, k8 to end of row. – 24sts
Row 17: Purl.
Row 18 (inc): K9, kfb, k4, kfb, k9 to

end of row, PM at on first and last stitch for Left and Right Neck Base Markers. – 26sts
Row 19: Purl.
Row 20 (inc): K1, kfb, k8, kfb, k4, kfb, k8, kfb, k1. – 30sts
Row 21: Purl.
Row 22 (inc): [K3, kfb] twice, k3, skpo, k4, k2tog, k3, [kfb, k3] twice. – 32sts
Row 23: Purl.
Row 24 (inc): [K3, kfb] twice, k4, skpo, k4, k2tog, k4, [kfb, k3] twice. – 34sts
Row 25: Purl.
Row 26 (inc): [K3, kfb] twice, k18, [kfb, k3] twice. – 38sts
Row 27: Purl.
Row 28 (inc): [K3, kfb] twice, k22, [kfb, k3] twice. – 42sts
Row 29: Purl.

Work short rows for Neck Base:
Short row 1: K32, W+Tk.
Short row 2: P22, W+Tp.
Short row 3: K21, W+Tk.
Short row 4: P20, W+Tp.
Short row 5: K19, W+Tk.
Short row 6: P18, W+Tp.
Short row 7: K17, W+Tk.
Short row 8: P16, W+Tp.
Short row 9: K29 to end of row.

Row 30: Purl.

Work short rows for Breast Side 1:
Short row 1: K13, W+Tk.
Short row 2: P13.
Short row 3: K12, W+Tk.
Short row 4: P12.
Short row 5: K11, W+Tk.
Short row 6: P11.
Short row 7: K10, W+Tk.
Short row 8: P10.
Short row 9: K9, W+Tk.
Short row 10: P9.
Short row 11: K8, W+Tk.
Short row 12: P8.
Short row 13: K7, W+Tk.
Short row 14: P7.
Short row 15: K6, W+Tk.
Short row 16: P6.
Short row 17: K5, W+Tk.
Short row 18: P5.
Short row 19: K4, W+Tk.
Short row 20: P4.

Row 31: Knit.

Work short rows for Breast Side 2:
Short row 1: P13, W+Tp.
Short row 2: K13.
Short row 3: P12, W+Tp.

"Madam, have you lost your way?" said he.
He had a long bushy tail which he was sitting
upon, as the stump was somewhat damp.

Short row 4: K12.
Short row 5: P11, W+Tp.
Short row 6: K11.
Short row 7: P10, W+Tp.
Short row 8: K10.
Short row 9: P9, W+Tp.
Short row 10: K9.
Short row 11: P8, W+Tp.
Short row 12: K8.
Short row 13: P7, W+Tp.
Short row 14: K7.
Short row 15: P6, W+Tp.
Short row 16: K6.
Short row 17: P5, W+Tp.
Short row 18: K5.
Short row 19: P4, W+Tp.
Short row 20: K4.

Row 32: Purl.

Work short rows for the Back:
Short row 1: K27, W+Tk.
Short row 2: P12, W+Tp.
Short row 3: K11, W+Tk.
Short row 4: P10, W+Tp.

Short row 5: K9, W+Tk.
Short row 6: P8, W+Tp.
Short row 7: K25 to end of row.

Row 33: Purl, PM on first and last stitch for Left and Right Front Markers.
Row 34: K2tog, k16, kfb, k4, kfb, k16, k2tog.
Row 35: Purl.
Rows 36-43: Repeat last two rows four times.
Rows 44-47: Beginning with a knit row, work four rows stocking stitch, PM on first and last stitch of last row for Left and Right Foot Markers.

Separate Wings from Body
The wings are knitted and when joined together create folded wings that look as though they are tucked inside at the centre of the Back and in between the left and right sides of the body.
Row 48 (dec): K18, k2tog, k1, turn (flip

work over so purl-side faces).
Row 49: P10, turn (flip work over so knit-side faces) to work on Left Wing only as follows (leave the Body Sides sts and Right Wing sts on the needle as you work in between them).

Left Wing
Row 1 (dec): K2tog, k8, turn. – 9sts for Left Wing
Row 2: P9, turn.
Row 3 (dec): K2tog, k7, turn. – 8sts
Row 4: P8, turn.
Row 5 (dec): K2tog, k6, turn. – 7sts
Row 6: P7, turn.
Row 7 (dec): K2tog, k5, turn. – 6sts
Row 8: P6, turn.
Row 9 (dec): K2tog, k4, turn. – 5sts
Row 10: P5, turn.
Row 11 (dec): K2tog, k3, turn. – 4sts
Row 12: P4, turn.
Row 13 (dec): K2tog, k2, turn. – 3sts
Row 14 (dec): P3tog. – 1st
Fasten off for Left Wing Point.

RS facing, rejoin yarn BCC to 21 sts on your LH needle.
Row 48 (dec): K1, k2tog, k8, turn.
Row 49: P10, turn (flip work over so knit-side faces) to work on Right Wing only as follows (leave the Left and Right Sides of the Body sts on the needle as you work in between them) as follows:

Right Wing
Row 1 (dec): K8, k2tog, turn. – 9sts for Right Wing
Row 2: P9, turn.
Row 3 (dec): K7, k2tog, turn. – 8sts
Row 4: P8, turn.
Row 5 (dec): K6, k2tog, turn. – 7sts
Row 6: P7, turn.
Row 7 (dec): K5, k2tog, turn. – 6sts
Row 8: P6, turn.
Row 9 (dec): K4, k2tog, turn. – 5sts
Row 10: P5, turn.
Row 11 (dec): K3, k2tog, turn. – 4sts
Row 12: P4, turn.
Row 13 (dec): K2, k2tog, turn. – 3sts
Row 14 (dec): P3tog. – 1st
Fasten off for Right Wing Point.

Join Wings Seam
1. RS together match the Left and Right Wing Points together and back

stitch to join the two straight edges at the inside of the wings from the wing points up to the split.
2. Turn out to RS.

Body Sides
Now the wings have been sewn you can return to completing each side of the body starting with the Right Side as follows:

Right Side
RS facing, rejoin yarn BCC to 10 sts on your LH needle ready to work Right Side as follows:
Row 1 (inc): K9, kfb. – 11sts for Right Side
Row 2: Purl.
Row 3 (inc): K10, kfb. – 12sts
Rows 4-14: Beginning with a purl row, work 11 rows stocking stitch.
Row 15 (inc): Kfb, knit to end of row. – 13sts
Row 16: Purl.
Rows 17-20 (inc): Repeat last two rows twice, PM on last stitch of last purl row for Right Wing Tip Marker. – 15sts
Cut yarn but leave all 15 Right Side sts on the knitting needle for now.

Left Side
WS facing, rejoin yarn BCC to 10 sts on your LH needle ready to work Left Side as follows:
Row 1 (inc): P9, pfb. – 11sts for Left Side
Row 2: Knit.
Row 3 (inc): P10, pfb. – 12sts
Rows 4-13: Beginning with a knit row, work ten rows stocking stitch.
Row 14 (inc): K11, kfb. – 13sts
Row 15: Purl.
Row 16 (inc): K12, kfb. – 14sts
Row 17: Purl.
Row 18 (inc): K13, kfb. – 15sts
Row 19: Purl, PM on first st for Left Wing Tip Marker.
Do not cut yarn.

Join Left Side and Right Side
Row 1 (RS): Knit across all 15 Left Side sts; knit across all 15 Right Side sts. – 30sts
Row 2: Purl.

Work short rows for Tail:
Short row 1: K24, W+Tk.
Short row 2: P18, W+Tp.
Short row 3: K17, W+Tk.
Short row 4: P16, W+Tp.
Short row 5: K15, W+Tk.
Short row 6: P14, W+Tp.
Short row 7: K13, W+Tk.
Short row 8: P12, W+Tp.
Short row 9: K11, W+Tk.
Short row 10: P10, W+Tp.
Short row 11: K9, W+Tk.
Short row 12: P8, W+Tp.
Short row 13: K19 to end of row.

Cast off all 30 sts for Tail purl-wise, PM on first cast-off st and last cast-off st for Left and Right Tail Seam Markers.

Join Tail Seam
WS together fold the Tail Cast-Off Edge in half, matching the Left and Right Tail Seam Markers together, and mattress stitch to join the halves of the cast-off edge from markers to the fold.
Remove one of the Tail Seam Markers.

Join Wing Outer Edges to the Body Sides
Refer to Body D, **Fig. 26** in Making Up.

1. WS together match the end of the Wing Seam (at the Wing Points) to the Wing Tip Markers.
2. Working on one side at a time, mattress stitch along the wing outer edge row ends to the row ends from the body side (left wing outer edge to left body side for example). Join Left Side, dotted line A to dotted line B; Right side, dotted line C to dotted line D.
Remove the Wing Tip Markers.
3. Thread all your yarn endings into the WS of the knitting and tuck them into the tail.

Abdomen
WS of knitting/inside of duck's Back facing, and Tail Seam towards your left, beginning at the duck's Left Breast Marker (on your right) with the larger 3.75mm needles and yarn BCC, pick up and knit 12 sts evenly along Left-Side row ends to the Tail

Seam Marker; from the Tail Seam pick up and knit 12 sts evenly along Right-Side row ends to the duck's Right Breast Marker – 24sts
Remove remaining Tail Seam Marker.
Row 1: Purl.
Row 2 (dec): K9, skpo, k2, k2tog, k9. – 22sts
Row 3: Purl.
Row 4 (dec): K8, skpo, k2, k2tog, k8. – 20sts
Row 5: Purl.
Row 6 (dec): K7, skpo, k2, k2tog, k7. – 18sts
Row 7: Purl, PM on first and last stitches for Left and Right Abdomen Markers.

Work short rows for Abdomen:
Short row 1: K17, W+Tk.
Short row 2: P16, W+Tp.
Short row 3: K15, W+Tk.
Short row 4: P14, W+Tp.
Short row 5: K13, W+Tk.
Short row 6: P12, W+Tp.
Short row 7: K11, W+Tk.
Short row 8: P10, W+Tp.
Short row 9: K9, W+Tk.
Short row 10: P8, W+Tp.
Short row 11: K7, W+Tk.
Short row 12: P6, W+Tp.
Short row 13: K12 to end of row.

Rows 8-18: Beginning with a purl row, work 11 rows stocking stitch for Front, PM on first and last stitch of last purl row for Left and Right Lower Front Markers.
Row 19 (dec): K6, skpo, k2, k2tog, k6. – 16sts
Row 20: Purl.
Row 21 (dec): K5, skpo, k2, k2tog, k5. – 14sts
Row 22: Purl.
Row 23 (dec): K4, skpo, k2, k2tog, k4. – 12sts
Row 24: Purl.
Row 25 (dec): K3, skpo, k2, k2tog, k3. – 10sts
Row 26: Purl.
Row 27 (dec): K3, skpo, k2tog, k3. – 8sts
Row 28: Purl.
Row 29 (dec): K3, k2tog, k3. – 7sts
Rows 30-40: Beginning with a purl row, work 11 rows stocking stitch.
Row 41 (dec): K2tog, k3, k2tog. – 5sts
Rows 42-50: Beginning with a purl row, work nine rows stocking stitch, PM on first and last stitch of last purl row for Left and Right Lower Front Markers.
Rows 51-62: Beginning with a knit row, work 12 rows stocking stitch for Neck Front.
Row 63 (dec): K2tog, k1, k2tog. – 3sts
Cast-off purl-wise for Lower Bill Seam.

Join Neck to Lower Neck
Working on one side at a time, WS together match Neck Base Marker to Lower Neck Base Marker, ease together and work mattress stitch to join Neck Front Seam so joining neck and neck front row ends from Neck Marker to Neck Base/Lower Neck Base Markers.
Remove Neck and Lower Neck Base Markers.

Join Back to Front
Working on one side at a time, WS together match Front to Lower Front Markers, ease seam together and work mattress stitch to join Back and Front Seam so joining Back to Breast and Front along rows ends from Front to Lower Front markers to Neck Base markers, it's quite a long seam so you may wish to pin together first.
Remove Neck Base and Lower Front Markers.
At this stage you can add stuffing into the head, neck and breast.
Add a little at a time using the stuffing to pad out the shaping at the head and breast, making sure the head isn't overly stuffed.

Join Bill Seam
Refer to Body D, **Fig. 25** in Making Up.

WS together join the bill row ends all along from bill seam to the colour change at the head.

Join Bill to Neck
WS together, find the centre of the Lower Bill Seam Cast-Off Edge and match it to the bottom of the Bill Seam that you've just sewn. Work a couple of stitches to hold in place then working on each side of the cast-off edge match the corner of the cast-off edge to the Neck Marker and mattress stitch the tiny seams either side of the lower bill seam cast-off edge. Carefully and neatly work mattress stitch or whip stitch to join the flattened end of the bill across the tip.
The bill is stuffed but only a little; I used the yarn endings.

Add Eyes
Working on one eye at a time, WS together push the toy eye into the side of the head, from front/knit-side to back/purl-side, referring to the photographs for placement and making sure you are happy with the position before securing it firmly in place with the plastic or metal backing.

Join Head Back Seam
Refer to Body A, **Fig. 13** in Making Up.

WS together, working on one side at a time, work mattress stitch to join the Head Back Seam Cast-Off Edge to the row ends at the back of the head, at the same time adding a little stuffing to pad out the head back.

Create Indents for Head Shaping
Refer to Body D, **Fig. 27** in Making Up.

Thread up some yarn C and secure one end.
Pass the tip of the sewing needle into one side of the head just to the side of the eye.

NOTE: If you're planning to embroider the eyes then insert the sewing needle where you want the eyes to be, work this shaping technique then, with black yarn or thread, work French Knots inside the indents.

Pass the thread through the head to emerge to the side of the other eye on the other side of the head. Pass the thread back in, near where you have you have just pulled through to emerge back where you started. Gently tug the yarn to create indents at each side. When you are happy with the shapes then secure the thread – in at A; out at B; in at C; out at A.

BILL DETAIL
Refer to Body D, **Fig. 28** in Making Up.

With a doubled length yarn A, secure the end then embroider two 'V's

either side of the bill over already knitted stitches to duplicate them so to add detail to the bill.

With a single strand of yarn D embroider three or four of straight stitches to resemble 'nostrils' on either side of the bill.

To flatten the bill a little press the bill with a warm iron.

WEBBED FEET

Refer to Body D, **Fig. 29** in Making Up.

The feet are picked up and knitted near where the Back joins the Abdomen as follows:

Left Foot

RS and duck's back towards you, beginning at duck's Left Foot Marker, with yarn AA and smaller 3.5mm knitting needles, pick up and knit 6 sts along abdomen row ends to duck's Left Abdomen Marker.

*Foot Sole

Row 1: Purl.
Row 2: Knit.
Row 3 (inc): P1, k2, m1, k2, p1. – 7sts
Row 4 (inc): Kfb, p2, k1, p2, kfb. – 9sts
Row 5: P1, k3, p1, k3, p1.
Row 6 (inc): Kfb, p3, k1, p3, kfb. – 11sts
Row 7: P1, k4, p1, k4, p1.
Row 8 (inc): Kfb, p4, k1, p4, kfb. – 13sts
Row 9: P1, k5, p1, k5, p1, PM at each end of last row for Foot Fold Markers.

Foot Upper

Row 10 (dec): K2tog, p4, k1, p4, k2tog. – 11sts
Row 11: P1, k4, p1, k4, p1.
Row 12 (dec): K2tog, p3, k1, p3, k2tog. – 9sts
Row 13: P1, k3, p1, k3, p1.
Row 14 (dec): K2tog, p1, k3tog, p1, k2tog. – 5sts
Row 15: [P1, k1] twice, p1.
Row 16 (dec): K1, k2tog, p1, k1. – 4sts
Row 17: Purl.
Row 18 (inc): Kfb, k2, kfb. – 6sts
Cast off all 6 sts purl-wise for Foot Front.**

Right Foot

RS and duck's tail towards you, beginning at duck's Right Abdomen Marker, with yarn AA and smaller 3.5mm knitting needles, pick up and knit 6 sts along abdomen row ends to duck's Left Foot Marker.

Work as Left Foot Sole and Upper from * to **.

Join Foot Seam

Working on one foot at a time, WS facing, fold the foot at the Foot Fold Markers so that the side with most of the knitting is WS. Join along the two diagonal edges joining Foot Sole to Foot Upper, leaving the cast-off edge unsewn for now.

Remove Foot, Foot Fold and Abdomen Markers.

The feet aren't stuffed but they are lightly pressed with an iron to flatten them out a little more.

Join Abdomen Seam

Stuff the remainder of the body and tail (and a little into the leg part of the foot – the two rows stocking stitch) before closing these last two seams. With WS together, working on one side at a time, work mattress stitch to join the seam that joins the Back to the Abdomen from the Lower Front Marker to the top of the foot. Ease the rows ends from the Back and Abdomen around the top of the foot so joining the foot cast-off edge to the abdomen and back.

I then sewed the two inner corners of the foot to either side of the abdomen to stop the feet from flailing outwards. Remove Lower Front Markers.

NOTE: To make Jemima sit, gently bend her back a little so that she sits over her abdomen with her tail as counter-balance and with her neck slightly leaning backwards.

Bonnet

You will need no more than one ball of each of:
- A: DROPS Alpaca shade 2917 Turquoise
- B: DROPS Alpaca shade 6205 Light Blue

Shawl

You will need no more than one ball of each of:
- A: DROPS Kid-Silk shade 09 Light Lavender

Unless otherwise stated, double strands of yarn are used together throughout this pattern. The exact combinations of yarn to be used are indicated by multiple letters (see How to Use this Book).

PATTERN NOTES
- Use cable cast-on unless otherwise stated
- General knitting abbreviations can be found in How to Use This Book

TENSION

Bonnet: 13 stitches and 16 rows over 5cm (2in)
Shawl: 13 stitches and 16 rows over 5cm (2in)

NEEDLES

Bonnet: 3.5mm (US 4) knitting needles
Shawl: 3.75mm (US 5) knitting needles

OTHER TOOLS AND MATERIALS
- Tapestry or darning needle and embroidery needle (with a largish eye)
- Scissors

Bonnet
- 40cm (15¾in) baby blue satin ribbon, 10mm (½in) wide

BONNET

With yarn AB cast on 49sts, PM on first and last cast-on st for Bonnet Trim.

Rows 1-3: Beginning with a purl row, work three rows stocking stitch.
Row 4 (dec): [K5, k2tog] seven times. – 42sts
Row 5: Purl.
Row 6 (dec): [K4, k2tog] seven times. – 35sts
Row 7: Purl.
Row 8 (dec): [K3, k2tog] seven times. – 28sts
Row 9: Purl.

Row 10 (dec): [K2, k2tog] seven times. – 21sts
Rows 11-15: Beginning with a purl row, work five rows stocking stitch.
Row 16: Purl on RS (to mark where the back of the bonnet begins).
Row 17 (dec): [P1, p2tog] seven times. – 14sts
Row 18: Knit.
Row 19 (dec): [K2tog] seven times. – 7sts
Row 20: Knit.
Row 21 (dec): P2tog, p3, p2tog. – 5sts
Cast off all 5 sts for Bonnet Back. Weave in all tail ends.

Bonnet Trim

With yarn AB RS and Bonnet back facing, begin at bonnet's Left Bonnet Trim Marker (on your right), pick up and knit 11 sts evenly along row ends to near the centre of Bonnet Back Cast-Off Edge; pick up one stitch at the centre; from near-centre pick up and knit 11 sts evenly along row ends to bonnet's Right Bonnet Trim Marker. – 23sts
Row 1: Purl.
Row 2 (inc): [K3, kfb] five times, k3. – 28sts
Row 3: Purl.
Row 4 (inc): [K4, kfb] five times, k3. – 33sts

Row 5: Purl.
Cast off all 33 sts for Bonnet Trim.

Block the Bonnet

To prevent the edges curling over, dampen the knitting then pin down the cast-on and the cast-off edges flat onto a few folded layers of cloth or a thick towel, leave to dry.

Ribbon Trimming

1. Find the centre of the ribbon.
2. Measure 10cm (4in) either side of the centre and either make a small mark or place a pin at these points.
3. With yarn B thread-up the embroidery sewing needle and work a running stitch in and out along the centre of the ribbon from mark/pin to mark/pin.
4. Gather up the ribbon until it becomes the same width as the Bonnet Trim.
5. Work a few stitches to join the gathered ribbon onto the bonnet trim – you should have two lengths of 10cm (4in) either side of the bonnet trim for tying the bonnet beneath Jemima's chin.
6. I sewed the back of the bonnet to the back of the head with a few small, discreet stitches.

SHAWL

The shawl is created by making a single increase into the centre of each stocking stitch row as follows:

With yarn AA (use other end of yarn ball A) cast on 2 sts for Shawl Corner.

Row 1 (inc): Kfb, k1. – 3sts
Row 2 (inc): P1, pfb, p1. – 4sts
Row 3 (inc): K2, m1, k2. – 5sts
Row 4 (inc): P2, pfb, p2. – 6sts
Row 5 (inc): K3, m1, k3. – 7sts
Row 6 (inc): P3, pfb, p3. – 8sts
Row 7 (inc): K4, m1, k4. – 9sts
Row 8 (inc): P4, pfb, p4. – 10sts
Row 9 (inc): K5, m1, k5. – 11sts
Row 10 (inc): P5, pfb, p5. – 12sts
Row 11 (inc): K6, m1, k5. – 13sts

Continue to work these pairs of increases over two rows of stocking stitch until your last pair of increases reads: P30, pfb, p30. – 62sts; K31, m1, k31. – 63sts

Cast off all 63 sts for Shawl Edge. Weave in all the tail ends.

Tassels

You're going to make nine tassels so cut nine lengths (about 20cm/8in) of yarn A.

1. Wrap the yarn around two fingers held together about ten times.

2. Slip the wound yarn carefully off your fingers.

3. Take one of the cut lengths and tie it securely around the wound bundle, approx. 6mm (¼in) from the top/near one of the loops created when you wound around your fingers – this will become the knotted top loop of the tassel, the looped end which you will sew onto the edge of the shawl.

4. At the other end trim the tassel. Each tassel you make should be the same length.

5. Make nine tassels and sew in place evenly spaced along the two row ends lengths of the shawl – four each side. Sew the ninth tassel at the Shawl Corner.

Add Pattern Detail

Thread-up the embroidery needle with yarn B, securing the end with a knot. Work double or triple Lazy Daisy motifs randomly over the shawl.

THE TAILOR OF GLOUCESTER™

THIS tale tells the story of a poor tailor trying to survive in his freezing workshop over a hard winter. He has a terribly important commission to complete before Christmas Day but is ill and tired. Luckily some very kind mice live in the dresser and set about helping the tailor with his work.

FINISHED SIZE
Approx. 9.5cm (3¾in) tall from feet to tip of ears

YARN
You will need no more than one ball of each of:
A: DROPS Alpaca shade 0618 Light Beige Mix
B: DROPS Kid-Silk shade 42 Almond
C: DROPS Kid-Silk shade 35 Chocolate
D: DROPS Nord shade 07 Light Beige Mix
E: DROPS Kid-Silk shade 01 Off White
F: DROPS Kid-Silk shade 40 Pink Pearl
PLUS: Length mid-tone pink lace-weight yarn for inner ear detail, I used DROPS Kid-Silk shade 04 Old Pink; and length dark brown lace-weight yarn for the mouth/nose detail, I used DROPS Kid-Silk shade 15 Dark Brown
Unless otherwise stated, double and triple strands of yarn are used together throughout this pattern. The exact combinations of yarn to be used are indicated by multiple letters (see How to Use This Book).

TENSION
15 stitches and 17.5 rows over 5cm (2in)

NEEDLES
3.25mm (US 3) knitting needles

OTHER TOOLS AND MATERIALS
- 1 small safety pin
- 16 coloured locking stitch markers (see How to Use This Book: Stitch Markers)
- 2 x 6mm (¼in) black toy safety eyes
- Toy stuffing or yarn/fabric scraps
- Tapestry or darning needle
- Optional Extra: Spectacles; the ones pictured measure 2.5cm (1in) across the front and 2.5cm (1in) in length. The height is 1cm (⅜in)

PATTERN NOTES
- Use cable cast-on unless otherwise stated
- General knitting abbreviations can be found in How to Use This Book

HEAD
Beginning at the Nose.
With yarn A cast on 5 sts for Nose Seam.
Row 1: Purl.
Row 2 (inc): K1, kfb, k1, kfb, k1. – 7sts
Row 3: Purl.
Row 4 (inc): Kfb, k1, kfb, k1, kfb, k1, kfb. – 11sts
Row 5: Purl, PM on first and last stitch of row for Left and Right Neck Markers.
Join yarn B, continue with yarn AB as follows:
Row 6 (inc): Kfb, k3, kfb, k1, kfb, k3, kfb. – 15sts
Row 7: Purl.
Row 8 (inc): K5, kfb, k3, kfb, k5 to end of row. – 17sts
Row 9: Purl.
Row 10 (inc): K5, kfb, k5, kfb, k5 to end. – 19sts

Row 11: Purl.
Row 12 (dec): K6, PM on last stitch (6th stitch) for Left Ear Position Marker, skpo, k3, k2tog, k1, PM on last stitch (1st stitch) for Right Ear Position Marker, k5 to end of row. – 17sts
Row 13: Purl.
Row 14 (dec): K5, skpo, k3, k2tog, k5 to end of row. – 15sts

Divide the Head Back to Create Head Back Seam
Row 15 (dec): Cast off 4 sts for Head Back Seam (Right-Side) purl-wise, purl next 6sts, cast off last 4 sts for Head Back Seam (Left-Side) purl-wise. – 7sts

Head Back
RS facing rejoin yarn AB to 7 sts for Head Back, continue as follows:
Rows 16-17: Beginning with a knit

row, work two rows stocking stitch.
Row 18 (dec): Skpo, k3, k2tog. – 5sts
Row 19: Purl.
Cut yarn, slip all 5 sts for Head Back onto a safety pin for now.

NECK AND BACK
Refer to Body A, **Fig. 2** in Making Up.

Join Left Side of Head
With yarn AB begin at mouse's Left Neck Marker, RS facing pick up and knit 4 sts evenly along row ends to the left-side corner of Head Back Seam Cast-Off Edge; slip all 5 Head Back sts from the safety pin onto a knitting needle then from corner of Head Back Cast-Off Edge dec) skpo, k1, k2tog.

Join Right Side of Head
Continue to pick up across the right side of the head, all onto the same needle as follows:
Pick up and knit 4 sts evenly along row ends from right corner of Head Back Seam Cast-Off Edge to Right Neck Marker – 11sts – pick up and knit from A to B; knit across from C to D; pick up and knit from E to F.
Row 1: Purl all 11 sts.

BODY
Back
Row 2 (inc): Kfb, k3, kfb, k1, kfb, k3, kfb. – 15sts
Row 3: Purl.
Row 4 (inc): Kfb, k4, PM on last knitted stitch for Left Foreleg Placement, knit next 6 sts, PM on last knitted stitch for Right Foreleg Placement, k3, kfb. – 17sts
Row 5: Purl.
Row 6: Kfb, k5, skpo, k1, k2tog, k5 to last st, kfb.
Row 7: Purl.
Row 8 (inc): K6, kfb, k3, kfb, k6 to end of row. – 19sts
Row 9: Purl.
Row 10 (inc): Kfb, k6, kfb, k3, kfb, k6, kfb. – 23sts
Row 11: Purl, PM on first and last stitch of row for Left and Right Thigh Markers.
Cut yarn B, join yarn C, continue to work with yarn AC as follows:

And out from under tea-cups and from under bowls and basins, stepped other and more little mice who hopped away down off the dresser and under the wainscot.

Hind Legs
Work short rows (see Techniques) for Left Hind Leg:
Short row 1 (inc): Cast on 4 sts, k5, W+Tk.
Short row 2: P2, W+Tp.
Short row 3: K3, W+Tk.
Short row 4: P4, W+Tp.
Short row 5: K5, W+Tk.
Short row 6: P6, W+Tp.
Short row 7 (dec): K6, skpo, k18 to end of row. – 26sts

Work short rows for Right Hind Leg:
Short row 1 (inc): Cast on 4 sts, p5, W+Tp.
Short row 2: K2, W+Tk.
Short row 3: P3, W+Tp.
Short row 4: K4, W+Tk.
Short row 5: P5, W+Tp.
Short row 6: K6, W+Tk.
Short row 7 (dec): P6, p2tog, p21 to end of row. – 29sts

Row 12 (dec): K2tog, k6, skpo, k9, k2tog, k6, k2tog. – 25sts

Row 13: Purl.
Row 14 (dec): K2tog, k5, skpo, k7, k2tog, k5, k2tog. – 21sts

Lower Back
Work short rows for Lower Back:
Short row 1: P14, W+Tp.
Short row 2: K7, W+Tk.
Short row 3: P6, W+Tp.
Short row 4: K5, W+Tk.
Short row 5: P4, W+Tp.
Short row 6: K3, W+Tk.
Short row 7 (dec): Cast off next 3 sts for Tail Space, purl next 8 to end of row (you should end up with 9 sts either side of the cast-off edge).

Row 15 (dec): K2tog, k6, k2tog, k6, k2tog. – 15sts
Row 16: Purl, PM on first and last stitch of row for Left and Right Belly Markers.
Row 17 (dec): Cast off 4 sts for Left Paw Edge, knit next 6 sts, cast off last 4 sts for Right Paw Edge. – 7sts

"But that does not hinder the little brown mice; they run in and out without any keys through all the old houses in Gloucester!"

Belly

WS facing, rejoin yarn DE to 7 sts on knitting needle.

Row 1: Purl across all 7 Belly sts.

Rows 2-5: Beginning with a knit row, work four rows stocking stitch, PM on first and last stitch of last row for Left and Right Inner Belly Markers.

Rows 6-11: Beginning with a knit row, work six rows stocking stitch.

Row 12 (inc): K1, kfb, k3, kfb, k1. – 9sts

Rows 13-15: Beginning with a purl row, work three rows stocking stitch.

Row 16 (inc): K2, kfb, k3, kfb, k2. – 11sts

Rows 17-19: Beginning with a purl row, work three rows stocking stitch.

Row 20 (dec): K2tog, knit to last 2 sts, k2tog. – 9sts

Row 21: Purl, PM on first and last stitch of row for Left and Right Inner Thigh Markers.

Work short rows for Breast:

Short row 1 (dec): K1, k2tog, k3, W+Tk.

Short row 2: P5, W+Tp.

Short row 3: K4, W+Tk.

Short row 4: P3, W+Tp.

Short row 5: K5 to end of row. – 8sts

Row 22 (dec): P2tog, p3, p2tog. – 5sts

Row 23: Knit.

Row 24 (dec): P2tog, p1, p2tog. – 3sts

Chin

Cut yarn D, join yarn E, continue with yarn EE (use other end of yarn ball E) as follows:

Rows 25-27: Beginning with a knit row, work three rows stocking stitch.

Row 28 (dec): P3tog, fasten off for Chin Point.

Join Thigh Front Seam

Refer to Body A, **Fig. 3** in Making Up.

Working on one side at a time, WS together match Inner Thigh to Thigh Markers, match Inner Belly to Belly Markers, work mattress stitch to join Thigh Front Seam so joining Thigh to Belly from Inner Thigh/Thigh Markers to Inner Belly/Belly markers – join as dotted line A to B.

Remove Inner Belly and Inner Thigh Markers.

Join Nose Seam

Refer to Body A, **Fig. 1** in Making Up.

RS together fold the Nose Cast-On Edge from the beginning of the pattern in half and join both halves together with back stitch – join dotted line A to B.

Turn out to RS.

Join Chin Seam

WS together match Chin Point to Nose Seam then, working on one side at a time, join muzzle to chin with mattress stitch (or over-sewing because they are such tiny seams), the seams from nose seam/chin point so joining chin row ends (from colour change) to muzzle rows ends (seam ends at Neck Markers).

Remove both Neck Markers.

Join Head Back Seam

Refer to Body A, **Fig. 13** in Making Up.

WS together, working on one side at a time, work mattress stitch to join the Head Back Seam Cast-Off Edge to the row ends at the back of the head, at the same time adding a little stuffing to pad out the head back. You can also add little bits of stuffing into the muzzle and nose to pad out those too.

At this stage you can add stuffing into the head and body. Add a little at a time using the stuffing to pad out the shaping at the head, belly, thighs and back.

Add Eyes

Push the toy eyes into the knitting from front/knit-side to back/purl-side at the place where the eyes are to be (refer to the photographs for placement) and secure them in place firmly with the plastic or metal backing.

Create Indents for Head Shaping

Refer to Body D, **Fig. 27** in Making Up.

Thread up some yarn C and secure one end.

Pass the tip of the sewing needle into one side of the head just to the side of the eye.

NOTE: If you're planning to embroider the eyes then insert the sewing needle where you want the eyes to be, work this shaping technique then, with black yarn or thread, work French Knots inside the indents.

Pass the thread through the head to emerge to the side of the other eye on the other side of the head. Pass the thread back in, near where you have you have just pulled through to emerge back where you started. Gently tug the yarn to create indents at each side. When you are happy with the shapes then secure the thread – in at A; out at B; in at C; out at A.

Join Belly to Back Seam
Refer to Body A, **Fig. 4** in Making Up.

Working on one side at a time, WS together match Neck Markers to the corners at Neck Cast-Off Edge (where you picked-up stitches for the Chin), ease seam together and work mattress stitch to join Belly and Breast Seam so joining Belly and Breast to Back from Neck Markers to Thigh Markers – join as dotted line A to B. Remove Neck and Thigh Markers.

HIND PAWS
Refer to Body A, **Fig. 14** in Making Up.

The Left and Right Hind Paws are picked up and knitted along the Hind Paw Cast-Off Edge, knitted into a paw shape, the seam is sewn all along the paw's heel, upper and sole, stuffing at the same time.
The details are embroidered on once the paw is completed.

Left Hind Paw
RS and mouse's Left Thigh facing, begin at Left Belly Marker, with yarn BF pick up and knit 3 sts along Left Paw Cast-Off Edge from Left Belly Marker to the other corner of the cast-off edge near the mouse's Back – pick up as dotted line from A to B. Remove Left Belly Marker.
Row 1: Purl.
Row 2 (inc): Cast on 4 sts for Left Paw Upper, knit across all 7 sts.
Row 3: Purl.

Work short rows for Left Paw Front Outer Edge:
Short row 1: K3, W+Tk.
Short row 2: P3.
Short row 3: K2, W+Tk.
Short row 4: P2.

Row 4: Knit.
Row 5: Purl.

Work short rows for Left Paw Front Inner Edge:
Short row 1: K3, W+Tk.

Short row 2: P3.
Short row 3: K2, W+Tk.
Short row 4: P2.

Row 6 (dec): Cast off 4 sts for Paw Upper Inside Edge, knit to end of row. – 3sts
Cast off all 3 sts purl-wise for Paw Inside Edge.

Right Hind Paw
RS and mouse's Right Thigh facing, begin at the opposite corner to Right Belly Marker, with yarn BF pick up and knit 3 sts along Right Paw Cast-Off Edge to Right Belly Marker. Remove Right Belly Marker.
Row 1 (inc): Cast on 4 sts for Right Paw Upper, purl across all 7 sts.
Rows 2-4: Beginning with a knit row, work three rows stocking stitch.

Work short rows for Right Paw Front Outer Edge:
Short row 1: P3, W+Tp.
Short row 2: K3.
Short row 3: P2, W+Tp.
Short row 4: K2.

Row 5: Purl.
Row 6: Knit.

Work short rows for Right Paw Inner Edge:
Short row 1: P3, W+Tp.
Short row 2: K3.
Short row 3: P2, W+Tp.
Short row 4: K2.

Row 7 (dec): Cast off 4 sts purl-wise for Paw/Upper Inside Edge, purl to end of row. – 3sts
Cast off all 3 sts for Paw/Inside Edge.

Join Hind Paw Seam
Refer to Body A, **Fig. 15** in Making Up.

Working on one paw at a time, WS together fold paw in half across the row ends at the heel.
Mattress stitch the Paw Inside Cast-Off Edge to the row ends at the Belly. Work mattress stitch to join the cast-on and cast-off edges of the paw upper and the row ends that will become the paw front.

Join Seam at Heel – the feet aren't stuffed.

TAIL
Refer to Body A, **Fig. 16** in Making Up.

The Tail is picked up and knitted along the Tail Cast-Off Edge, the under-tail edges are cast on either side of the picked-up and knitted stitches then the Tail is knitted in its entirety as i-cord, below is the i-cord technique using two single point needles. The cast-on edges are then joined to the Tail Cast-On Edge.
RS and mouse's Back facing, return to the Tail Cast-Off Edge. With yarn BF, begin at mouse's left side (your right side) of the cast-off edge, pick up and knit 3 sts into the cast-off edge, all along from your right to your left – Tail already picked up and knitted as dotted line from A to B.
Row 1 (inc): Cast on 1 st for Tail Underside 1, purl all 3 sts.
Row 2 (inc): Cast on 1 st for Tail Underside 2, knit all 4 sts.
Do not turn the work over to the purl-side.

You'll now work 'i-cord' on these 4 Tail sts as follows:

NOTE: Have RS/knit-side facing at all time.

i-cord row 1: RS facing, with the 4 sts on the needle in your right hand, slip the 4 sts off the RH needle onto the LH needle – keeping RS/knit-side facing and the working yarn pulled behind the work, k4.
Then, without turning the work so RS facing continue as follows:
i-cord row 2 (dec): RS facing, with the 4 sts on the needle in your right hand, slip the 4 sts off the RH needle onto the LH needle – keeping RS/knit-side facing and the working yarn pulled behind the work, k1, k2tog, k1. – 3sts
i-cord row 3: Slip the 3 sts off the RH needle onto the LH needle – keeping RS/knit-side facing and the working yarn pulled behind the work, k3.
Continue to work as i-cord row 3 until the tail, from where you picked up stitches for the tail, measures 7cm (2¾in).
Thread cut tail end back inside the i-cord.
Join the Under-Tail Cast-On Edges to the cast-on edge from Back to close the seam completely.

FORELEGS
The Left and Right Forelegs are knitted independently of the mouse's body and joined after stuffing onto the Back as directed with the pattern, using the Foreleg Placement Marker as a guide.
The details are embroidered on once the foreleg is completed.

Left Foreleg
With yarn AC cast on 3 sts.
Row 1: Purl.
Row 2 (inc): Kfb, knit to last st, kfb. – 5sts
Row 3: Purl, PM on first and last stitch of row for Shoulder Markers.
Row 4 (inc): Cast on 2 sts for Left Under-Foreleg Side 1, knit across all 7 sts.
Row 5 (inc): Cast on 2 sts for Left Under-Foreleg Side 2, purl across all 9 sts.
Rows 6-7: Beginning with a knit row, work two rows stocking stitch.

Work short rows for Left Elbow Joint:
Short row 1: K6, W+Tk.
Short row 2: P3, W+Tp.
Short row 3: K2, W+Tk.
Short row 4: P1, W+Tp.
Short row 5: K5 to end of row.

Rows 8-9: Beginning with a purl row, work two rows stocking stitch.
Cut yarn AC join yarn BF, continue to work with yarn BF as follows:
Row 10 (dec): P2tog, purl to last 2 sts, p2tog. – 7sts
Row 11 (dec): K2tog, knit to last 2 sts, k2tog. – 5sts

Work short rows for Left Paw:
Short row 1: K4 W+Tk.
Short row 2: P3, W+Tp.
Short row 3: K2, W+Tk.
Short row 4: P1, W+Tp.
Short row 5: K3 to end of row.
Cut yarn, thread end through all 5 sts, pull up and secure the end.

Right Foreleg
With yarn AC cast on 3 sts.
Row 1: Knit.
Row 2 (inc): Pfb, purl to last st, pfb. – 5sts

Row 3: Knit, PM on first and last stitch of row for Shoulder Markers.
Row 4 (inc): Cast on 2 sts for Right Under-Foreleg Side 1, purl across all 7 sts.
Row 5 (inc): Cast on 2 sts for Right Under-Foreleg Side 2, knit across all 9 sts.
Rows 6-7: Beginning with a purl row, work two rows stocking stitch.

Work short rows for Right Elbow Joint:
Short row 1: P6, W+Tp.
Short row 2: K3, W+Tk.
Short row 3: P2, W+Tp.
Short row 4: K1, W+Tk.
Short row 5: P5 to end of row.

Rows 8-9: Beginning with a knit row, work two rows stocking stitch.
Cut yarn AC join yarn BF, continue to work with yarn BF as follows:
Row 10 (dec): K2tog, knit to last 2 sts, k2tog. – 7sts
Row 11 (dec): P2tog, purl to last 2 sts, p2tog. – 5sts

Work short rows for Right Paw:
Short row 1: K4, W+Tk.
Short row 2: P3, W+Tp.
Short row 3: K2, W+Tk.
Short row 4: P3 to end of row.

Cut yarn, thread end through all 5 sts, pull up and secure the end.

Join Foreleg Seam
Refer to Body A, **Fig. 18** in Making Up.

Working on one foreleg at a time, WS together fold Paw Cast-Off Edge in half and mattress stitch to join the two halves.
Mattress stitch the row ends to join the Foreleg Seam up to the Shoulder Markers, so leaving the first five shoulder rows of free to join onto the body – join dotted line A to B.
Stuff the paw with the tiniest amount of stuffing (or just use yarn snippings) through the opening at the shoulder.
Remove the Shoulder Markers.
Flatten the front of the paw with your thumb and forefinger then with a doubled length

of yarn C work four lots of straight stitches to create toe sections, pulling the straight stitches as you sew them to make the paw indent a little.

Join Forelegs to the Back
Refer to Body A, **Fig. 19** in Making Up.

Find the centre of the Shoulder Cast-On Edge and mark with a pin. Working on one foreleg at a time and making sure you have the correct foreleg for the side of the body match the pin to the Foreleg Placement Marker and hold in place with a stitch or two.
Remove the placement marker. Mattress stitch each side of the cast-on edge, working either side of the centre of the shoulder – you're wanting to create a round shoulder shape. Then mattress stitch the few shoulder row ends joining the shoulder to the side of the body/onto the Back.
Complete the seam by joining, with mattress stitch, the Under-Foreleg Cast-On Edge to the body.

EARS
The Left and Right Ears are knitted independently of the mouse's body and joined after stuffing onto the Head as directed with the pattern, using the Ear Position Marker as a guide.

Left and Right Ears – Make 2 alike
With yarn D cast on 9 sts.
Row 1: Purl.

Jon yarn F, continue with yarn DF as follows:
Work short rows for Ear:
Short row 1: K8, W+Tk.
Short row 2: P7, W+Tp.
Short row 3: K6, W+Tk.
Short row 4: P5, W+Tp.
Short row 5: K4, W+Tk.
Short row 6: P3, W+Tp.
Short row 7: K2, W+Tk.
Short row 8: P1, W+Tp.
Short row 9: K5 to end of row.

Row 2: *P2tog, cast off 1 st purl-wise**, repeat from * to ** four times, fasten off last stitch for Ear to Head Edge.

" There was a snippeting of scissors, and snappeting of thread; and little mouse voices sang loudly "

Join Ears to Head
Refer to Body C, **Fig. 24** in Making Up.

Working on one ear at a time, shape the ear into a petal shape (the backs of the ears are the RS/knit-side) then use the tail ends to join the ear onto each side of the head at the marker by first joining the corners of the cast-on edge either side of the marker then joining all around the curved back of the ear onto the head – the cast-on edge become the outer edge of the ear.
Remove the Ear Markers.

As a final detail, thread up the length of mid-pink yarn and work straight stitches, similar to Satin Stitch, inside the ear.

FACE DETAIL
Refer to Body A, **Fig. 20** in Making Up.

With a single length of dark brown yarn, with embroidered straight stitches work a 'V' either side of the point of the nose then fill in the 'V' with yarn B to create a nose.

POSE
To pose him so that he looks like one of Beatrix's illustrations have his arms crossed a little at the front and join with a few discreet stitches to hold them in place, likewise, if he's to sit atop of a wooden cotton-spool have his feet crossed and join with a few discreet stitches to hold them in place. The spectacles are glued in place. I also made a small bundle of fancy threads for him to hold.

Mr. Tod™

WHILST never explicitly stated, we first meet Beatrix Potter's fox in *The Tale of Jemima Puddle-Duck*. Naïve Jemima believes him to be a foxy whiskered gentleman who offers her a nest at his house. Little does she know he intends to have her as roast duck. We next meet him in *The Tale of Mr. Tod*, in which Peter Rabbit and Benjamin Bunny must save Benjamin's young family.

FINISHED SIZE
Approx. 41cm (16in) tall from feet to top of head

YARN
You will need no more than one ball of each of:
A: DROPS Fabel shade 110 Rust
B: DROPS Baby Merino shade 55 Peanut
C: DROPS Kid-Silk shade 30 Curry
D: DROPS Alpaca shade 2925 Rust Mix
E: DROPS Kid-Silk shade 42 Almond
F: DROPS Flora shade 16 Pistachio
G: DROPS Nord shade 22 Chestnut
H: DROPS Alpaca shade 0100 Off White
I: DROPS Kid-Silk shade 01 Off White
J: You'll also need a very small amount dark brown yarn for the nose and ears – I used DROPS Kid-Silk shade 15 Dark Brown
Unless otherwise stated, double and triple strands of yarn are used together throughout this pattern. The exact combinations of yarn to be used are indicated by multiple letters (see How to Use This Book).

TENSION
11 stitches and 14 rows over 5cm (2in)

NEEDLES
4mm (US 6) knitting needles

OTHER TOOLS AND MATERIALS
- 2 large safety pins or stitch holders
- 3 x 10mm (½in) pearl-coloured, 4-hole buttons and sewing thread to match
- 26 coloured locking stitch markers (see How to Use This Book: Stitch Markers)
- 2 x 5mm (¼in) black toy safety eyes
- Toy stuffing or yarn/fabric scraps
- Tapestry or darning needle

PATTERN NOTES
- Use cable cast-on unless otherwise stated
- General knitting abbreviations can be found in How to Use This Book

HEAD
Beginning at the Nose.
With yarn ABC cast on 5 sts for Nose Seam.
Row 1: Purl.
Row 2 (inc): [Kfb, k1] twice, kfb. – 8sts
Row 3: Purl.
Row 4 (inc): Kfb, k3, m1, k3, kfb. – 11sts
Row 5: Purl.
Row 6 (inc): Kfb, k3, kfb, k1, kfb, k3, kfb. – 15sts

Row 7: Purl.
Row 8 (inc): [Kfb] twice, [k3, kfb] twice, k3, [kfb] twice. – 21sts
Row 9: Purl, PM on first and last stitch for Left and Right Nose Markers.

Work short rows (see Techniques) for Left Muzzle:
Short row 1: K7, W+Tk.
Short row 2: P7.
Short row 3: K6, W+Tk.
Short row 4: P4, W+Tp (this is correct).
Short row 5: K3, W+Tk.
Short row 6: P2, W+Tp.
Short row 7 (inc): K6, kfb, k1, kfb, k9 to end of row. – 23sts

Work short rows for Right Muzzle:
Short row 1: P7, W+Tp.
Short row 2: K7.
Short row 3: P6, W+Tp.
Short row 4: K4, W+Tk.
Short row 5: P3, W+Tp.
Short row 6: K2, W+Tk.

Short row 7: P20 to end of row.

Row 10 (inc): Kfb, k9, kfb, k1, kfb, k9, kfb. – 27sts
Row 11: Purl.

Forehead
Work short rows for Forehead:
Short row 1: K20, W+Tk.
Short row 2: P13, W+Tp.
Short row 3: K12, W+Tk.
Short row 4: P11, W+Tp.
Short row 5: K10, W+Tk.
Short row 6: P9, W+Tp.
Short row 7: K8, W+Tk.
Short row 8: P7, W+Tp.
Short row 9: K6, W+Tk.
Short row 10: P5, W+Tp.
Short row 11: K16 to end of row.

Row 12: Purl, PM on first and last stitch for Left and Right Neck Markers.
Row 13: K10, PM on last stitch for Left Ear Front Marker, knit next 8 sts,

PM on last stitch for Right Ear Front Marker, k9 to end of row.

Row 14: Purl.

Row 15 (dec): K8, skpo, k7, k2tog, k8. – 25sts

Row 16: Purl.

Row 17 (dec): K6, PM on last stitch for Left Ear Back Marker, knit next 2 sts, skpo, k5, k2tog, k3, PM on last stitch for Right Ear Back Marker, k5 to end of row. – 23sts

Row 18: Purl.

Row 19 (dec): K8, skpo, k3, k2tog, k8. – 21sts

Row 20: Purl.

Divide the Head Back to create Head Back Seam as follows:

Row 21 (dec): Cast off 5 sts for Head Back Seam, Left-Side, knit next 10 sts, cast off last 5 sts for Head Back Seam, Right-Side. – 11sts

Head Back

WS facing rejoin yarn ABC and to 11 sts for Head Back, continue as follows:

Row 22: Purl.

Row 23 (dec): K3, skpo, k1, k2tog, k3 to end of row. – 9sts

Row 24: Purl.

Row 25 (dec): K3, k3tog, k3 to end of row. – 7sts

Row 26: Purl.

Cut yarn, place all 7 sts for Head Back onto a large safety pin for now.

Join Head Seams

Refer to Body A, **Fig. 1** in Making Up.

WS together fold the Nose Cast-On Edge from the beginning of the pattern in half and join both halves together with mattress stitch – join A to B.

NECK AND BACK

Refer to Body A, **Fig. 2** in Making Up.

Joining Left Side of Head

With yarn ABC and begin at Left Neck Marker, RS facing pick up and knit 6 sts evenly along row ends to the left-side corner of Head Back Seam Cast-Off Edge; slip all 7 Head Back sts from the safety pin onto a knitting needle then from corner of

Head Back Cast-Off Edge knit across all 7 Head Back sts.

Joining Right Side of Head

Continue to pick up across the right side of the head, all onto the same needle as follows:

Pick up and knit 6 sts evenly along row ends from right corner of Head Back Seam Cast-Off Edge to Right Neck Marker – 19sts – pick up and knit from A to B; knit across from C to D; pick up and knit from E to F.

Row 1: Purl all 19 sts.

Row 2 (inc): Kfb, knit to last st, kfb. – 21sts

Row 3: Purl.

Row 4 (inc): Kfb, knit to last st, kfb. – 23sts

Row 5: Purl.

Cut yarn BC, join yarn DE, continue to work with ADE as follows:

WAISTCOAT/BODY
Back

Row 6 (inc): Kfb, knit to last st, kfb. – 25sts

Rows 7-11: Beginning with a purl row, work five rows stocking stitch.

Row 12 (inc): K4, PM on last stitch for Left Foreleg Placement, knit next 6 sts, kfb, k3, kfb, k7, PM on last stitch for Right Foreleg Placement, k3 to end of row. – 27sts

Rows 13-15: Beginning with a purl row, work three rows stocking stitch.

Row 16 (inc): K11, kfb, k3, kfb, k11 to end of row. – 29sts

Rows 17-19: Beginning with a purl row, work three rows stocking stitch.

Row 20 (inc): K12, kfb, k3, kfb, k12 to end of row. – 31sts

Rows 21-23: Beginning with a purl row, work three rows stocking stitch.

Row 24 (inc): Kfb, k12, kfb, k3, kfb, k12, kfb. – 35sts

> *He made his way up the hill; his temper was not improved by noticing unmistakable marks of badger.*

Rows 25-27: Beginning with a purl row, work three rows stocking stitch. Cut yarn AD, join yarn BF, continue with yarn BEF as follows:
Row 28 (inc): Kfb, k13, kfb, k5, kfb, k13, kfb. – 39sts
PM on first and last stitch of last row for Left and Right Thigh Markers.

TROUSER/BODY
Trouser/Hind Legs
Work short rows for Left Hind Leg:
Short row 1 (inc): Cast on 8 sts, k9, W+Tk.
Short row 2: P2, W+Tp.
Short row 3: K3, W+Tk.
Short row 4: P4, W+Tp.
Short row 5: K5, W+Tk.
Short row 6: P6, W+Tp.
Short row 7: K7, W+Tk.
Short row 8: P8, W+Tp.
Short row 9: K9, W+Tk.
Short row 10: P10, W+Tp.
Short row 11: K11, W+Tk.
Short row 12: P12, W+Tp.
Short row 13: K13, W+Tk.
Short row 14: P14, W+Tp.
Short row 15 (inc): K15, kfb, k30 to end of row. – 48sts

Work short rows for Right Hind Leg:
Short row 1 (inc): Cast on 8 sts, p9, W+Tp.

Short row 2: K2, W+Tk.
Short row 3: P3, W+Tp.
Short row 4: K4, W+Tk.
Short row 5: P5, W+Tp.
Short row 6: K6, W+Tk.
Short row 7: P7, W+Tp.
Short row 8: K8, W+Tk.
Short row 9: P9, W+Tp.
Short row 10: K10, W+Tk.
Short row 11: P11, W+Tp.
Short row 12: K12, W+Tk.
Short row 13: P13, W+Tp.
Short row 14: K14, W+Tk.
Short row 15 (inc): P15, kfb, p39 to end of row. – 57sts

Row 29: Knit.
Row 30: Purl.
Row 31 (dec): K23, skpo, k7, k2tog, k3, k23. – 55sts
Row 32: Purl.
Row 33 (dec): K22, skpo, k7, k2tog, k3, k22. – 53sts
Row 34: Purl.
Row 35 (dec): K2tog, k19, skpo, k7, k2tog, k19 to last 2 sts, k2tog. – 49sts
Row 36: Purl.
Row 37 (dec): K2tog, k17, skpo, k7, k2tog, k17 to last 2 sts, k2tog. – 45sts
Row 38: Purl.
Row 39 (dec): K2tog, k15, skpo, k7, k2tog, k15 to last 2 sts, k2tog. – 41sts
Row 40: Purl.

Row 41 (dec): K2tog, k13, skpo, k7, k2tog, k13 to last 2 sts, k2tog. – 37sts
Row 42: Purl.
Row 43 (dec): K2tog, k11, skpo, k7, k2tog, k11 to last 2 sts, k2tog. – 33sts
Row 44: Purl.
Row 45 (dec): K13, cast off 7 sts for Under Tail Space, k12 to end of row. – 26sts
Row 46 (inc): P13, cast on 6 sts for Under Tail Space, p13 to end of row. – 32sts
Row 47: K2tog, k13, [kfb] twice, k13, k2tog.
Row 48: Purl, PM on first and last stitch of row for Leg Divide Markers.

Divide for Trouser Seam
You'll now divide the trousers into two legs as follows:
Row 49 (inc): K15, kfb, turn (flip work over so purl-side faces) continue to work on Trouser Side 1.
Row 50: Purl all 17 sts.
Row 51: K17, turn.

Trouser Side 1
Rows 52-58: Beginning with a purl row, work seven rows stocking stitch on just 17 sts for Trouser Side 1.
Row 59 (dec): K1, k2tog, k2, k2tog, k3, k2tog, k2, k2tog, k1, turn. – 13sts
Row 60: P13.
Row 61 (dec): K2tog, k9, k2tog, turn. – 11sts
Row 62: P11.
Row 63 (dec): K2tog, k2, k3tog, k2, k2tog, turn. – 7sts
Row 64: P7, PM on first and last stitch of row for Trouser Marker.
Cut yarn F, join yarn G, continue with yarn BEG as follows:

Left Leg
Row 65: Knit all 7 sts.
Row 66: Purl.
Row 67 (inc): Cast on 6 sts for Left Leg Back, knit all 13 sts.
Rows 68-72: Beginning with a purl row, work five rows stocking stitch.

Shape Front and Back of Leg
Row 73: K2tog, k3, kfb, k1, kfb, k3, k2tog.
Row 74: Purl.
Rows 75-78: Repeat last two rows twice.

Work short rows for Foot Front:
Short row 1: K10, W+Tk.
Short row 2: P7, W+Tp.
Short row 3: K6, W+Tk.
Short row 4: P5, W+Tp.
Short row 5: K4, W+Tk.
Short row 6: P3, W+Tp.
Short row 7: K2, W+Tk.
Short row 8: P1, W+Tp.
Short row 9: K7 to end of row.

Row 79 (dec): [P2tog, cast off 1 st] six times, fasten off last stitch for Foot Edge.

Trouser Side 2
Rejoin yarn BEF to 16 sts on LH needle, continue to work on Trouser Side 2 as follows:
Row 49 (inc): Kfb, knit to end. – 17sts
Rows 50-58: Beginning with a purl row, work nine rows stocking stitch.
Row 59 (dec): K1, k2tog, k2, k2tog, k3, k2tog, k2, k2tog, k1. – 13sts
Row 60: Purl.
Row 61 (dec): K2tog, k9, k2tog. – 11sts
Row 62: Purl.
Row 63 (dec): K2tog, k2, k3tog, k2, k2tog, turn. – 7sts
Row 64: Purl, PM on first and last stitch of row for Trouser Marker. Cut yarn F, join yarn G, continue with yarn BEG as follows:

Right Leg
Row 65: Knit all 7 sts.
Row 66 (inc): Cast on 6 sts for Right Leg Back, purl all 13 sts.
Rows 67-72: Beginning with a knit row, work six rows stocking stitch.

Shape Front and Back of Leg
Row 73: K2tog, k3, kfb, k1, kfb, k3, k2tog.
Row 74: Purl.
Rows 75-78: Repeat last two rows twice.

Work short rows for Foot Front:
Short row 1: K10, W+Tk.
Short row 2: P7, W+Tp.
Short row 3: K6, W+Tk.
Short row 4: P5, W+Tp.
Short row 5: K4, W+Tk.
Short row 6: P3, W+Tp.

Short row 7: K2, W+Tk.
Short row 8: P1, W+Tp.
Short row 9: K7 to end of row.

Row 79 (dec): [P2tog, cast off 1 st] six times, fasten off last stitch for Foot Edge.

Join Leg Seams
Working on one leg at a time, WS together, fold the Foot Cast-Off Edge in half and join both halves together with mattress stitch to create the Foot Seam, then work mattress stitch to join the leg seam row ends from the foot seam up to the colour change near Trouser Markers.
You can stuff your yarn endings into the legs but there's no need to completely stuff the legs at moment – you'll be able to do that later.

Trouser Inside Legs and Front
The completion of the Trouser begins with the Inside Legs which are picked-up and knitted across the cast-on edge from Leg Back as follows:

Left Trouser Inside Leg
Return to Left Leg Back Cast-On Edge – you should have the RS of the Left Leg Back facing (the Trouser Back is facing you with WS/purl-side showing).

*Beginning at Trouser Marker on your right with yarn BEF pick up and knit 8 sts across the Leg Back Cast-On Edge from the marker on your right to the marker on your left.
Row 1: Purl across all 8 Inside Leg sts.
Row 2 (inc): [K2, kfb] twice, k2. – 10sts
Row 3: Purl.
Row 4 (inc): Kfb, knit to last st, kfb. – 12sts
Row 5: Purl.
Row 6 (inc): [K2, kfb] four times. – 16sts
Row 7: Purl.
Row 8 (inc): [K3, kfb] four times. – 20sts
Rows 9-13: Beginning with a purl row, work five rows stocking stitch.
Row 14 (dec): [K3, k2tog] four times. – 16sts**

Row 15: Purl, PM on last stitch of row for Left Inner Belly Marker.
Cut yarn, slip all 16 sts for Left Inside Leg onto a large safety pin.

Right Trouser Inside Leg
Return to Right Trouser Leg Back Cast-On Edge – you should have the RS of the Right Leg Back facing (the Trouser Back is facing you with WS/purl-side showing).
Continue to Work as Left Leg from * to **.
Row 15: Purl, PM on first stitch of row for Right Inner Belly Marker.
Cut yarn, slip all 16 sts for Right Inside Leg onto a large safety pin.

Join Trouser Inside Leg to Trouser Back
Working on one trouser leg at a time and working on one side seam at a time, WS together match Inner Belly Marker with Leg Divide Marker and work mattress stitch to join the row ends seam from the top of the Leg at Trouser Marker to the Inner Belly/Leg Divide Markers.
Then join the other Inside Leg Seam working mattress stitch to join row ends from the top of the leg up to

where you divided for the trouser legs, near the tail gap.
Remove Trouser and Leg Divide Markers.

Trouser Front/Belly
RS facing, slip Left Inside Leg sts off the safety pin and onto a knitting needle ready to knit across, rejoin yarn BEF knit 13, skpo, k1, slip Right Inside Leg sts off the safety pin and onto the knitting needle ready to knit across, knit 1, k2tog, k13 to end. – 30sts

Row 1: Purl across all 30 Trouser Front/Belly sts.
Row 2 (dec): K11, cast off next 8 sts for Gusset Seam, knit 10 to end of row. – 22sts
Row 3 (dec): Purl 10, p2tog, PM on last stitch for Gusset Marker, p10 to end. – 21sts
Row 4 (dec): K4, skpo, k9, k2tog, k4 to end of row. – 19sts
Rows 5-7: Beginning with a purl row, work three rows stocking stitch.
Row 8 (dec): K4, skpo, k7, k2tog, k4 to end of row. – 17sts
Rows 9-11: Beginning with a purl row, work three rows stocking stitch.
Row 12 (dec): K4, skpo, k5, k2tog, k4 to end of row. – 15sts
Rows 13-17: Beginning with a purl row, work five rows stocking stitch.

Incorporate the Waistcoat Front into the Trouser Front
In this section you are working with two different yarn combinations in the same rows. The yarn not in use should be carried across the back on the work to the next place it is needed.

NOTE: I found it easier to cut about 1 metre (1 yard) lengths of yarn ADE (cut yarn E from the other end of the ball) and strand that as I continued to work with yarn BEF.

Row 18: K3 in BEF; k1 in ADE; k7 in BEF; k1 in ADE; k3 in BEF.
Row 19: P2 in BEF; p3 in ADE; p5 in BEF; p3 in ADE; p2 in BEF.
Row 20: K1 in BEF; k5 in ADE; k3 in BEF; k5 in ADE; k1 in BEF.
Row 21: P7 in ADE; p1 in BEF; p7 in ADE.
Cut yarn BEF, continue to work in yarn ADE only as follows:
Rows 22-26: Beginning with a knit row, work five rows stocking stitch, PM on first and last stitch of last row for Left and Right Inner Thigh Markers.
Rows 27-33: Beginning with a purl row, work seven rows stocking stitch.
Row 34 (dec): K2tog, knit to last 2 sts, k2tog. – 13sts
Rows 35-39: Beginning with a purl row, work five rows stocking stitch.
Row 40 (dec): K2tog, knit to last 2 sts, k2tog. – 11sts
Rows 41-43: Beginning with a purl row, work three rows stocking stitch.
Row 44 (dec): K2tog, knit to last 2 sts, k2tog. – 9sts
Rows 45-47: Beginning with a purl row, work three rows stocking stitch.

Cut yarn ADE, join yarn HHI (use the other end of yarn ball H), continue with the Neck as follows:

Neck
Row 48 (inc): Kfb, knit to last st, kfb. – 11sts
Row 49: Purl.
Row 50 (inc): Kfb, k2, kfb, k3, kfb, k2, kfb. – 15sts
Row 51: Purl.
Row 52 (inc): K5, kfb, k3, kfb, k5. – 17sts
Row 53: Purl.
Cast off all 17 sts for Neck Edge, PM on first and last cast-off stitch for Left and Right Inner Neck Markers.

Join Thigh Front Seam
Refer to Body A, **Fig. 3** in Making Up.

Working on one side at a time, WS together match Inner Thigh to Thigh Markers and work mattress stitch to join Thigh Front Seam so joining Thigh to Trouser Front/Belly from Inner Thigh/Thigh Markers to Inner Belly Marker – join as dotted line A to B. Remove Inner Belly and Inner Thigh Markers.

Join Belly to Back Seam
Refer to Body A, **Fig. 4** in Making Up.

Working on one side at a time, WS together match Inner Neck to Neck Markers, ease seam together and work mattress stitch to join Belly and Breast Seam so joining Belly to Back from Inner Neck/Neck Markers to Thigh Markers – join as dotted line A to B.

NOTE: Also make sure the colour change row ends match up when you join the tops of waistcoat back and front.

Remove Inner Neck and Thigh Markers.

Join Nose Seams
WS together match both Left and Right Nose Markers and mattress stitch to join the Nose from the markers to the Nose Seam. Remove Nose Markers.

Join Gusset Seam

WS together work mattress stitch to join small gusset seam from Gusset Marker to the split, also if there is a small hole where you divided for the trouser legs work a few stitches to close it.
Remove Gusset Marker.
At this stage you can add stuffing into the body and legs.
Add a little at a time using the stuffing to pad out the shaping at the thighs, belly, back and feet.

CHIN

Return to the Neck Cast-Off Edge.
RS and Belly facing, with yarn HHI (use the other end of yarn ball H), starting at Left Neck Marker (on your right), pick up and knit 14 sts across row ends and cast-off edge from Left Neck Marker to Right Neck Marker. Remove both Neck Markers.
Row 1: Purl.
Row 2: Kfb, k3, skpo, k2, k2tog, k3, kfb.
Row 3: Purl.
Rows 4-5: Repeat last two rows.
Row 6 (inc): Kfb, knit to last st, kfb. – 16sts
Row 7: Purl.
Rows 8-9 (inc): Repeat last two rows once. – 18sts
Row 10 (dec): K2tog, knit to last 2 sts, k2tog. – 16sts
Row 11: Purl.
Row 12 (dec): K2tog, k1, skpo, k6, k2tog, k1, k2tog. – 12sts
Row 13: Purl.
Row 14 (dec): K2tog, k1, skpo, k2, k2tog, k1, k2tog. – 8sts
Row 15 (dec): P1, p2tog, p2, p2tog, p1. – 6sts
Row 16 (dec): K2tog, k2, k2tog. – 4sts
Row 17: Purl.
Row 18 (dec): [K2tog] twice. – 2sts
Cut yarn, thread end through both Chin sts, pull up to gather for Chin Point.

Complete the Head

Push the toy eyes into the head, either side of the nose, referring to the photographs for placement, from front/knit-side to back/purl-side and secure it in place firmly with the plastic or metal backing.

Join Chin to Muzzle Seam

Refer to Body A, **Fig. 5** in Making Up.

Stuff the head a little to make it easier to join the seams.
Bring the Chin Point over the Nose Seam and place it beneath the Nose Seam. Work a small stitch or two to hold in place whilst you join the chin to both sides of the Nose and Muzzle as follows:
Working on one side at a time join the nose and the muzzle to the chin with mattress stitch, easing the seam together as you do – in other words you are joining the chin over the nose seam (the chin seam completely covers nose seam), and also joining the chin to the row ends at the muzzle all the way down to where you picked up for the chin sts.

Sew on Waistcoat Buttons

To complete the body, sew the buttons evenly down the front of the Waistcoat.

EARS
Left Outer Ear

Refer to Body A, **Fig. 8** in Making Up.

RS and with the top of the head facing, begin near Left Ear Front Marker and with yarn GJ pick up and knit 7 sts into the knitted stitches at the top of the head in a straight line across to Left Ear Back Marker – pick up and knit as dotted line from A to B. Remove Left Front Ear Marker.
Row 1 (inc): Cast on 7 sts, purl across all 14 sts.
Row 2 (dec): K2tog, k2, skpo, k2, k2tog, k2, k2tog. – 10sts
Row 3: Purl.
Row 4 (dec): K2, skpo, k2, k2tog, k2. – 8sts
Row 5: Purl.
Row 6 (dec): K1, skpo, k2, k2tog, k1. – 6sts
Row 7: Purl.
Row 8 (dec): K2tog, k2, k2tog. – 4sts
Row 9 (dec): [P2tog] twice. – 2sts
Cut yarn, thread end through all 2 sts for Left Ear, pull up to gather for Ear Point.
Weave the tail end in and out along ear edge.

> *Mr. Tod turned his back towards the bed, and undid the window. It creaked; he turned round with a jump.*

Right Outer Ear

RS and with the top of the head facing, begin near Right Ear Back Marker and with yarn GJ pick up and knit 7 sts into the knitted stitches at the top of the head in a straight line across to Right Ear Front Marker – stitches shown picked up and knitted as dotted line from A to B. Remove Right Front Ear Marker.
Row 1: Purl.
Row 2 (inc): Cast on 7 sts, knit across all 14 sts.
Row 3 (dec): P2tog, p2, p2tog, p2, p2tog, p2, p2tog. – 10sts
Row 4: Knit.
Row 5 (dec): P2, p2tog, p2, p2tog, p2. – 8sts
Row 6: Knit.

Row 7 (dec): P1, p2tog, p2, p2tog, p1. – 6sts
Row 8: Knit.
Row 9 (dec): P2tog, p2, p2tog. – 4sts
Row 10 (dec): [K2tog] twice. – 2sts
Cut yarn, thread end through all 2 sts for Right Ear, pull up to gather for Ear Point.
Weave the tail end in and out along ear edge.

Left Inner Ear Side 1
Refer to Body A, **Fig. 9** in Making Up.

RS facing, with yarn EE (use the other end of yarn ball E) starting at the corner of Left Ear Outer Edge pick up and knit 7 sts evenly along rows ends up to Left Ear Point – stitches shown picked up and knitted as dotted line from A to B
Row 1: Purl.
Row 2 (dec): Knit to last 2 sts, k2tog. – 6sts
Row 3: Purl.
Cast off all 6 sts for Left Inner Ear Centre Side 1.

Left Inner Ear Side 2
RS facing, with yarn EE (use the other end of yarn ball E) starting at Left Ear Point pick up and knit 7 sts evenly along rows ends to the corner of Left Ear Inner Edge – stitches shown picked up and knitted as dotted line from C to D
Row 1: Purl.
Row 2 (dec): K2tog, knit to end. – 6sts
Row 3: Purl.
Cast off all 6 sts for Left Inner Ear Centre Side 2.

Right Inner Ear Side 1
RS facing, with yarn EE (use the other end of yarn ball E) starting at the corner of Right Ear Inner Edge pick up and knit 7 sts evenly along rows ends up to Right Ear Point.
Row 1: Purl.
Row 2 (dec): Knit to last 2 sts, k2tog. – 6sts
Row 3: Purl.
Cast off all 6 sts for Right Inner Ear Centre Side 1.

Right Inner Ear Side 2
RS facing, with yarn EE (use the other end of yarn ball E) starting at Right Ear Point pick up and knit 7 sts evenly along rows ends to the corner of Right Ear Outer Edge.
Row 1: Purl.
Row 2 (dec): K2tog, knit to end. – 6sts
Row 3: Purl.
Cast off all 6 sts for Right Inner Ear Centre Side 2.

Join Inner Ear Seam
Refer to Body A, **Fig. 10** in Making Up.

Working on one Inner Ear at a time, with RS together, match Inner Ear Centre Side 1 to Inner Ear Centre Side 2 and work back stitch to join along both cast-off edges, continue to join the seam along the diagonal row ends up to the Ear Point. Leave the straight edges at the base of the ear inner open for turning through – join dotted lines A to B.
Turn out to RS and trim the tail ends (it's best not to have any stuffing for inside the ears).

Refer to Body B, **Fig. 22** in Making Up.

Then, WS facing, carefully over-sew to join the straight edges from the Inner Ears to the base of the outer ear/the picked-up edge and the cast-on edge from outer ear.

For a little detailing inside the ear, thread up yarn JJ and work horizontal straight lines, similar to satin stitch, just inside the ear making sure the stitches aren't seen on the backs of the ear nor the ear edges. I then gently brushed the inner ears towards the tops of the ears with a soft, clean, nail brush to make them extra fluffy!

Join Ears to the Head
Refer to Body A, **Fig. 12** in Making Up.

Join each Ear Back onto the head by curving it around in a kind of arc, the corner of the Ear Back should almost join with the Ear Back Marker. Pin in place and when you are happy with your placement, make a stitch or two to hold the corner of the ear in place and then securely sew down the ear back onto the head – either with mattress stitch or by over-sewing – join as shown.
Remove Ear Back Markers.

Join Head Back Seam
Refer to Body A, **Fig. 13** in Making Up.

WS together, working on one side at a time, work mattress stitch to join the Head Back Seam Cast-Off Edge to the row ends at the back of the head, at the same time adding a little stuffing to pad out the head back.

You can also add little bits of stuffing into the muzzle and nose to pad out those too.

TAIL
Refer to Body A, **Fig. 16** in Making Up.

The Tail is picked up and knitted along the Tail Cast-Off Edge, the under-tail edges are cast on either side of the picked-up and knitted stitches then the Tail is knitted in its entirety.

The seam is sewn all along the tail from tip to cast-on edges. The cast-on edges are then joined to the Tail Cast-On Edge.

Add any more stuffing (also stuff your yarn snippings) through the tail opening.

RS and fox's Back facing, return to the Tail Cast-Off Edge. With yarn ABCC (use the other end of yarn ball C), begin at fox's left side (your right side) of the cast-off edge, pick up and knit 9 sts into the cast-off edge, all along from your right to your left – Tail already picked up and knitted as dotted line from A to B.

Row 1 (inc): Cast on 3 sts for Tail Underside 1, purl all 12 sts.
Row 2 (inc): Cast on 3 sts for Tail Underside 2, knit all 15 sts.
Row 3: Purl.
Row 4 (inc): [Kfb, k2] five times. – 20sts
Rows 5-9: Beginning with a purl row, work five rows stocking stitch.
Row 10 (inc): [Kfb, k3] five times. – 25sts
Rows 11-17: Beginning with a purl row, work seven rows stocking stitch.
Row 18 (dec): [k2tog, k3] five times. – 20sts
Rows 19-25: Beginning with a purl row, work seven rows stocking stitch.
Row 26 (dec): [k2tog, k2] five times. – 15sts
Rows 27-29: Beginning with a purl row, work three rows stocking stitch.
Cut yarn ABCC, join yarn EHHI (use the other end of yarn ball H), continue as follows:
Rows 30-33: Beginning with a knit row, work four rows stocking stitch.
Row 34 (dec): K2tog, knit to last 2 sts, k2tog. – 13sts
Row 35: Purl.

Work short rows for Tail Tip:
Short row 1: K12, W+Tk.
Short row 2: P11, W+Tp.
Short row 3: K10, W+Tk.
Short row 4: P9, W+Tp.
Short row 5: K8, W+Tk.
Short row 6: P7, W+Tp.
Short row 7: K6, W+Tk.
Short row 8: P5, W+Tp.
Short row 9: K9 to end of row.

Cast off all 13 sts purl-wise for Tail End.

Join Tail Seam
Refer to Body A, **Fig. 17** in Making Up.

WS together fold tail in half at Tail End Cast-Off Edge, mattress stitch to join the cast-off edge.
Match row ends together and mattress stitch to join along the tail to cast-on edges at Tail Underside.
Join Tail Underside Cast-On Edges to the Cast-On Edge created at the Body/at Tail Gap.

NOTE: Just before closing the seam completely you can also add more stuffing, if needs be, to the body and head.

FORELEGS
The Left and Right Forelegs are knitted independently of the body and joined after stuffing onto the Back as directed with the pattern, using the Foreleg Placement Marker as a guide. The details are embroidered on once the foreleg is completed.

Left Foreleg
With yarn AEG cast on 5 sts.
Row 1: Purl.
Row 2: Kfb, knit to last st, kfb. – 7sts
Row 3: Purl.
Row 4: Knit.
Row 5: Purl, PM on first and last stitch of row for Shoulder Markers.
Row 6 (inc): Cast on 2 sts for Left Under-Foreleg Side 1, knit across all 9 sts.
Row 7 (inc): Cast on 2 sts for Left Under-Foreleg Side 2, purl across all 11 sts.
Rows 8-13: Beginning with a knit row, work six rows stocking stitch.

Work short rows for Left Knee Joint:
Short row 1: K8, W+Tk.
Short row 2: P5, W+Tp.
Short row 3: K4, W+Tk.
Short row 4: P3, W+Tp.
Short row 5: K2, W+Tk.
Short row 6: P1, W+Tp.
Short row 7: K6 to end of row.

Rows 14-22: Beginning with a purl row, work nine rows stocking stitch.

Work short rows for Left Paw Front:
Short row 1: K6, W+Tk.
Short row 2: P5, W+Tp.
Short row 3: K4, W+Tk.
Short row 4: P3, W+Tp.
Short row 5: K2, W+Tk.
Short row 6: P1, W+Tp.
Short row 7: K8 to end of row.

Row 23: Purl all 11 sts.
Row 24 (dec): [K2tog, k1] three times, k2tog. – 7sts
Row 25 (dec): P2tog, purl to last 2 sts, p2tog. – 5sts
Row 26 (dec): K2tog, k1, k2tog. – 3sts
Cut yarn, thread end through all 3 sts for Left Paw, pull up to gather for Paw Point.

Right Foreleg
With yarn AEG cast on 5 sts.
Row 1: Knit.
Row 2: Pfb, purl to last st, pfb. – 7sts
Row 3: Knit.
Row 4: Purl.
Row 5: Knit, PM on first and last stitch of row for Shoulder Markers.
Row 6 (inc): Cast on 2 sts for Right Under-Foreleg Side 1, purl across all 9 sts.
Row 7 (inc): Cast on 2 sts for Right Under-Foreleg Side 2, knit across all 11 sts.
Rows 8-13: Beginning with a purl row, work six rows stocking stitch.

Work short rows for Right Knee Joint:
Short row 1: P8, W+Tp.
Short row 2: K5, W+Tk.
Short row 3: P4, W+Tp.
Short row 4: K3, W+Tk.
Short row 5: P2, W+Tp.
Short row 6: K1, W+Tk.
Short row 7: P6 to end of row.

14-22: Beginning with a knit row, work nine rows stocking stitch.

Work short rows for Right Paw Front:
Short row 1: P6, W+Tp.
Short row 2: K5, W+Tk.
Short row 3: P4, W+Tp.
Short row 4: K3, W+Tk.
Short row 5: P2, W+Tp.

Short row 6: K1, W+Tk.
Short row 7: P8 to end of row.

Row 23: Knit all 11 sts.
Row 24 (dec): [P2tog, p1] three times, k2tog. – 7sts
Row 25 (dec): K2tog, knit to last 2 sts, k2tog. – 5sts
Row 26 (dec): P2tog, p1, p2tog. – 3sts
Cut yarn, thread end through all 3 sts for Right Paw, pull up to gather for Paw Point.

Join Foreleg Seam
Refer to Body A, **Fig. 18** in Making Up.

Working on one foreleg at a time, WS together fold Paw Cast-Off Edge in half and mattress stitch to join the two halves.
Mattress stitch the row ends to join the Foreleg Seam up to the Shoulder Markers, so leaving the first five shoulder rows of free to join onto the body – join dotted line A to B.
Stuff the paw through the opening at the shoulder.
Remove the Shoulder Markers.
Flatten the front of the paw with your thumb and forefinger then with a doubled length of yarn C work four lots of straight stitches to create toe sections, pulling the straight stitches as you sew them to make the paw indent a little.

Join Forelegs to the Back
Refer to Body A, **Fig. 19** in Making Up.

Find the centre of the Shoulder Cast-On Edge and mark with a pin.
Working on one foreleg at a time and making sure you have the correct foreleg for the side of the body, match the pin to the Foreleg Placement Marker and hold in place with a stitch or two.
Remove the placement marker.
Mattress stitch each side of the cast-on edge, working either side of the centre of the shoulder – you're wanting to create a round shoulder shape. Then mattress stitch the few shoulder row ends joining the shoulder to the side of the body/onto the Back.
Complete the seam by joining, with mattress stitch, the Under-Foreleg Cast-On Edge to the body.

FACE DETAIL
Refer to Body A, **Fig. 20** in Making Up.

With a doubled-up length of dark brown yarn G with embroidered straight stitches work a 'V' either side of the Nose then work smaller straight stitches to fill in the nose a little.
Work a single thread embroidered line for a mouth dividing it in the centre by working a small upward/ vertical embroidered line from the centre of the mouth to the nose.
For the detail around the eyes, with yarn H work a simple detail around the eye – similar to embroidering a single Lazy Daisy Petal that sits beneath the toy eye.

NOTE: Use Mr. Tod's Tail to aid his standing.

MR. TOD'S CLOTHES

OTHER TOOLS AND MATERIALS

Coat
- 23 x 23cm (9 x 9in) green wool felt, approx.
  1–1.5mm (1⁄32in) thick, and sewing thread to match
- Sharp hand sewing needle
- Scissors

COAT
Trace Mr. Tod's Coat (see Templates) and cut two Front/Backs, two Sleeves and two Pocket Flaps, all from green felt.

1. Match the Back Seams together and with 3mm (1⁄8in) seam, and either hand- or machine sew to join all along from the collar to the back opening (from A to B).

2. Working on one sleeve at a time, fold and match the long Underarm Seam ends together.

3. Either hand- or machine-sew along the underarm seam to join the long ends together.

4. Turn out to the RS.

5. Push the sleeve into the armhole. The underarm seam should lie at the bottom of the armhole.

6. Carefully hand work small back stitches to join the edges of the sleeve to the armhole allowing for roughly a 3mm (1⁄8in) seam. Repeat for the other sleeve.

7. Position the pocket flap as the grey outline on the template shows, and work small running stitches across the Flap Top Edge to sew it down. Repeat for the other pocket flap.

TOMMY BROCK™

WHEN food is scarce, Tommy Brock is partial
to some rabbit pie, so he kidnaps Flopsy and
Benjamin's children. Peter Rabbit and his cousin Benjamin
Bunny follow the unmistakable smell of Badger all the way
to Mr. Tod's house to rescue them. When Mr. Tod arrives a
"terrific battle" ensues between him and Tommy, allowing
the rabbits to escape unseen.

FINISHED SIZE
Approx. 26cm (10¼in) tall from feet to top of head

YARN
You will need no more than one ball of each of:
A: DROPS Alpaca shade 0100 Off White
B: DROPS Kid-Silk shade 01 Off White
C: DROPS Alpaca shade 0506 Dark Grey Mix
D: DROPS Kid-Silk shade 22 Ash Grey
E: DROPS Alpaca shade 3620 Red
F: DROPS Alpaca shade 3900 Tomato
G: DROPS Kid-Silk shade 31 Mauve
H: DROPS Alpaca shade 9028 Lemon Pie
Unless otherwise stated, double and triple strands of
yarn are used together throughout this pattern. The
exact combinations of yarn to be used are indicated by
multiple letters (see How to Use This Book).

TENSION
11 stitches and 14 rows over 5cm (2in)

NEEDLES
4mm (US 6) knitting needles

OTHER TOOLS AND MATERIALS
• 2 large safety pins or stitch holder
• 2 x 6mm (¼in) brown- or tortoiseshell-coloured,
  4-hole buttons and sewing thread to match
• 27 coloured locking stitch markers (see How to Use
  This Book: Stitch Markers)
• 2 x 5mm (¼in) black toy safety eyes
• Toy stuffing or yarn/fabric scraps
• Tapestry or darning needle

PATTERN NOTES
• Use cable cast-on unless otherwise stated
• General knitting abbreviations can be found in
  How to Use This Book

HEAD
Beginning at the Head Right Side.
With yarn AAB (use other end of
yarn ball A) cast on 11 sts for Nose
Seam, PM on 6th cast-on stitch for
Right Neck Marker and last cast-on
stitch for Right Head Back Marker.
Row 1 (RS): Knit.
Row 2: Purl.

Work short rows (see Techniques) for
Right Front Nose:
Short row 1: K4, W+Tk.
Short row 2: P3, W+Tp.
Short row 3: K10 to end of row.

Work short rows for Right Head Side:
Short row 1: P4, W+Tp.
Short row 2: K3, W+Tk.
Short row 3: P2, W+Tp.
Short row 4: K3 to end of row.

Row 3: Purl.
Row 4 (inc): Cast on 3 sts for Nose,
PM on last stitch (3rd stitch) for Right
Nose Marker, k4, turn (flip work over
so purl-side faces), continue to work

on 4 Nose sts as follows:
Row 5: P4, turn (flip work over so
knit-side faces).
Row 6: K4, turn.
Row 7: P4, turn.
Slip all 4 Nose sts off knitting needle
and onto a safety pin.

Add Right Black Stripe
Join yarn CCD (use other end of
yarn ball C) to 10 sts on LH needle,
continue with Right Black Stripe
as follows:
Row 4: Knit.
Row 5 (inc): Pfb, purl to end. – 11sts
Row 6 (inc): Kfb, knit to end. – 12sts

Work short rows for the Right Stripe:
Short row 1 (inc): Pfb, p4, W+Tp.
Short row 2: K6.
Short row 3: P5, W+Tp.
Short row 4: K5. – 13sts

Row 7: Purl all 13 Right Stripe sts.
Cut yarn CCD and leave all 13 sts on
the knitting needle.

> *Upon the top of the wall*
> *there were again the*
> *marks of badger; and*
> *some ravellings of a sack*
> *had caught on a briar*

Forehead

Slip all 4 Nose sts off the safety pin and onto the knitting needle in your left hand (therefore in front of the black stripe sts) ready to knit across. With yarn AAB continue with 17 Forehead sts as follows:

Row 8: Knit all 4 Nose sts, then knit across all 13 Stripe sts. – 17sts

Rows 9-11: Beginning with a purl row, work three rows stocking stitch.

Work short rows for Forehead:

Short row 1: K12, W+Tk.
Short row 2: P4, W+Tp.
Short row 3: K3, W+Tk.
Short row 4: P2, W+Tp.
Short row 5: K8 to end of row.

Rows 12-14: Beginning with a purl row, work three rows stocking stitch.

Nose

You will now work on just the Nose sts as follows:

Row 15: K4, turn.
Row 16: P4, turn.
Row 17: K4, turn.
Row 18: P4, turn.
Slip all 4 Nose sts off knitting needle and onto a small safety pin.

Add Left Black Stripe

Join yarn CCD to 13 sts on LH needle, continue with Left Black Stripe as follows:

Row 15: Knit.

Work short rows for the Left Stripe:

Short row 1 (dec): P2tog, p3, W+Tp.
Short row 2: K4.
Short row 3: P5, W+Tp.
Short row 4: K5. – 12sts

Row 16: Purl all 12 Left Stripe sts.
Row 17 (dec): K2tog, knit to end. – 11sts
Row 18 (dec): P2tog, purl to end. – 10sts
Cut yarn CCD and leave all 10 sts on the knitting needle.

Left Head Side

Slip 4 Nose sts off the safety pin and onto the knitting needle in your left hand (so in front of the black stripe

sts) ready to knit across.
With yarn AAB continue with 14 Left Side sts as follows:

Row 19: Knit all 4 Nose sts, then knit across all 10 Stripe sts. – 14sts
Row 20: Purl.

Work short rows for Left Head Side:

Short row 1 (dec): PM for Left Nose Marker in first stitch of row then cast off 3 Nose sts, k9, W+Tk.
Short row 2: P3, W+Tp.
Short row 3: K2, W+Tk.
Short row 4: P9 to end of row. – 11sts

Work short rows for Left Front Nose:

Short row 1: K4, W+Tk.
Short row 2: P3, W+Tp.
Short row 3: K10 to end of row.

Row 21: Purl.
Row 22: Knit.
Row 23 (dec): Cast off all 11 sts for Left Side purl-wise, PM on first cast-off stitch for Left Head Back Marker and on 6th cast-off stitch for Left Neck Marker.

Head Back

With yarn AAD and beginning at Left Head Back Marker at the corner of the Left Side Cast-Off edge, RS facing pick up and knit 23 sts evenly along row ends to the right-side corner of Right-Side Cast-On Edge (from the beginning of the pattern).

Row 1: Purl.
Row 2: K6, PM on last stitch for Left Ear Position Marker, knit next 12 sts, PM on last stitch for Right Ear Position Marker, k5 to end of row.
Row 3: Purl.

Divide the Head Back to create Head Back Seam as follows:

Row 4 (dec): Cast off 5 sts for Head Back Seam, Left-Side, knit next 12sts, cast off last 5 sts for Head Back Seam, Right-Side. – 13sts

WS facing rejoin yarn AAD to 13 sts for Head Back, continue as follows:

Rows 5-7: Beginning with a purl row, work three rows stocking stitch.
Cut yarn, place all 13 Head Back sts onto a safety pin for now.
Remove Head Back Markers.

NECK AND BACK
Refer to Body A, **Fig. 2** in Making Up.

Join Left Side of Head
With yarn AAD begin at Left Neck Marker, RS facing pick up and knit 5 sts evenly along row ends to the left-side corner of Head Back Seam Cast-Off Edge; slip all 13 Head Back sts from the safety pin onto a knitting needle then from corner of Head Back Cast-Off Edge knit across all 13 Head Back sts.

Join Right Side of Head
Continue to pick up across the right side of the head, all onto the same needle as follows:
Pick up and knit 5 sts evenly along row ends from right corner of Head Back Seam Cast-Off Edge to Right Neck Marker – 23sts – pick up and knit from A to B; knit across from C to D; pick up and knit from E to F.
Row 1: Purl all 23 sts.

BODY
Back
Row 2 (inc): K10, kfb, k1, kfb, k10 to end of row. – 25sts
Cut yarn AAD, join yarn EFG continue with Waistcoat Back as follows:
Row 3: Purl.

Work short rows for Waistcoat/Body Back:
Short row 1: K6, PM on last stitch for Left Foreleg Placement, knit next 14 sts, PM on last stitch for Right Foreleg Placement, k4, W+Tk.
Short row 2: P23, W+Tp.
Short row 3: K22, W+Tk.
Short row 4: P21, W+Tp.
Short row 5: K20, W+Tk.
Short row 6: P19, W+Tp.
Short row 7: K18, W+Tk.
Short row 8: P17, W+Tp.
Short row 9: K16, W+Tk.
Short row 10: P15, W+Tp.
Short row 11: K14, W+Tk.
Short row 12: P13, W+Tp.
Short row 13: K12, W+Tk.
Short row 14: P11, W+Tp.
Short row 15: K18 to end of row.

Row 4: Purl.
Row 5 (inc): Kfb, knit to last st, kfb. – 27sts
Row 6: Purl.
Row 7 (inc): Kfb, knit to last st, kfb. – 29sts
Rows 8-10: Beginning with a purl row, work three rows stocking stitch, PM on first and last stitch of last (purl) row for Left and Right Thigh Markers. Cut yarn EFG, join yarn BHH continue with yarn BHH (use other end of yarn ball H) for Trousers/Hind Legs and Back as follows:

Hind Legs
Work short rows for Left Hind Leg:
Short row 1 (inc): Cast on 5 sts, k6, W+Tk.
Short row 2: P2, W+Tp.
Short row 3: K3, W+Tk.
Short row 4: P4, W+Tp.
Short row 5: K5, W+Tk.
Short row 6: P6, W+Tp.
Short row 7: K7, W+Tk.
Short row 8: P8, W+Tp.
Short row 9: K33 to end of row. – 34sts

Work short rows for Right Hind Leg:
Short row 1 (inc): Cast on 5 sts, p6, W+Tp.
Short row 2: K2, W+Tk.
Short row 3: P3, W+Tp.
Short row 4: K4, W+Tk.
Short row 5: P5, W+Tp.
Short row 6: K6, W+Tk.
Short row 7: P7, W+Tp.
Short row 8: K8, W+Tk.
Short row 9: P38 to end of row. – 39sts

Rows 11-16: Beginning with a knit row, work six rows stocking stitch.
Row 17 (dec): K2tog, k6, k2tog, k6, skpo, k3, k2tog, k6, k2tog, k6, k2tog. – 33sts
Row 18: Purl.
Row 19 (dec): K5, k2tog, k6, skpo, k3, k2tog, k6, k2tog, k5 to end of row. – 29sts
Row 20: Purl.
Row 21 (dec): K4, k2tog, k5, skpo, k3,

" Then Mr. Tod rushed upon Tommy Brock, and Tommy Brock grappled with Mr. Tod amongst the broken crockery, and there was a terrific battle all over the kitchen. "

k2tog, k5, k2tog, k4 to end of row.
– 25sts
Row 22: Purl.
Row 23 (inc): K10, kfb, k3, kfb, k10 to end of row. – 27sts
Row 24: Purl.
Row 25 (inc): K10, kfb, k5, kfb, k10 to end of row. – 29sts
Row 26: Purl.
Row 27 (inc): K11, kfb, k2, kfb, k2, kfb, k11 to end of row. – 32sts
Row 28: Purl, PM on first and last stitch of row for Leg Divide Markers.

Divide for Trouser Seam
You'll now divide the trousers into two legs as follows:
Row 29 (inc): K15, kfb, turn (flip work over so purl-side faces) and continue to work on Trouser Side 1.
Row 30: Purl.
Row 31: K17, turn.
Row 32: Purl.
Row 33 (dec): K1, k2tog, k2, k2tog, k3, k2tog, k2, k2tog, k1, turn. – 13sts
Row 34: Purl.
Row 35 (dec): K2tog, k9, k2tog, turn. – 11sts
Row 36: Purl.
Row 37 (dec): K2tog, k2, k3tog, k2, k2tog, turn. – 7sts
Row 38: Purl, PM on first and last stitch of row for Trouser Markers. Cut yarn BHH, join yarn CCD, continue with yarn CCD as follows:

Left Leg
Row 39: Knit all 7 sts.
Row 40: Purl.
Row 41 (inc): Cast on 6 sts for Left Leg Back, knit all 13 sts.
Row 42: Purl.

Work short rows for Foot Front:
Short row 1: K10, W+Tk.
Short row 2: P7, W+Tp.
Short row 3: K6, W+Tk.
Short row 4: P5, W+Tp.
Short row 5: K4, W+Tk.
Short row 6: P3, W+Tp.
Short row 7: K2, W+Tk.
Short row 8: P1, W+Tp.
Short row 9: K7 to end of row.

Row 43 (dec): [P2tog, cast off 1 st] 3 times, fasten off last stitch for Foot Edge.

Trouser Side 2
Rejoin yarn BHH to 16 sts on LH needle, continue to work on Trouser Side 2 as follows:
Row 29 (inc): Kfb, knit to end. – 17sts
Rows 30-32: Beginning with a purl row, work three rows stocking stitch.
Row 33 (dec): K1, k2tog, k2, k2tog, k3, k2tog, k2, k2tog, k1. – 13sts
Row 34: Purl.
Row 35 (dec): K2tog, k9, k2tog. – 11sts
Row 36: Purl.
Row 37 (dec): K2tog, k2, k3tog, k2, k2tog. – 7sts
Row 38: Purl, PM on first and last stitch of row for Trouser Markers. Cut yarn BHH, join yarn CCD, continue with yarn CCD as follows:

Right Leg
Row 39: Knit all 7 sts.
Row 40 (inc): Cast on 6 sts for Right Leg Back, purl all 13 sts.
Rows 41-42: Beginning with a knit row, work two rows stocking stitch.

Work short rows for Foot Front:
Short row 1: K10, W+Tk.
Short row 2: P7, W+Tp.
Short row 3: K6, W+Tk.
Short row 4: P5, W+Tp.
Short row 5: K4, W+Tk.
Short row 6: P3, W+Tp.
Short row 7: K2, W+Tk.
Short row 8: P1, W+Tp.
Short row 9: K7 to end of row.

Row 43 (dec): [P2tog, cast off 1 st] 3 times, fasten off last stitch for Foot Edge.

Join Leg Seams
Working on one leg at a time, WS together, fold the Foot Cast-Off Edge in half and join both halves together with mattress stitch to create the Foot Seam, then work mattress stitch to join the leg seam row ends from the foot seam up to the colour change near Trouser Markers.
You can stuff your yarn endings into the legs but there's no need to completely stuff the legs at moment – you'll be able to do that later.

Trouser Inside Legs and Front
The completion of the Trousers begins with the Inside Legs which are picked-up and knitted across the cast-on edge from Leg Back as follows:

Left Trouser Inside Leg
Return to Left Leg Back Cast-On Edge – you should have the RS of the Left Leg Back facing (the Trouser Back is facing you with WS/purl-side showing).

*Beginning at Trouser Marker on your right with yarn BHH pick up and knit 8 sts across the Leg Back Cast-On Edge from the marker on your right to the marker on your left.
Row 1: Purl across all 8 Inside Leg sts.
Row 2 (inc): [K2, kfb] twice, k2. – 10sts
Row 3: Purl.
Row 4 (inc): Kfb, knit to last st, kfb. – 12sts
Row 5: Purl.
Row 6 (inc): [K2, kfb] four times. – 16sts
Row 7: Purl.
Row 8 (inc): [K3, kfb] four times. – 20sts

Rows 9-11: Beginning with a purl row, work three rows stocking stitch.
Row 12 (dec): K2tog, knit to last 2 sts, k2tog. – 18sts**

Row 13: Purl, PM on last stitch of row for Left Inner Belly Marker.
Cut yarn, slip all 18 Left Inside Leg sts onto a large safety pin.

Right Trouser Inside Leg
Return to Right Trouser Leg Back Cast-On Edge – you should have the RS of the Right Leg Back facing (the Trouser Back is facing you with WS/purl-side showing).
Continue to Work as Left Leg from * to **.
Row 13: Purl, PM on first stitch of row for Right Inner Belly Marker.
Cut yarn, slip all 18 Right Inside Leg sts onto a large safety pin.

Join Trouser Inside Leg to Trouser Back
Working on one trouser leg at a time and working on one side seam at a time, WS together match Inner Belly Marker with Leg Divide Marker and work mattress stitch to join the row ends seam from the top of the Leg at Trouser Marker to the Inner Belly/Leg Divide markers.
Then join the other Inside Leg

Seam working mattress stitch to join row ends from the top of the leg up to where you divided for the trouser legs.
Remove Trouser and Leg Divide Markers.

Trouser Front/Belly
RS facing, slip Left Inside Leg sts off the safety pin and onto a knitting needle ready to knit across, rejoin yarn BHH k15, skpo, k1; slip Right Inside Leg sts off the safety pin and onto the knitting needle ready to knit across, k1, k2tog, k15 to end. – 34sts

Row 1: Purl across all 34 Trouser Front/Belly sts.
Row 2 (dec): K13, cast off next 8 sts for Gusset Seam, k12 to end of row. – 26sts
Row 3 (dec): P12, p2tog, PM on last stitch for Gusset Seam Marker, p12 to end. – 25sts
Rows 4-7: Beginning with a knit row, work four rows stocking stitch.
Row 8 (dec): K6, skpo, k9, k2tog, k6 to end of row. – 23sts
Rows 9-11: Beginning with a purl row, work three rows stocking stitch.
Row 12 (dec): K6, skpo, k7, k2tog, k6 to end of row. – 21sts
Row 13: Purl.

Incorporate the Waistcoat Front into the Trouser Front
In this section you are working with two different yarn combinations in the same rows. The yarn not in use should be carried across the back on the work to the next place it is needed.

NOTE: I found it easier to cut about 1 metre (1 yard) lengths of yarn EFG and strand that as I continued to work with yarn BHH.

Row 14: K6 in BHH; k1 in EFG; k7 in BHH; k1 in EFG; k6 in BHH.
Row 15: P5 in BHH; p3 in EFG; p5 in BHH; p3 in EFG; p5 in BHH.
Row 16: K4 in BHH; k5 in EFG; k3 in BHH; k5 in EFG; k4 in BHH.
Row 17: P3 in BHH; p7 in EFG; p1 in BHH; p7 in EFG; p3 in BHH.
Row 18: K2 in BHH; k17 in EFG; k2 in BHH.
Row 19: P1 in BHH; p19 in EFG; p1 in BHH.
Cut yarn BHH, continue to work in yarn EFG only as follows:
Rows 20-25: Beginning with a knit row, work six rows stocking stitch, PM on first and last stitch of last row for Left and Right Inner Thigh Markers.
Rows 26-27: Beginning with a knit row, work two rows stocking stitch.
Row 28 (dec): K2tog, knit to last 2 sts, k2tog. – 19sts
Row 29: Purl.
Row 30 (dec): K2tog, knit to last 2 sts, k2tog. – 17sts
Row 31: Purl.
Row 32 (dec): K2tog, knit to last 2 sts, k2tog. – 15sts
Cut yarn EFG, join yarn AAD, continue with the Neck as follows:

Neck
Row 33: Purl.
Row 34 (dec): K2tog, knit to last 2 sts, k2tog. – 13sts
Row 35: Purl.
Row 36 (dec): K2tog, knit to last 2 sts, k2tog. – 11sts

Work short rows for Chin:
Short row 1: P10, W+Tp.
Short row 2: K9, W+Tk.
Short row 3: P8, W+Tp.
Short row 4: K7, W+Tk.

Short row 5: P9 to end of row.
Cast off all 11 sts for Chin Edge.

Join Thigh Front Seam
Refer to Body A, **Fig. 3** in Making Up.

Working on one side at a time, WS together match Inner Thigh to Thigh Markers, mattress stitch Thigh Front Seam so joining Thigh to Trouser Front/Belly from Inner Thigh/Thigh markers to Inner Belly marker – join as dotted line A to B.
Remove Inner Belly and Inner Thigh Markers.

Join Belly to Back Seam
Refer to Body A, **Fig. 4** in Making Up.

Working on one side at a time, WS together match colour change at waistcoat from Waistcoat Back to Waistcoat Front, ease seam together and work mattress stitch to join Belly to Back Seam from red waistcoat colour change to Thigh Markers.
Remove Thigh Markers.

Join Nose Seam
RS together fold the Nose row ends matching left and right Nose Markers and work back stitch the seam from markers to the fold.

Join Muzzle Seam
RS together working on one side at a time, match the corner of the Head Side cast-on edge from the beginning of the pattern to the Nose Marker/ Nose Seam and back stitch the tiny muzzle seam so joining Head Sides Rows ends to Nose Cast-On Edge from corner of head side cast-on edge/nose cast-on edge to the split.
Turn out to RS.
Then carefully mattress stitch the tiny gaps at the nose sides and stripes – use doubled black yarn, yarn CC, to complete this tiny seam.
Remove the Nose Markers.
Push your little finger and the white yarn endings into the nose seam to enhance and shape the nose.

Join Chin Seam
WS match the Neck Markers and mattress stitch to join both Head

Sides Cast-On Edges together to create Chin Seam from markers to the Nose Seam.
Remove Neck Markers.

Join Gusset Seam
WS together work mattress stitch to join small gusset seam from Gusset Marker to the split, also if there is a small hole where you divided for the trouser legs work a few stitches to close it.
Remove Gusset Marker.
At this stage you can add stuffing into the body and legs.
Add a little at a time using the stuffing to pad out the shaping at the thighs, belly, back and feet.

Complete the Head
Push the toy eye into the head, either side of the nose, referring to the photographs for placement, from front/knit-side to back/purl-side and secure it in place firmly with the plastic or metal backing.

Join Chin Seam
Refer to Body A, **Fig. 5** in Making Up.

Ease the Chin Cast-Off edge and row ends to the neck. Matching the centre of the chin cast-off edge to the chin, seam beneath the nose then ease the seam together and mattress stitch either side of the chin and neck.

NOTE: The chin is barely stuffed/ only lightly, giving him a slightly baggy double chin!

Sew on Waistcoat Buttons
To complete the body sew the buttons evenly down the front of the Waistcoat.

FORELEGS
The Left and Right Forelegs are knitted independently of the body and joined after stuffing onto the Back as directed with the pattern, using the Foreleg Placement Marker as a guide. The details are embroidered on once the foreleg is completed.

Left Foreleg
With yarn CCD cast on 5 sts.

Row 1: Purl.
Row 2 (inc): Kfb, knit to last st, kfb. – 7sts
Row 3: Purl.
Row 4: Knit.
Row 5: Purl, PM on first and last stitch of row for Shoulder Markers.
Row 6 (inc): Cast on 2 sts for Left Under-Foreleg Side 1, knit across all 9 sts.
Row 7 (inc): Cast on 2 sts for Left Under-Foreleg Side 2, purl across all 11 sts.
Rows 8-11: Beginning with a knit row, work four rows stocking stitch.

Work short rows for Left Knee Joint:
Short row 1: K8, W+Tk.
Short row 2: P5, W+Tp.
Short row 3: K4, W+Tk.
Short row 4: P3, W+Tp.
Short row 5: K2, W+Tk.
Short row 6: P1, W+Tp.
Short row 7: K6 to end of row.

Rows 12-16: Beginning with a purl row, work five rows stocking stitch.

Work short rows for Left Paw Front:
Short row 1: K6, W+Tk.
Short row 2: P5, W+Tp.
Short row 3: K4, W+Tk.
Short row 4: P3, W+Tp.
Short row 5: K2, W+Tk.
Short row 6: P1, W+Tp.
Short row 7: K8 to end of row.

Row 17: Purl all 11 sts.
Row 18 (dec): [K2tog, k1] three times, k2tog. – 7sts
Row 19 (dec): P2tog, purl to last 2 sts, p2tog. – 5sts

Row 20 (dec): K2tog, k1, k2tog. – 3sts
Cut yarn, thread end through all 3
sts for Left Paw, pull up to gather for
Paw Point.

Right Foreleg
With yarn CCD cast on 5 sts.
Row 1: Knit.
Row 2 (inc): Pfb, purl to last st, pfb.
– 7sts
Row 3: Knit.
Row 4: Purl.
Row 5: Knit, PM on first and last stitch
of row for Shoulder Markers.
Row 6 (inc): Cast on 2 sts for Right
Under-Foreleg Side 1, purl across
all 9 sts.
Row 7 (inc): Cast on 2 sts for Right
Under-Foreleg Side 2, knit across all
11 sts.
Rows 8-11: Beginning with a purl row,
work four rows stocking stitch.

Work short rows for Right Knee Joint:
Short row 1: P8, W+Tp.
Short row 2: K5, W+Tk.
Short row 3: P4, W+Tp.
Short row 4: K3, W+Tk.
Short row 5: P2, W+Tp.
Short row 6: K1, W+Tk.
Short row 7: P6 to end of row.

Rows 12-16: Beginning with a knit
row, work five rows stocking stitch.

Work short rows for Right Paw Front:
Short row 1: P6, W+Tp.
Short row 2: K5, W+Tk.
Short row 3: P4, W+Tp.
Short row 4: K3, W+Tk.
Short row 5: P2, W+Tp.
Short row 6: K1, W+Tk.
Short row 7: P8 to end of row.

Row 17: Knit all 11 sts.
Row 18 (dec): [P2tog, p1] three times,
k2tog. – 7sts
Row 19 (dec): K2tog, knit to last 2 sts,
k2tog. – 5sts
Row 20 (dec): P2tog, p1, p2tog. – 3sts
Cut yarn, thread end through all 3 sts
for Right Paw, pull up to gather for
Paw Point.

Join Foreleg Seam
Refer to Body A, **Fig. 18** in Making Up.

Working on one foreleg at a time,
WS together fold Paw Cast-Off Edge
in half and mattress stitch to join the
two halves.
Mattress stitch the row ends to join
the Foreleg Seam up to the Shoulder
Markers, so leaving the first five
shoulder rows of free to join onto the
body – join dotted line A to B.
Stuff the paw through the opening at
the shoulder.
Remove the Shoulder Markers.
Flatten the front of the paw with your
thumb and forefinger then with a
doubled length of yarn C work four
lots of straight stitches to create toe
sections, pulling the straight stitches
as you sew them to make the paw
indent a little.

Join Forelegs to the Back
Refer to Body A, **Fig. 19** in Making Up.

Find the centre of the Shoulder Cast-
On Edge and mark with a pin.
Working on one foreleg at a time
and making sure you have the correct
foreleg for the side of the body match
the pin to the Foreleg Placement
Marker and hold in place with a stitch
or two.
Remove the Foreleg Placement Marker.
Mattress stitch each side of the
cast-on edge, working either side of
the centre of the shoulder – you're
wanting to create a round shoulder
shape. Then mattress stitch the
few shoulder row ends joining the
shoulder to the side of the body/onto
the Back.

Complete the seam by joining, with
mattress stitch, the Under-Foreleg
Cast-On Edge to the body.
With a doubled length of yarn A work
4 small straight stitches at each paw
edge for claws.

EARS
The Left and Right Ears are knitted
independently of the body and
joined after stuffing onto the Head as
directed with the pattern, using the
Ear Position Marker as a guide.

Left and Right Ears – Make 2 alike
With yarn AB cast on 10 sts.
Row 1: Purl.
Cut yarn AB, join yarn CD continue
with yarn CD as follows:
Rows 2-3: Beginning with a purl row,
work two rows stocking stitch.
Cut yarn, thread end through all 10
sts, pull up tightly and secure the
gathered up sts.

Join Ears to Head
Refer to Body C, **Fig. 24** in Making Up.

1. Use the tail ends to join each ear
onto each side of the head – the
backs of the ears are the RS/knit-side
which lie against the head.
2. Working on one ear at a time,
pinch the corners of the cast-on edge
together, hold in place with a stitch or
two then and sit the ear over the Ear
Position Marker. Remove the marker
as you carefully over-sew to join the
base of the ear onto the head.

FACE DETAIL
Refer to Body A, **Fig. 20** in Making Up.

With a doubled length of yarn D,
using embroidered straight stitches
work about 5 or 6 approx. 1cm (³⁄₈in)
long straight lines across the tip of the
nose.
Work a single thread embroidered
line for a mouth dividing it in the
centre by working a small upward/
vertical embroidered line from the
centre of the mouth to the nose.

TOMMY BROCK'S CLOTHES

OTHER TOOLS AND MATERIALS
- Sharp hand sewing needle
- Scissors

Coat
- 23 x 23cm (9 x 9in) royal-blue wool felt, approx. 1–1.5mm (⅛₂in) thick, and sewing thread to match

Waistcoat Collar
- 10 x 2cm (4 x ¾in) red wool felt, approx. 1–1.5mm (⅛₂in) thick, and sewing thread to match

COAT
Trace Tommy Brock's Coat (see Templates) and cut two Front/Backs and two Sleeves, all from royal-blue felt.

1. Match the Back Seams together and either hand- or machine-sew with a 3mm (⅛in) seam to join all along from the collar to the back opening – from A to B.

2. Working on one sleeve at a time, fold and match the long Underarm Seam ends together.

3. Either hand- or machine-sew along the underarm seam to join the long ends together.

4. Turn out to the RS.

5. Push the sleeve into the armhole. The underarm seam should lie at the bottom of the armhole.

6. Carefully hand work small back stitches to join the edges of the sleeve to the armhole allowing for roughly a 3mm (⅛in) seam. Repeat for the other sleeve.

WAISTCOAT COLLAR
Trace Tommy Brock's Waistcoat Collar (see Templates) and cut one from red felt.

1. Place the collar over the front of the knitted waistcoat making sure it's symmetrical.

2. Join the collar by whip-stitching in place all along the short sides and the top edge.

SAMUEL WHISKERS™

THE first farm that Beatrix Potter owned, Hill Top, was
an old house with thick walls and many hiding places
for rats and mice. In this tale the farmhouse is Tom Kitten's
home and the story tells what happens when Tom
accidentally comes upon the rat Samuel Whiskers living in a
secret hideout behind the attic walls.

FINISHED SIZE
Approx. 13cm (5¼in) tall from feet to top of head

YARN
You will need no more than one ball of each of:
A: DROPS Alpaca shade 0618 Light Beige Mix
B: DROPS Kid-Silk shade 42 Almond
C: DROPS Kid-Silk shade 15 Dark Brown
D: DROPS Flora shade 17 Yellow
E: DROPS Kid-Silk shade 29 Vanilla
F: DROPS Kid-Silk shade 35 Chocolate
G: Very small amount brown DK yarn for his boots –
I used DROPS Nord (doubled) shade 22 Chestnut

Unless otherwise stated, double and triple strands of
yarn are used together throughout this pattern. The
exact combinations of yarn to be used are indicated by
multiple letters (see How to Use This Book).

TENSION
13 stitches and 16 rows over 5cm (2in)

NEEDLES
3.5mm (US 4) knitting needles

OTHER TOOLS AND MATERIALS
• 1 small safety pin
• 16 coloured locking stitch markers (see How to Use
  This Book: Stitch Markers)
• 2 x 6mm (¼in) black toy safety eyes
• Toy stuffing or yarn/fabric scraps
• Tapestry or darning needle

PATTERN NOTES
• Use cable cast-on unless otherwise stated
• General knitting abbreviations can be found in
  How to Use This Book

HEAD
Beginning at the Nose.
With yarn A cast on 7 sts for
Nose Seam.
Row 1: Purl.
Row 2 (inc): K2, kfb, k1, kfb, k2 to end
of row. – 9sts
Row 3: Purl.
Row 4 (inc): Kfb, k2, kfb, k1, kfb, k2,
kfb. – 13sts
Row 5: Purl.
Join yarn B, continue with yarn AB
as follows:
Row 6 (inc): [Kfb, k3] three times, kfb.
– 17sts

Row 7: Purl, PM on first and last
stitch of row for Left and Right
Neck Markers.
Row 8 (inc): Kfb, k5, kfb, k3, kfb, k5,
kfb. – 21sts
Row 9: Purl.
Row 10 (inc): Kfb, k5, [kfb] twice, k5,
[kfb] twice, k5, kfb. – 27sts
Row 11: Purl.
Cut yarn B, join yarn C continue with
yarn AC as follows:
Rows 12-15: Beginning with a knit
row, work four rows stocking stitch.
Row 16: K12, PM on last stitch for Left
Ear Position Marker, knit next 4 sts,
PM on last stitch for Right Ear Position
Marker, k11 to end of row.
Row 17: Purl.
Row 18 (dec): K2tog, k8, skpo, k3,
k2tog, k8, k2tog. – 23sts
Row 19: Purl.

Divide the Head Back to Create Head Back Seam
Row 20 (dec): Cast off 5 sts for Head
Back Seam, Left-Side, knit next 12sts,
cast off last 5 sts for Head Back Seam,
Right-Side. – 13sts

Head Back
WS facing rejoin yarn AC to 13 sts for
Head Back, continue as follows:
Rows 21-23: Beginning with a purl
row, work three rows stocking stitch.
Cut yarn, leave all 13 sts for Head
Back on the knitting needle for now.

NECK AND BACK
Refer to Body A, **Fig. 2** in Making Up.

Join Left Side of head
With yarn AB begin at rat's Left Neck
Marker, RS facing pick up and knit
5 sts evenly along row ends to the
left-side corner of Head Back Seam
Cast-Off Edge; knit across all 13 Head
Back sts then from corner of Head
Back Cast-Off Edge knit across all 13
Head Back sts.

Join Right Side of Head
Continue to pick up across the right
side of the head, all onto the same
needle as follows:
Pick up and knit 5 sts evenly along
row ends from right corner of Head
Back Seam Cast-Off Edge to Right
Neck Marker – 23sts – pick up and

128

knit from A to B; knit across from C to D; pick up and knit from E to F.
Row 1: Purl all 23 sts.

BODY
Back
Row 2 (inc): K10, kfb, k1, kfb, k10 to end of row. – 25sts
Cut yarn AC, join yarn DE continue with Waistcoat Back as follows:
Row 3: Purl.

Work short rows (see Techniques) for Waistcoat/Body Back:
Short row 1: K6, PM on last stitch for Left Foreleg Placement, knit next 14 sts, PM on last stitch for Right Foreleg Placement, k4, W+Tk.
Short row 2: P23, W+Tp.
Short row 3: K22, W+Tk.
Short row 4: P21, W+Tp.
Short row 5: K20, W+Tk.
Short row 6: P19, W+Tp.
Short row 7: K18, W+Tk.
Short row 8: P17, W+Tp.
Short row 9: K16, W+Tk.
Short row 10: P15, W+Tp.
Short row 11: K14, W+Tk.
Short row 12: P13, W+Tp.
Short row 13: K12, W+Tk.
Short row 14: P11, W+Tp.
Short row 15: K18 to end of row.

Row 4: Purl.
Row 5 (inc): Kfb, knit to last st, kfb. – 27sts
Row 6: Purl.
Row 7 (inc): Kfb, knit to last st, kfb. – 29sts
Row 8: Purl, PM on first and last stitch of row for Left and Right Thigh Markers.

Cut yarn DE, join yarn AC continue with Hind Legs and Back as follows:

Hind Legs
Work short rows for Left Hind Leg:
Short row 1 (inc): Cast on 5 sts, k6, W+Tk.
Short row 2: P2, W+Tp.
Short row 3: K3, W+Tk.
Short row 4: P4, W+Tp.
Short row 5: K5, W+Tk.
Short row 6: P6, W+Tp.
Short row 7: K7, W+Tk.

Short row 8: P8, W+Tp.
Short row 9: K33 to end of row.
– 34sts

Work short rows for Right Hind Leg:
Short row 1 (inc): Cast on 5 sts, p6, W+Tp.
Short row 2: K2, W+Tk.
Short row 3: P3, W+Tp.
Short row 4: K4, W+Tk.
Short row 5: P5, W+Tp.
Short row 6: K6, W+Tk.
Short row 7: P7, W+Tp.
Short row 8: K8, W+Tk.
Short row 9: P38 to end of row.
– 39sts

Row 9 (dec): K2tog, k6, k2tog, k6, skpo, k3, k2tog, k6, k2tog, k6, k2tog. – 33sts
Row 10: Purl.
Row 11 (dec): K5, k2tog, k6, skpo, k3, k2tog, k6, k2tog, k5 to end of row. – 29sts
Row 12: Purl.
Row 13 (dec): K4, k2tog, k5, skpo, k3, k2tog, k5, k2tog, k4 to end of row. – 25sts
Row 14: Purl.
Row 15 (dec): K3, k2tog, k15, k2tog, k3 to end of row. – 23sts
Row 16: Purl.
Row 17 (dec): K10, cast off next 3 sts for Tail Space, knit next 9 to end of row. – 20sts

Row 18 (inc): P10, cast on 2 sts for Under Tail Space, p10 to end of row. – 22sts
Row 19 (dec): K8, skpo, k2, k2tog, k8 to end of row. – 20sts
Row 20: Purl, PM on first and last stitch of row for Left and Right Belly Markers.
Row 21 (dec): Cast off 4 sts for Left Paw Edge, knit next 11 sts, cast off last 4 sts for Right Paw Edge. – 12sts

Belly
WS facing, rejoin yarn AC to 12 sts on knitting needle.
Row 1: Purl across all 12 Belly sts.
Rows 2-5: Beginning with a knit row, work four rows stocking stitch. PM on first and last stitch of last row for Left and Right Inner Belly Markers.
Rows 6-11: Beginning with a knit row, work six rows stocking stitch.
Row 12 (inc): K1, kfb, k8, kfb, k1. – 14sts
Rows 13-15: Beginning with a purl, row work three rows stocking stitch.
Row 16 (inc): K2, kfb, k8, kfb, k2. – 16sts
Rows 17-19: Beginning with a purl row, work three rows stocking stitch.
Row 20 (inc): K3, kfb, k8, kfb, k3. – 18sts
Row 21: Purl, PM on first and last stitch of row for Left and Right Inner Thigh Markers.

" *Oh! Mother, Mother, there has been an old man rat in the dairy—a dreadful 'normous big rat, mother; and he's stolen a pat of butter and the rolling-pin.* "

Rows 22-23: Beginning with a knit row, work two rows stocking stitch. Cast off all 18 sts for Belly.

Waistcoat/Belly
RS facing, begin at rat's Left Inner Thigh Marker, with yarn DE pick up and knit 14 sts across from Left Inner Thigh Marker to Right Inner Thigh Marker.

Work short rows for Waistcoat/Belly:
Short row 1: P13, W+Tp.
Short row 2: K12, W+Tk.
Short row 3: P11, W+Tp.
Short row 4: K10, W+Tk.
Short row 5: P9, W+Tp.
Short row 6: K8, W+Tk.
Short row 7: P11 to end of row.

Rows 1-2: Beginning with a knit row, work two rows stocking stitch.
Row 3 (dec): K2tog, knit to last 2 sts, k2tog. – 12sts
Row 4: Purl.

Row 5 (dec): K2tog, knit to last 2 sts, k2tog. – 10sts
Row 6: Purl.
Cut yarn DE, join yarn AB continue with Chin as follows:
Row 7 (dec): K2tog, k2, k2tog, k2, k2tog. – 7sts
Row 8: Purl.
Row 9 (dec): [K2tog] three times, k1. – 4sts
Row 10: Purl.
Row 11 (dec): K1, k2tog, k1. – 3sts
Row 12: Purl.
Row 13: K3tog, fasten off for Chin Point.

Join Thigh Front Seam
Refer to Body A, **Fig. 3** in Making Up.

Working on one side at a time, WS together match Inner Thigh to Thigh Markers, match Inner Belly to Belly Markers, work mattress stitch to join Thigh Front Seam so joining Thigh to Belly from Inner Thigh/Thigh Markers to Inner Belly/Belly markers – join as dotted line A to B.
Remove Inner Belly and Inner Thigh Markers.

Join Waistcoat Front to Waistcoat Back
Refer to Body A, **Fig. 4** in Making Up.

Working on one side at a time, WS together match colour change for Waistcoat at the neck, ease seam together and work mattress stitch to join Belly and Breast Seam so joining Belly and Breast to Back from colour change at waistcoat to Thigh Markers. Remove Thigh Markers.
At this stage you can add stuffing into the head and body.
Add a little at a time using the stuffing to pad out the shaping at the head (although not too much, you want the jowls to remain flabby not filled-out); thighs, breast, belly (adding quite a bit of stuffing into the belly at the short row shaping) and back.

Add Eyes
Push the toy eyes into the knitting from front/knit-side to back/purl-side at the place where the eyes are to be (refer to the photographs for placement) and secure them in place firmly with the plastic or metal backing.

Create Indents for Head Shaping
Refer to Body D, **Fig. 27** in Making Up.

Thread up some yarn C and secure one end.
Pass the tip of the sewing needle into one side of the head just to the side of the eye.

NOTE: If you're planning to embroider the eyes then insert the sewing needle where you want the eyes to be, work this shaping technique then, with black yarn or thread, work French Knots inside the indent.

Pass the thread through the head to emerge to the side of the other eye on the other side of the head. Pass the thread back in, near where you

have you have just pulled through
to emerge back where you started.
Gently tug the yarn to create indents
at each side. When you are happy
with the shapes then secure the
thread – in at A; out at B; in at C;
out at A.

Join Chin Seam
Refer to Body C, **Fig. 23** in Making Up.

1. RS together fold the Nose Cast-
On Edge from the beginning of the
pattern in half and join both halves
together with back stitch.
2. Turn out to RS.
3. WS together match both Neck
Markers together, work mattress stitch
to join seam under the nose from
markers to the Nose Seam you've
just sewn – join dotted line A to B.
Remove the Neck Markers.
4. Match the fastened-off Chin Point
from belly stitches to the seam
under the nose you've just sewn and
mattress stitch to join both sides
of the triangle that was created at
the chin.

Join Head Back Seam
Refer to Body A, **Fig. 13** in Making Up.

WS together, working on one side at
a time, work mattress stitch to join
the Head Back Seam Cast-Off Edge
to the row ends at the back of the
head, at the same time adding a little
stuffing to pad out the head back.
You can also add little bits of stuffing
into the muzzle and nose to pad out
those too.

HIND PAWS
Refer to Body A, **Fig. 14** in Making Up.

The Left and Right Boots/Hind Paws
are picked up and knitted along the
Hind Paw Cast-Off Edge, knitted into
a boot shape, then the seam is sewn
all along the boot's heel, upper and
sole, stuffing at the same time.

Left Boot/Hind Paw
RS and rat's Left Thigh facing, begin at
Left Belly Marker, with yarn G pick up
and knit 3 sts along Left Paw Cast-Off
Edge from Left Belly Marker to the

other corner of the cast-off edge near
the rat's Back – pick up as dotted line
from A to B.
Remove Left Belly Marker.
Row 1: Purl.
Row 2 (inc): Cast on 5 sts for Left
Paw Upper, knit across all 8 sts.
Rows 3-5: Beginning with a purl row,
work three rows stocking stitch.

Work short rows for Left Paw/Boot
Front Outer Edge:
Short row 1: K3, W+Tk.
Short row 2: P3.
Short row 3: K2, W+Tk.
Short row 4: P2.

Row 6: Knit.
Row 7: Purl.

Work short rows for Left Paw/Boot
Front Inner Edge:
Short row 1: K3, W+Tk.
Short row 2: P3.
Short row 3: K2, W+Tk.
Short row 4: P2.

Rows 8-9: Beginning with a knit row,
work two rows stocking stitch.
Row 10 (dec): Cast off 5 sts for Paw/
Boot Upper Inside Edge, knit to end
of row. – 3sts
Cast off all 3 sts purl-wise for Paw/
Boot Inside Edge.

Right Boot/Hind Paw
RS and rat's Right Thigh facing, begin
at the opposite corner to Right Belly
Marker, with yarn G pick up and knit 3
sts along Right Paw Cast-Off Edge to
Right Belly Marker.
Remove Right Belly Marker.
Row 1 (inc): Cast on 5 sts for Right
Paw/Boot Upper, purl across all 8 sts.
Rows 2-4: Beginning with a knit row,
work three rows stocking stitch.

Work short rows for Right Paw/Boot
Outer Edge:
Short row 1: P3, W+Tp.
Short row 2: K3.
Short row 3: P2, W+Tp.
Short row 4: K2.

Row 5: Purl.
Row 6: Knit.

Work short rows for Right Paw/Boot
Inner Edge:
Short row 1: P3, W+Tp.
Short row 2: K3.
Short row 3: P2, W+Tp.
Short row 4: K2.

Rows 7-8: Beginning with a purl row,
work two rows stocking stitch.
Row 9 (dec): Cast off 5 sts purl-wise
for Paw/Boot Upper Inside Edge, purl
to end of row. – 3sts
Cast off all 3 sts for Paw/Boot
Inside Edge.

Join Boot Seam/Hind Paw Seam
Refer to Body A, **Fig. 15** in Making Up.

Working on one paw at a time, WS
together fold paw in half across the
row ends at the heel.
Mattress stitch the Paw Inside Cast-
Off Edge to the row ends at the Belly.
Work mattress stitch to join the
cast-on and cast-off edges of the paw
upper and the row ends that will
become the paw front.
Stuff the paw through the last seam at
the heel before closing that seam with
mattress stitch.

Flatten the front of the paw with your thumb and forefinger then with a doubled length of yarn C work four lots of straight stitches to create toe sections, pulling the straight stitches as you sew them to make the paw indent a little.

TAIL
Refer to Body A, **Fig. 16** in Making Up.

The Tail is picked up and knitted along the Tail Cast-Off Edge, the under-tail edges are cast on either side of the picked-up and knitted stitches then the Tail is knitted in its entirety as i-cord, below is the i-cord technique using two single point needles. The cast-on edges are then joined to the Tail Cast-On Edge.

RS and rat's Back facing, return to the Tail Cast-Off Edge. With yarn AC, begin at rat's left side (your right side) of the cast-off edge, pick up and knit 3 sts into the cast-off edge, all along from your right to your left –

Tail already picked up and knitted as dotted line from A to B.
Row 1 (inc): Cast on 2 sts for Tail Underside 1, purl all 5 sts.
Row 2 (inc): Cast on 2 sts for Tail Underside 2, knit all 7 sts.
Do not turn the work over to the purl-side.
You'll now work 'i-cord' on these 7 Tail sts as follows:

NOTE: Have RS/knit-side facing at all time.

i-cord row 1: RS facing, with the 7 sts on the needle in your right hand, slip the 7 sts off the RH needle onto the LH needle – keeping RS/knit-side facing and the working yarn pulled behind the work, k7.
Then, without turning the work so RS facing continue as follows:
i-cord row 2 (dec): RS facing, with the 7 sts on the needle in your right hand, slip the 7 sts off the RH needle onto the LH needle – keeping RS/knit-side facing and the working yarn

pulled behind the work, K2tog, k3, k2tog. – 5sts
i-cord row 3: Slip the 5 sts off the RH needle onto the LH needle – keeping RS/knit-side facing and the working yarn pulled behind the work, k5.
Continue to work as i-cord row 3 until the tail, from where you picked up stitches for the tail, measures 7cm (2¾in).
Next i-cord row (dec): RS facing, with the 5 sts on the needle in your right hand, slip the 5 sts off the RH needle onto the LH needle – keeping RS/knit-side facing and the working yarn pulled behind the work, K2tog, k1, k2tog. – 3sts
Next i-cord row: Slip the 3 sts off the RH needle onto the LH needle – keeping RS/knit-side facing and the working yarn pulled behind the work, k3.
Repeat this row another four times.
Next i-cord row (dec): RS facing, with the 3 sts on the needle in your right hand, slip the 3 sts off the RH needle onto the LH needle – keeping RS/knit-side facing and the working yarn pulled behind the work, k3tog, fasten off for Tail Point.
Thread cut tail end back inside the i-cord. Entire Tail measures approx. 8cm (3¼in).
Join the Under-Tail Cast-On Edges to the cast-on edge from Back under the tail to close the seam completely.

FORELEGS
The Left and Right Forelegs are knitted independently of the body and joined after stuffing onto the Back as directed with the pattern, using the Foreleg Placement Marker as a guide. The details are embroidered on once the foreleg is completed.

Left Foreleg
With yarn AC cast on 3 sts.
Row 1: Purl.
Row 2 (inc): Kfb, knit to last st, kfb. – 5sts
Row 3: Purl, PM on first and last stitch of row for Shoulder Markers.
Row 4 (inc): Cast on 2 sts for Left Under-Foreleg Side 1, knit across all 7 sts.
Row 5 (inc): Cast on 2 sts for Left

Under-Foreleg Side 2, purl across
all 9 sts.
Rows 6-7: Beginning with a knit row,
work two rows stocking stitch.

Work short rows for Left Elbow Joint:
Short row 1: K6, W+Tk.
Short row 2: P3, W+Tp.
Short row 3: K2, W+Tk.
Short row 4: P1, W+Tp.
Short row 5: K5 to end of row.

Rows 8-11: Beginning with a purl row
work, four rows stocking stitch.
Cut yarn A, join yarn EE (use the
other end of yarn ball E), continue to
work with yarn CEE as follows:
Row 12 (dec): P2tog, purl to last 2 sts,
p2tog. – 7sts
Cut yarn C, continue to work with
yarn EE for Left Paw as follows:
Row 13: Knit.
Row 14: Purl.

Work short rows for Left Paw:
Short row 1: K6, W+Tk.
Short row 2: P5, W+Tp.
Short row 3: K4, W+Tk.
Short row 4: P3, W+Tp.
Short row 5: K5 to end of row.

Row 15 (dec): [P2tog] three times,
p1. – 4sts
Cut yarn, thread end through all 4 sts,
pull up and secure the end.

Right Foreleg
With yarn AC cast on 3 sts.
Row 1: Knit.
Row 2 (inc): Pfb, purl to last st, pfb.
– 5sts
Row 3: Knit, PM on first and last st of
row for Shoulder Markers.
Row 4 (inc): Cast on 2 sts for Right
Under-Foreleg Side 1, purl across all
7 sts.
Row 5 (inc): Cast on 2 sts for Right
Under-Foreleg Side 2, knit across
all 9 sts.
Rows 6-7: Beginning with a purl row,
work two rows stocking stitch.

Work short rows for Right Knee Joint:
Short row 1: P6, W+Tp.
Short row 2: K3, W+Tk.
Short row 3: P2, W+Tp.
Short row 4: K1, W+Tk.

*" I saw Mr. Samuel Whiskers and his wife on
the run, with big bundles on a little wheel-
barrow, which looked very like mine. "*

Short row 5: P5 to end of row.

Rows 8-11: Beginning with a knit row,
work four rows stocking stitch.
Cut yarn A, join yarn EE (use the
other end of yarn ball E), continue to
work with yarn CEE as follows:
Row 12 (dec): K2tog, knit to last 2 sts,
k2tog. – 7sts
Cut yarn C, continue to work with
yarn EE for Left Paw as follows:
Row 13: Purl.
Row 14: Knit.

Work short rows for Right Paw:
Short row 1: P6, W+Tp.
Short row 2: K5, W+Tk.
Short row 3: P4, W+Tp.
Short row 4: K3, W+Tk.
Short row 5: P5 to end of row.

Row 15 (dec): [K2tog] three times,
k1. – 4sts
Cut yarn, thread end through all 4 sts,
pull up and secure the end.

Join Foreleg Seam
Refer to Body A, **Fig. 18** in Making Up.

Working on one foreleg at a time,
WS together fold Paw Cast-Off Edge
in half and mattress stitch to join the
two halves.
Mattress stitch the row ends to join
the Foreleg Seam up to the Shoulder
Markers, so leaving the first five
shoulder rows free to join onto the
body – join dotted line A to B.
Stuff the paw with the tiniest amount
of stuffing (or just use yarn snippings)
through the opening at the shoulder.

Remove the Shoulder Markers. Flatten the front of the paw with your thumb and forefinger then with a doubled length of yarn C work four lots of straight stitches to create toe sections, pulling the straight stitches as you sew them to make the paw indent a little.

Join Forelegs to the Back
Refer to Body A, **Fig. 19** in Making Up.

Find the centre of the Shoulder Cast-On Edge and mark with a pin. Working on one foreleg at a time and, making sure you have the correct foreleg for the side of the body, match the pin to the Foreleg Placement Marker and hold in place with a stitch or two.
Remove the placement marker. Mattress stitch each side of the cast-on edge, working either side of the centre of the shoulder – you're wanting to create a round shoulder shape. Then mattress stitch the few shoulder row ends joining the shoulder to the side of the body/onto the Back.
Complete the seam by joining, with mattress stitch, the Under-Foreleg Cast-On Edge to the body.

EARS
The Left and Right Ears are knitted independently of the rat's body and joined after stuffing onto the Head as directed with the pattern, using the Ear Position Marker as a guide.

Left and Right Ears – Make 2 alike
With yarns AE cast on 10 sts.
Rows 1-5: Beginning with a purl row, work five rows stocking stitch.
Cut yarn, thread end through all 10 sts, pull up and secure the gathered-up sts.

Join Ears to Head
Refer to Body C, **Fig. 24** in Making Up.

1. Use the tail ends to join each ear onto each side of the head – the backs of the ears are the RS/knit-side which lie against the head.
2. Working on one ear at a time, pinch the corners of the cast-on edge together, hold in place with a stitch or two then and sit the ear over the Ear Position Marker. Remove the marker as you carefully over-sew to join the base of the ear onto the head.

FACE DETAIL
Refer to Body A, **Fig. 20** in Making Up.

With a doubled length of yarn F, with embroidered straight stitches work a 'V' either side of the point of the nose then fill in the 'V' to create a nose.

POSE
To pose him so that he looks like one of Beatrix's illustrations have his arms crossed a little at the front and join with a few discreet stitches to hold them in place.

OTHER TOOLS AND MATERIALS
- Sharp hand sewing needle
- Scissors

Coat
- 20 x 20cm (8 x 8in) green wool felt, approx. 1mm (1⁄32in) thick, and sewing thread to match

Trousers
- 20 x 20cm (8 x 8in) yellow wool felt, approx. 1mm (1⁄32in) thick, and sewing thread to match

COAT
Trace Samuel's Coat (see Templates) and cut one Front/Back, two Sleeves and two Pocket Linings, all from green felt.

1. Working on one sleeve at a time, fold and match the long Underarm Seam edges together.
2. Either hand- or machine-sew along the underarm seam to join the long ends together.
3. Turn out to the RS.
4. Push the sleeve into the armhole. The underarm seam should lie at the bottom of the armhole.
5. Carefully hand work small back stitches to join the edges of the sleeve to the armhole, allowing for roughly a 2mm (1⁄16in) seam. Repeat for the other sleeve.
6. Working on one pocket at a time, position the pocket lining behind the slit, on the WS of the coat as shown by the grey outline on the template, and then work tiny, almost-invisible-on-right-side whip stitches all around the edges of the rectangular pocket lining. Repeat for the other pocket lining.

TROUSERS
Trace Samuel's Trousers (see Templates) and cut one Front/Back and two Legs, all from yellow felt.

1. Working on one leg at a time, fold and match the short leg seam ends together, so joining A to B.
2. Either hand- or machine-sew the seam for each leg allowing for a 2mm (1⁄16in) seam either end.
3. Working on one side at a time, fold and match the Trouser Front and Trouser Back together, so joining C to D and E to F.
4. Either hand- or machine-sew the seams along the straight edges for each side allowing for a 2mm (1⁄16in) seam and leaving the Leg Opening Edges open.

5. Turn out to the RS.
6. Push the leg into the leg opening edge. The seam should lie at the side/outer edge of the leg.
7. Carefully hand work small back stitches to join the edges of the leg to the leg opening edge allowing for roughly a 2mm (1⁄16in) seam. Repeat for the other leg.
8. Fold the pleat, folding line A onto line B, and secure in place with a couple of stitches. The other pleat is made by folding in the opposite direction.
9. When dressing Samuel Whiskers, the Tail Opening slit determines which side is the trouser back.

MAKING UP

REFER TO these step photographs when making up pieces of your characters; in other words, when you are sewing seams and joining pieces. When the pattern says, for example, 'Refer to Body A, Fig. 1', turn to this section of the book, find the body type (A, B, C, D or E) and the figure number (for example Fig. 1), and follow the annotations as described within the patterns.

For example: In the pattern for Peter Rabbit it says: 'Join Inner Ear Seam Refer to Body A, Fig. 10 in Making Up', then the direction to 'join dotted lines A to B' – in this section of the book you'll see listed: Body A, Fig. 10 and on that step photograph two dotted lines labelled A and B which you will join together.

Tip: Using the Marker Guide worksheet – which you can download from www.davidandcharles.com – will really help because the colours listed on the guide will match the marker colours on the step photographs.

BODY A

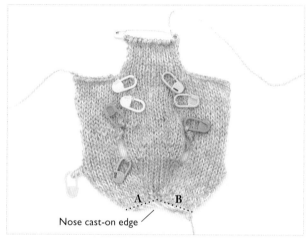

Figure 1: Join Nose Seam

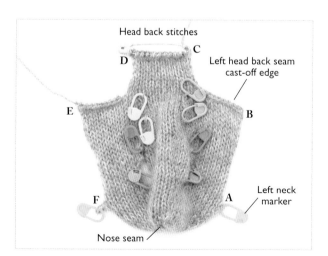

Figure 2: Join Right and Left Head Sides

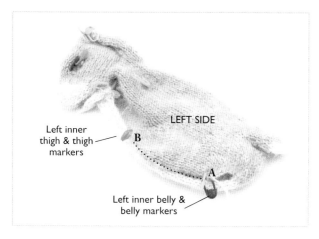

Figure 3: Join Thigh Front Seam

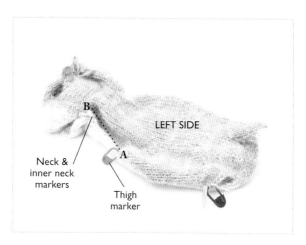

Figure 4: Join Belly to Back Seam

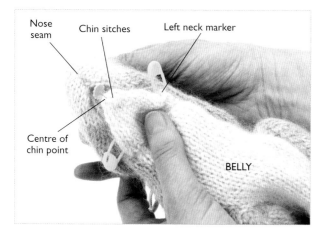

Figure 5: Join Chin to Muzzle Seam

Figure 6: Join Eye Sockets

Figure 7: Insert Eyes – push safety eye into centre of knitted eye socket, then join eye socket into the eye space

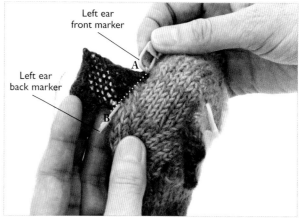

Figure 8: Pick up Outer Ear stitches

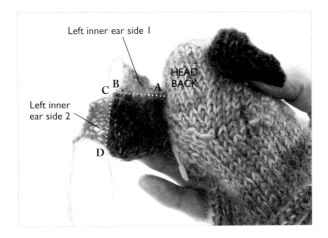

Figure 9: Pick up Inner Ear stitches

Figure 10: Join Inner Ear Seam – join A to B but leave straight edges unsewn

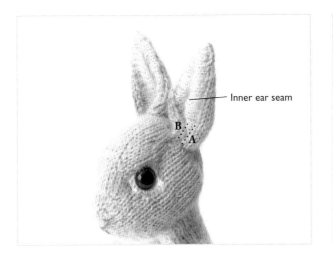

Figure 11: Join Ears at the Ear Base

Figure 12: Join Ear Back onto the Head

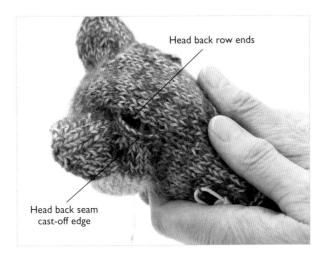

Figure 13: Join Head Back Seam

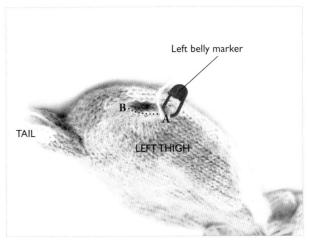

Figure 14: Pick up for Left Hind Paw

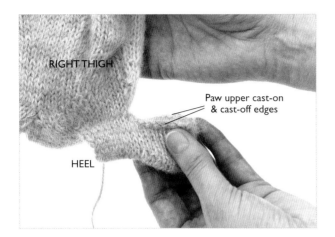

Figure 15: Join Hind Paw Seam

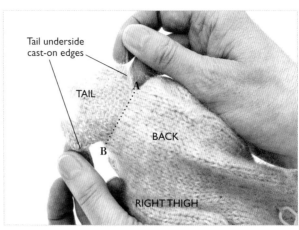

Figure 16: Pick up Tail Stitches – tail picked up into knitted stitches from A to B

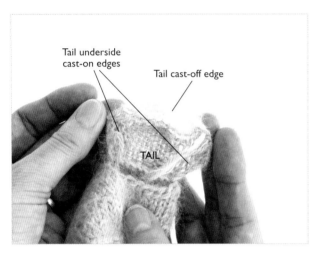

Figure 17: Join Tail Seam

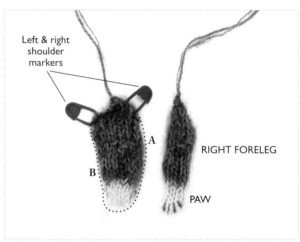

Figure 18: Join Foreleg Seam

Figure 19: Join Shoulder Seam – create as rounded a shoulder as you can when joining the Forelegs

Figure 20: Face detail

MAKING UP

BODY B

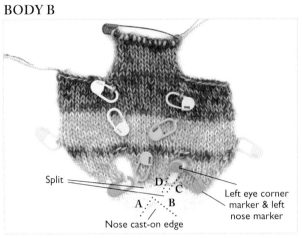

Figure 21: Join Head Seams

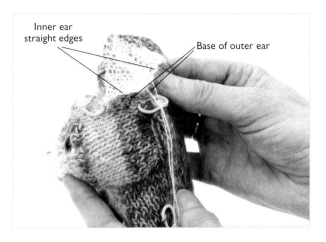

Figure 22: Join Inner Ears to Outer Ears

BODY C

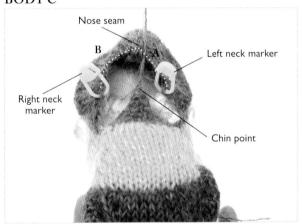

Figure 23: Join Chin Seam – join chin 'triangle', matching chin point to seam created when A & B are joined

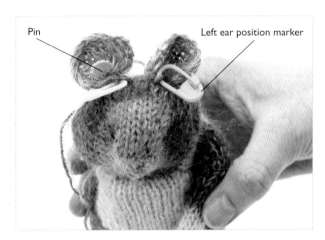

Figure 24: Join the Ears to the Head – pin ear before joining the base of the ear to the head

140

BODY D

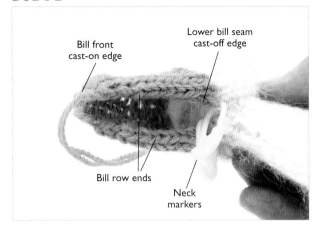

Figure 25: Join Bill Seam

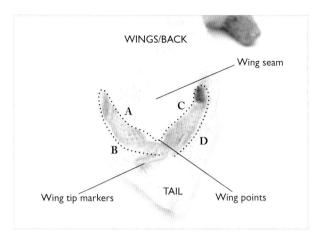

Figure 26: Join Wing Seam

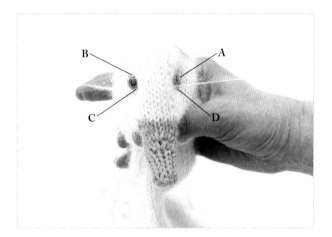

Figure 27: Create Eye Indents

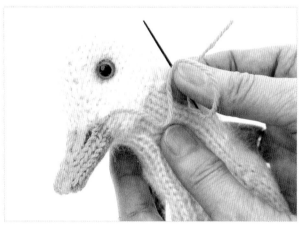

Figure 28: Bill Detail – at the side of the Bill, work a couple of stitches to copy the knitted 'V' shape

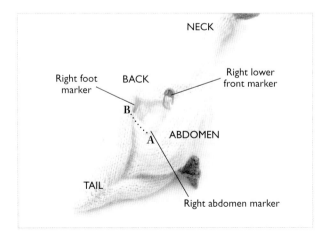

Figure 29: Webbed-Feet – for right foot pick up as dotted line from A to B

BODY E

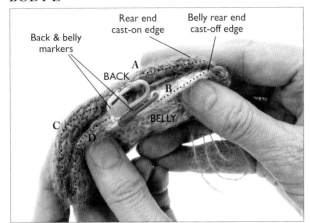

Figure 30: Join Body Seam

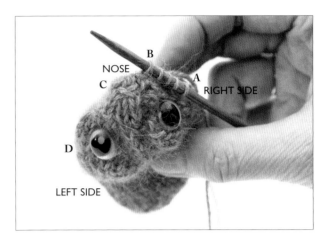

Figure 31: Pick up and knit Mouth

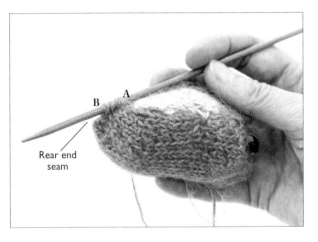

Figure 32: Pick up stitches for Left Hind Leg

Figure 33: Join Hind Leg Seam – join dotted lines to join top of the inside Leg to the Belly

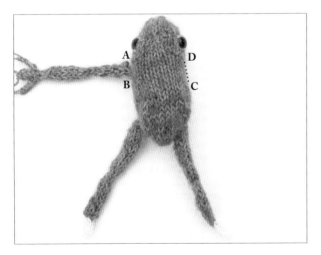

Figure 34: Pick up stitches for Forelegs at Back/Belly Seam - Left Foreleg sts from A to B and Right Foreleg sts from C to D

TEMPLATES

THESE TEMPLATES can be used to make the clothes for your characters. They are scaled at 100% so you can trace them directly onto paper, cut out and draw around them onto pieces of felt with a water-soluble pen, marking off any buttonholes or guides as the template directs. When you've completed the sewing up of the item, simply dab any visible lines away with a damp cloth. Printable versions of these templates can also be downloaded from www.davidandcharles.com.

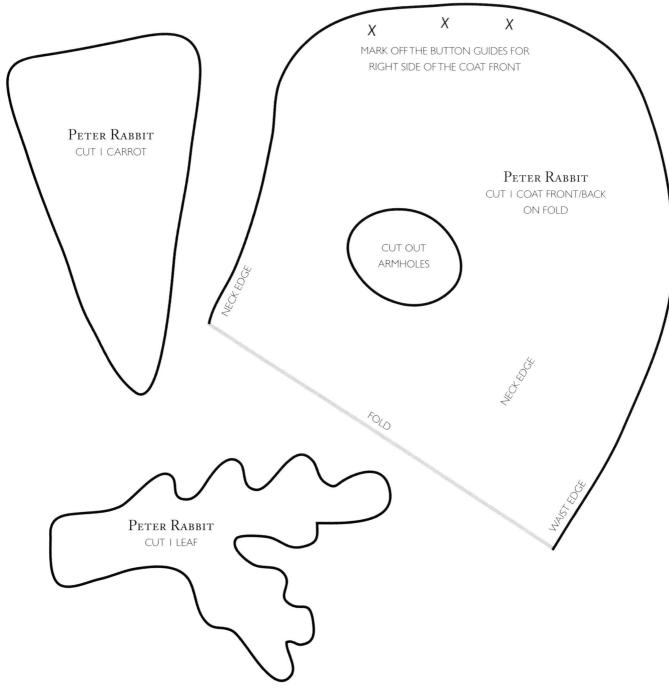

Peter Rabbit
CUT 1 CARROT

MARK OFF THE BUTTON GUIDES FOR
RIGHT SIDE OF THE COAT FRONT

Peter Rabbit
CUT 1 COAT FRONT/BACK
ON FOLD

CUT OUT
ARMHOLES

NECK EDGE

NECK EDGE

FOLD

WAIST EDGE

Peter Rabbit
CUT 1 LEAF

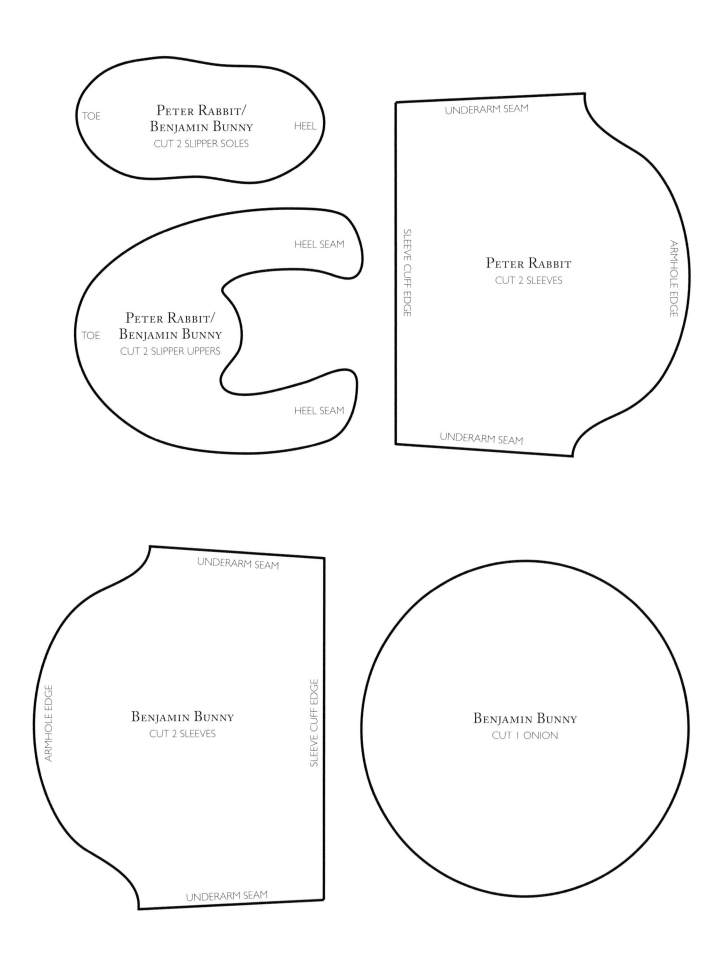

PETER RABBIT/
BENJAMIN BUNNY
CUT 2 SLIPPER SOLES

TOE

HEEL

PETER RABBIT/
BENJAMIN BUNNY
CUT 2 SLIPPER UPPERS

TOE

HEEL SEAM

HEEL SEAM

UNDERARM SEAM

SLEEVE CUFF EDGE

ARMHOLE EDGE

PETER RABBIT
CUT 2 SLEEVES

UNDERARM SEAM

UNDERARM SEAM

ARMHOLE EDGE

SLEEVE CUFF EDGE

BENJAMIN BUNNY
CUT 2 SLEEVES

UNDERARM SEAM

BENJAMIN BUNNY
CUT 1 ONION

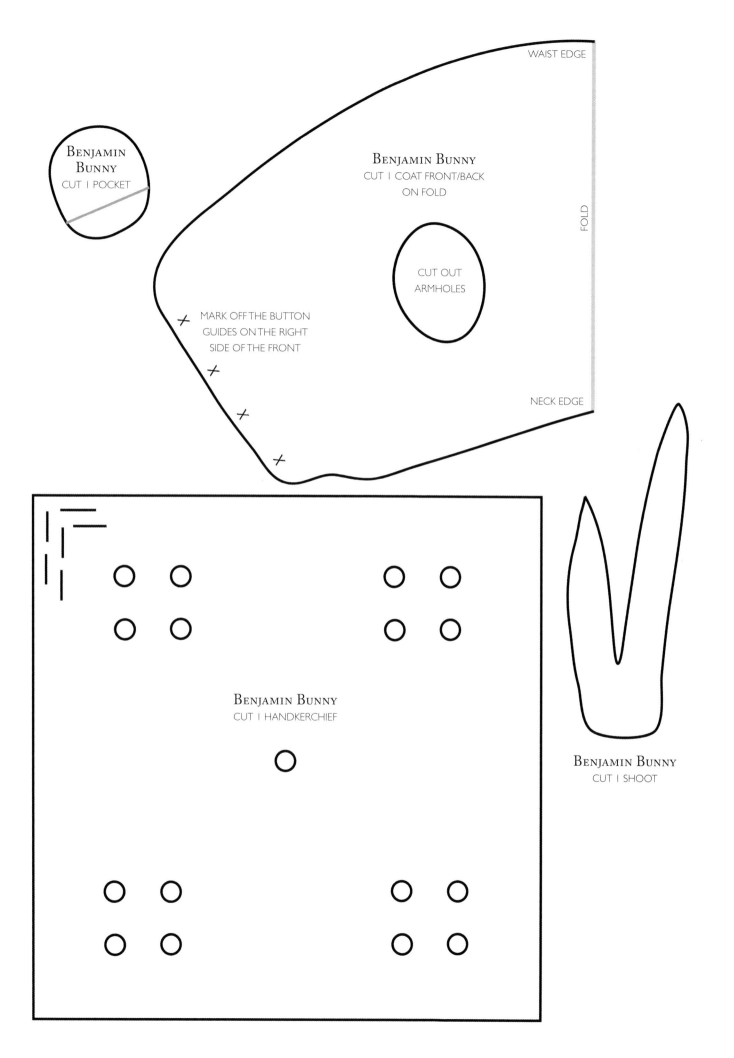

Benjamin
Bunny
CUT 1 POCKET

Benjamin Bunny
CUT 1 COAT FRONT/BACK
ON FOLD

WAIST EDGE

FOLD

CUT OUT
ARMHOLES

MARK OFF THE BUTTON
GUIDES ON THE RIGHT
SIDE OF THE FRONT

NECK EDGE

Benjamin Bunny
CUT 1 HANDKERCHIEF

Benjamin Bunny
CUT 1 SHOOT

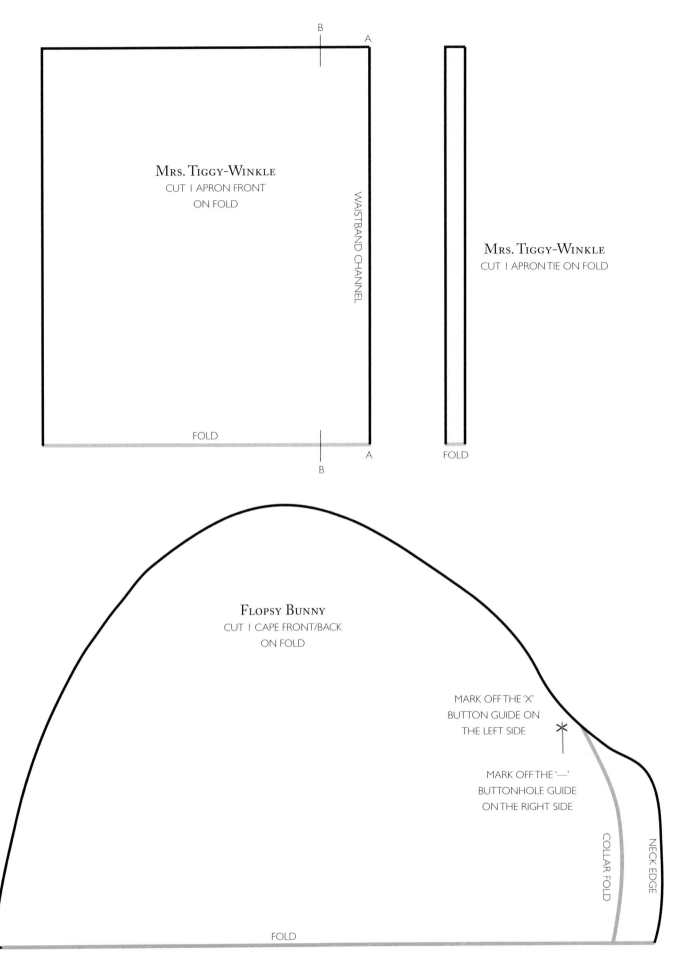

MRS. TIGGY-WINKLE
CUT 1 APRON FRONT
ON FOLD

WAISTBAND CHANNEL

FOLD

B

A

A

B

MRS. TIGGY-WINKLE
CUT 1 APRON TIE ON FOLD

FOLD

FLOPSY BUNNY
CUT 1 CAPE FRONT/BACK
ON FOLD

MARK OFF THE 'X'
BUTTON GUIDE ON
THE LEFT SIDE

MARK OFF THE '—'
BUTTONHOLE GUIDE
ON THE RIGHT SIDE

COLLAR FOLD

NECK EDGE

FOLD

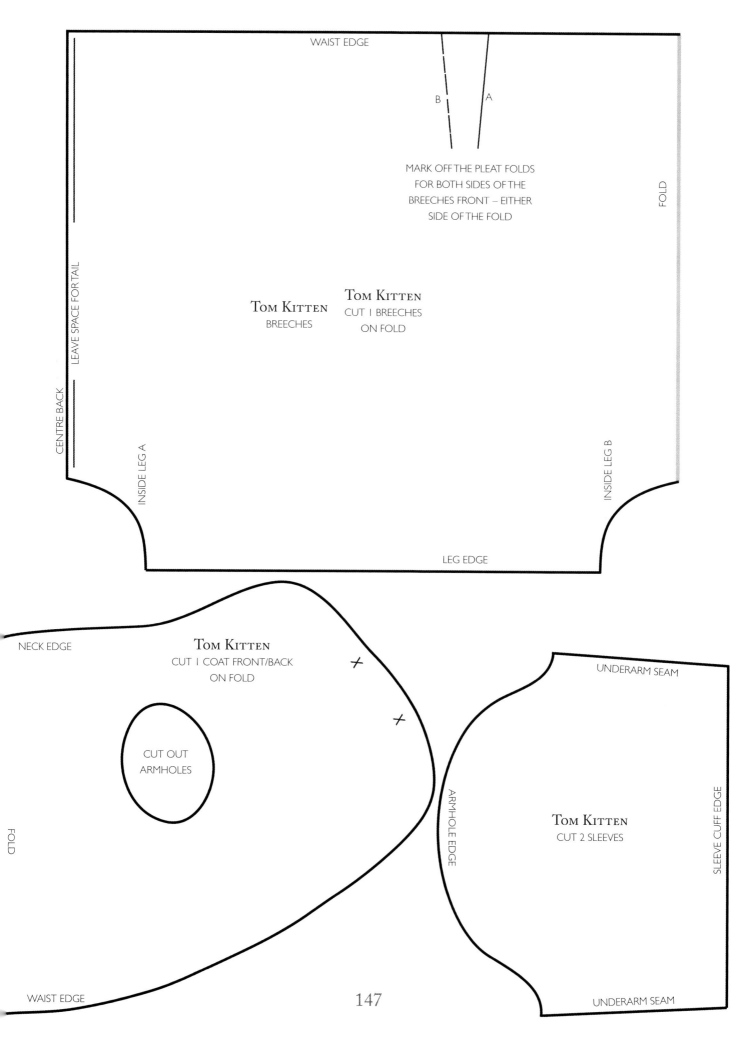

WAIST EDGE

B   A

MARK OFF THE PLEAT FOLDS
FOR BOTH SIDES OF THE
BREECHES FRONT – EITHER
SIDE OF THE FOLD

FOLD

LEAVE SPACE FOR TAIL

CENTRE BACK

TOM KITTEN
BREECHES

TOM KITTEN
CUT 1 BREECHES
ON FOLD

INSIDE LEG A

INSIDE LEG B

LEG EDGE

NECK EDGE

TOM KITTEN
CUT 1 COAT FRONT/BACK
ON FOLD

UNDERARM SEAM

CUT OUT
ARMHOLES

FOLD

ARMHOLE EDGE

TOM KITTEN
CUT 2 SLEEVES

SLEEVE CUFF EDGE

WAIST EDGE

147

UNDERARM SEAM

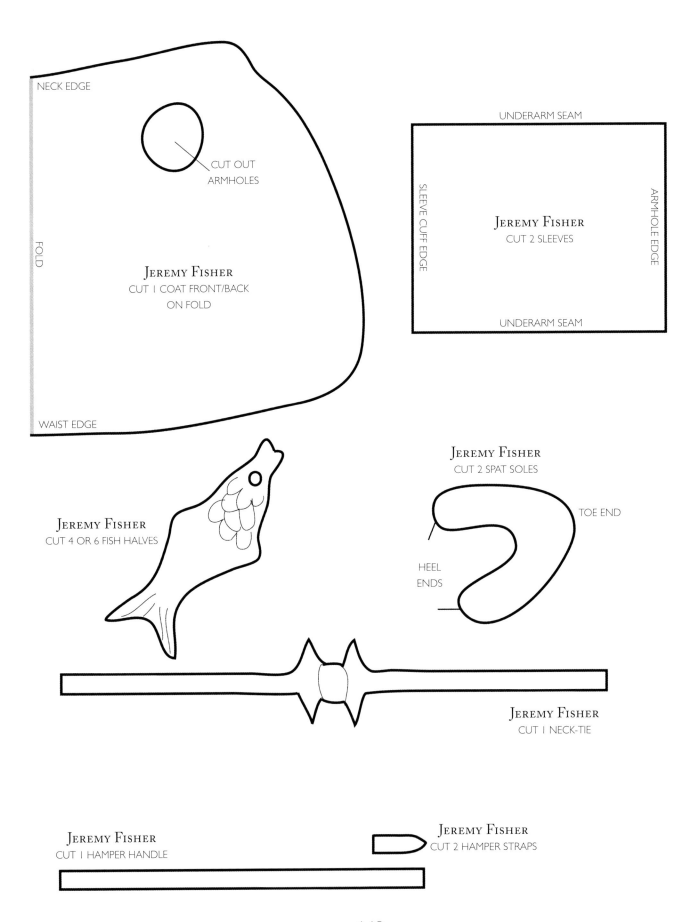

NECK EDGE

CUT OUT
ARMHOLES

FOLD

Jeremy Fisher
CUT 1 COAT FRONT/BACK
ON FOLD

WAIST EDGE

UNDERARM SEAM

SLEEVE CUFF EDGE

Jeremy Fisher
CUT 2 SLEEVES

ARMHOLE EDGE

UNDERARM SEAM

Jeremy Fisher
CUT 4 OR 6 FISH HALVES

Jeremy Fisher
CUT 2 SPAT SOLES

TOE END

HEEL
ENDS

Jeremy Fisher
CUT 1 NECK-TIE

Jeremy Fisher
CUT 1 HAMPER HANDLE

Jeremy Fisher
CUT 2 HAMPER STRAPS

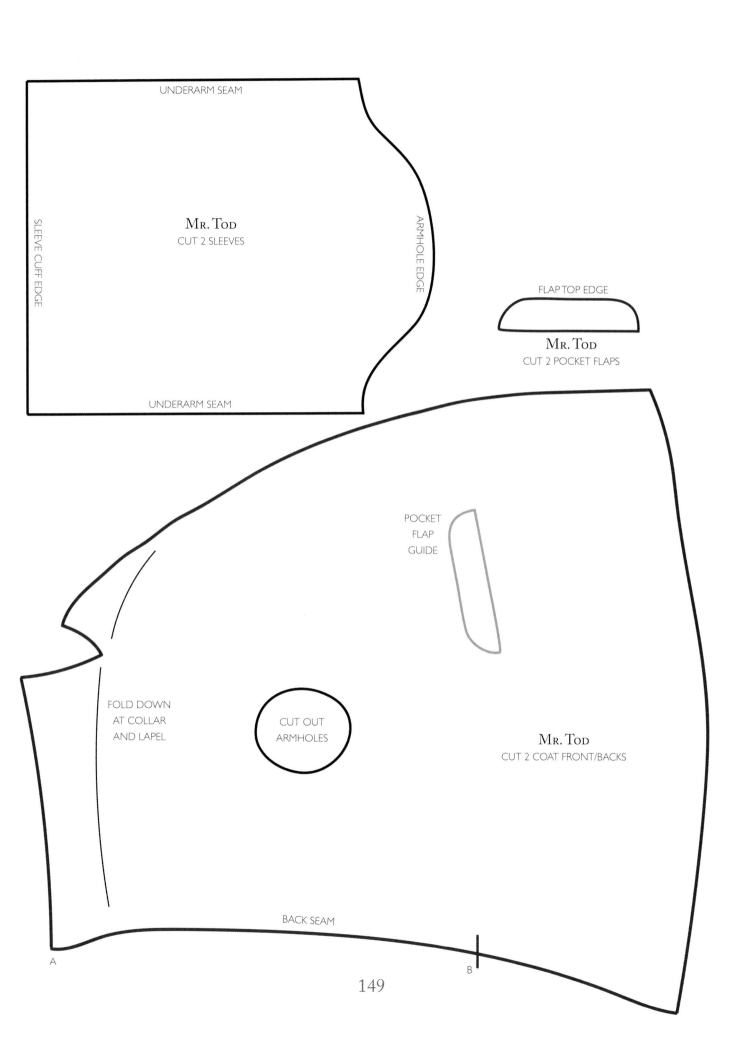

UNDERARM SEAM

SLEEVE CUFF EDGE

Mr. Tod
CUT 2 SLEEVES

ARMHOLE EDGE

UNDERARM SEAM

FLAP TOP EDGE

Mr. Tod
CUT 2 POCKET FLAPS

POCKET
FLAP
GUIDE

FOLD DOWN
AT COLLAR
AND LAPEL

CUT OUT
ARMHOLES

Mr. Tod
CUT 2 COAT FRONT/BACKS

BACK SEAM

A

B

149

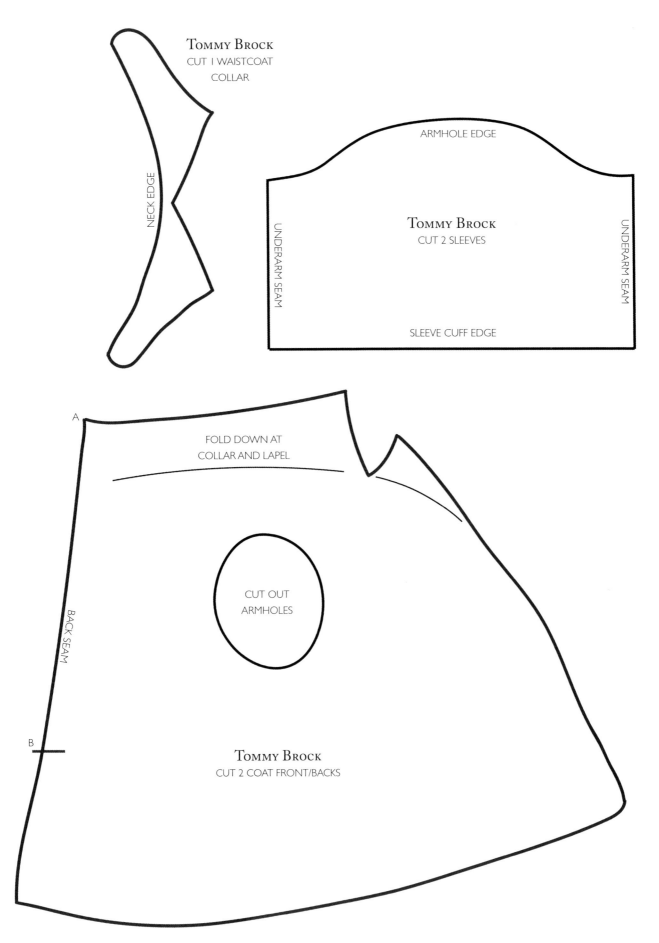

Tommy Brock
CUT 1 WAISTCOAT
COLLAR

NECK EDGE

ARMHOLE EDGE

Tommy Brock
CUT 2 SLEEVES

UNDERARM SEAM

UNDERARM SEAM

SLEEVE CUFF EDGE

A

FOLD DOWN AT
COLLAR AND LAPEL

CUT OUT
ARMHOLES

BACK SEAM

B

Tommy Brock
CUT 2 COAT FRONT/BACKS

150

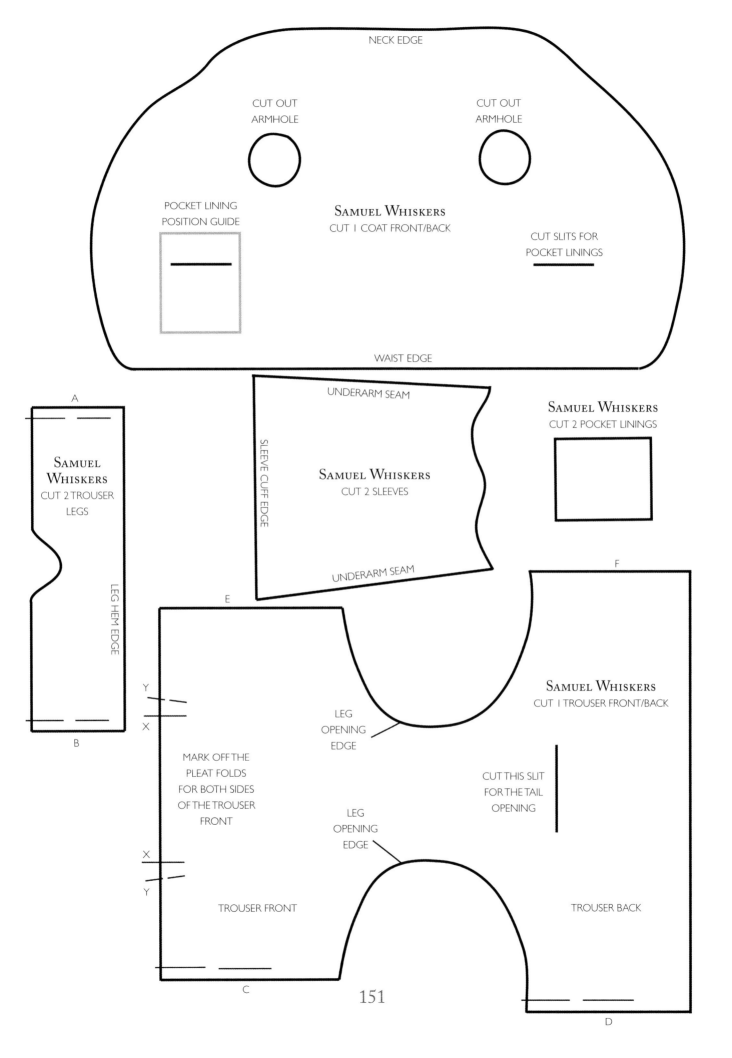

TECHNIQUES

IF YOU are new to knitting or need to brush up on your skills, the following pages provide guidance on the techniques you'll need to create the characters, including shaping, seaming, finishing and those extra touches including embroidery. Take the time to review the techniques you need, as the finished project will benefit from working the stitches and seaming correctly.

GENERAL

Cable Cast-On
While you can use your own favourite method for casting on, the cable cast-on gives a firm start. Begin with a slip knot and first stitch as for the knit cast-on method then for each new st, insert RH needle between the last 2 sts on LH needle, catch the new loop of yarn and pull it through, then place this new st on LH needle.

Knit Stitch
1. Insert RH needle tip from front to back through first st on LH needle.
2. Wrap the yarn from clockwise around tip of RH needle.
3. Pull the loop of yarn to front of work through original st, keeping new st on RH needle and allowing original st to fall from LH needle.

Purl Stitch
1. Insert RH needle tip from right to left through front of st on LH needle.
2. Wrap yarn anticlockwise (counter-clockwise) around tip of RH needle.
3. Pull the loop of yarn through original st, keeping new st on RH needle and allowing original st to fall from LH needle.

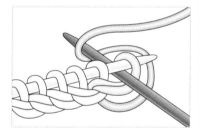

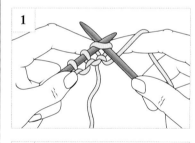

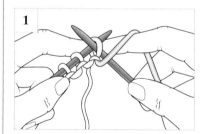

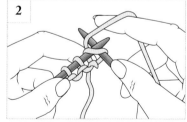

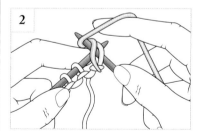

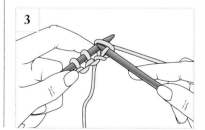

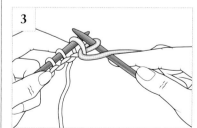

Pick Up and Knit
With right side of work facing:
1. Insert RH needle into appropriate space as instructed at the edge of the knitting from front to back.
2. Loop yarn around the needle.
3. Pull the yarn through, just as though you are knitting.
Repeat steps 1-3 until the required number of stitches have been picked up.

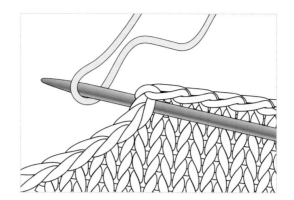

SHAPING

k2tog (Knit 2 stitches together)
Knit through the next two stitches as though they were one stitch. This decreases by one stitch.

skpo (Slip 1, knit 1, pass slipped stitch over)
1. Slip the next stitch (unknitted) from left to RH needle. Knit the next stitch on LH needle.
2. Lift the slipped stitch over the knitted stitch and off the RH needle. This decreases by one stitch.

M1 (Make one stitch)
1. Use the tip of RH needle to pick up the horizontal bar of last stitch worked, then slip the picked-up stitch onto LH needle.
2. Knit the picked-up stitch on LH needle. This increases by one stitch.

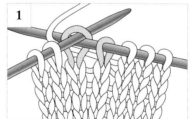

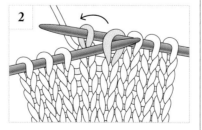

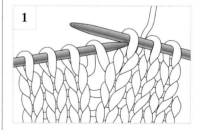

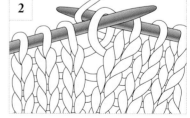

kfb (Knit into the front and back)
Knit into the front of the next stitch on LH needle. Instead of slipping the original stitch off the needle, knit into it again through the back loop. Then slip the original stitch off LH needle. This increases by one stitch.

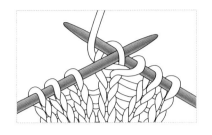

pfb (Purl into the front and back)
Purl into the front of the next stitch on LH needle. Instead of slipping the original stitch off the needle, take the working yarn to the back of the work and knit into the stitch through the back loop. Then slip original st off LH needle. This increases by one stitch.

Short Rows – Wrap and Turn
On a knit row:
1a. Bring working yarn to front of work, slip next stitch purl-wise onto RH needle. Take working yarn to back of work.
2a. Slip the wrapped stitch back onto LH needle. Turn the knitting to work back in the other direction.
Note: There is no need to pick up the wraps on subsequent rows for these patterns.

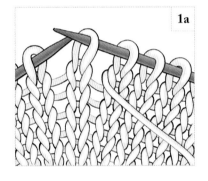
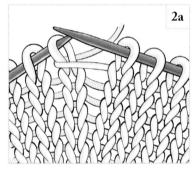

On a purl row:
1b. Take working yarn to back of work, slip next stitch purl-wise onto RH needle. Bring working yarn to the front of the work.
2b. Slip the wrapped stitch back onto LH needle. Turn the knitting to work back in the other direction.
Note: There is no need to pick up the wraps on subsequent rows for these patterns.

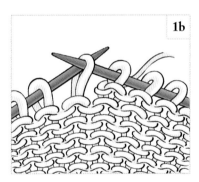
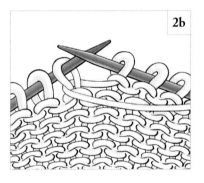

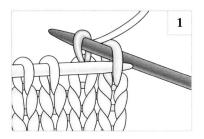

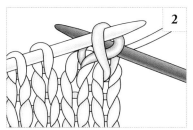

Cast-off

Work the first stitch on LH needle as if making a regular knit stitch. Then knit the second stitch.
1. Insert LH needle into the first stitch on RH needle.
2. Pass this stitch over the second loop on RH needle and drop it off the needle. This makes the first cast-off stitch.
To continue, knit the next stitch. Use LH needle to pass the new first stitch over the second stitch and drop it off the needle. Carry on until all the stitches in the row have been cast off.

Weaving in ends

The best way to weave in the loose ends so they will be invisible is to thread the yarn end through a tapestry or darning needle and sew it into the edge of the knitting by passing the needle through the 'bumps' of the stitches on the wrong side of the work. Sew the end in for about 2.5–5cm (1–2in) and then snip off any excess yarn.

SEAMING

Tip: For ease and effect I use fine mohair yarn for joining seams to lessen the bulkiness and to create a virtually invisible seam

Mattress Stitch

Put the two pieces of knitting next to each other, knit sides up and seams matching. Bring the yarn up through the centre of the first stitch on one piece of knitting, then under the legs of the first stitch on the other piece of knitting. Next go back down through the centre of the first stitch on the first piece of knitting. Continue in this way along the row, pulling up the stitches fairly tightly.

Back Stitch

Put both knit sides (right sides) together so the wrong side faces you. Carefully make small stitches along the edge, taking the needle down for each stitch behind the end of the previous stitch. Make sure you are sewing in a straight line as close to the edge as possible. It might sound obvious, but it is very easy to pick up stitches that are further away from the edge than you think. You want the sewing to be as invisible as possible.

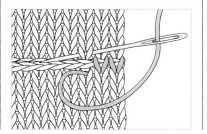

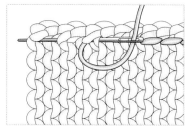

Whip Stitch / Over-Sewing

Work with a threaded-up length of yarn. Have the two pieces to be joined pinned or held together. Secure the yarn at the back of the work with a small knot. Bring the needle through the fabric from bottom to top as the seam allowance directs (for example, if the seam allowance is 6mm/¼in then start the stitch 6mm/¼in from the edge), then work a stitch over the edge from top to bottom. The needle should exit at the same hole where you started. This will give you your first stitch and secure the end of your row of stitching. Bring the needle through the same hole at the bottom once more but this time bring it up to the top edge at a diagonal next to your first stitch.

Then, bring the needle up from the bottom in line right underneath your last stitch (this is directly underneath the stitch at no angle). Angle the needle so the thread comes up next to the last stitch at the same diagonal distance as the previous step. Continue to work diagonal stitches over both edges of the two pieces needing to be joined, securing the end when the seam is complete.

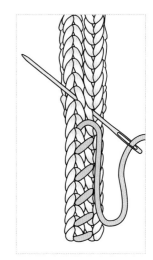

Extra touches

These are the methods I use to add that all-important extra detail to the knitted piece, in the case of the characters a few additional face markings make all the difference to achieving that final character, be it a stripe or two for tabby Tom Kitten or a little extra marking here and there for Jemima's bill.

Intarsia

Intarsia knitting is used for designs where there are blocks of colour or where you wish to switch colour to add stripes or animal fur detail. You will need a separate ball of yarn for each colour, and you will often have to change colours in the middle of a row. Knit along the row until the new colour is needed. Drop the first colour and pick up the second colour underneath the first one, crossing the two yarns over before knitting the next stitch in the second colour. The crossing of the yarns ensures that no holes are created between colours.

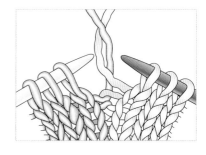

Swiss Darning

This is a simple way of adding small areas of contrasting colour and forms duplicate stitches over the knitted stitches. Thread a tapestry or darning needle with yarn and bring it up from the back of the work to the front through the middle of a knitted stitch where you want the contrast patch to be. Weave the contrasting thread to duplicate and cover the knitted stitch. Repeat, to cover as many knitted stitches as you wish. Secure the ends of yarn at the back of the contrasting patch.

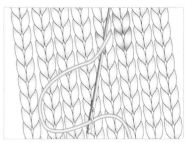

Spend time making the facial features perfect and full of character. You can use any stitches to create these features, although simple straight stitches are as effective as any. You can adapt them to make features of the noses or mouths for the characters and working a few simple stitches at the paws instantly create claws. Just remember, you need the stitches to look neat and be as firm as possible so that they don't undo.

Note: The simple petal pattern of Jemima's shawl is created using Lazy Daisy stitch and adding a line of running stitch and a few straight stitches gives an illustrative effect on Benjamin Bunny's handkerchief!

Straight Stitch

This is the simplest of stitches. Thread a tapestry or darning needle with the new colour of yarn and insert it from the back of the work to the front where you want the stitch to start. Take the yarn over at least a couple of knitted stitches and insert it back through the knitting where you want the stitch to end. Work as many stitches as you wish and then secure the ends at the back of the work. You can adapt these stitches endlessly, for example sewing them close together, on top of each other or splayed apart.

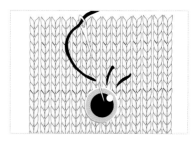

Lazy Daisy Stitch

Work with a threaded-up length of yarn. Secure the yarn at the back/purl-side of the knitting. Bring the needle through at the point where the bottom of the petal is to be, re-insert the needle very close to the starting point. Draw the yarn through to create a loop on the surface/knit-side of the knitting and hold the loop down with your finger. Make a straight stitch the length of the required petal on the purl-side and bringing the tip of the needle through to the knit-side and through the loop of yarn at the top of the petal, pull the thread until the loop lies flat and creates an attractive petal shape. Anchor the stitch with a small straight stitch. Continue to make similar petals scattered randomly over the knitting.

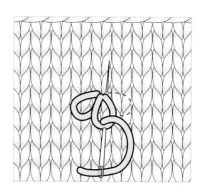

Running Stitch

Work with a threaded-up length of thread. Secure the thread and, working from left to right, pass the needle in and out of the fabric to make a line of short stitches, keeping the stitches and the spaces between them even.

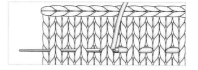

French Knots

Bring the needle from the back to the front of the work.
1. Wind yarn twice round the needle. Pull needle through the twists, bringing yarn through too to create the knot. Twist the yarn round the needle more times for a bigger knot if desired.
2. Insert needle from front to back at centre of knot and secure on wrong side.

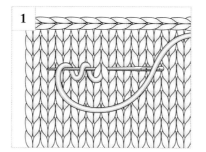
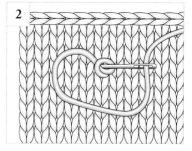

ABOUT THE AUTHOR

If there's one constant throughout Claire Garland's life, it's her need to create. Claire lives with her family, in a little white cottage tucked away in a corner of Cornwall, surrounded by woods and fields. Here she knits at her kitchen table, inspired by the fauna which surrounds her home.

Claire started knitting toys many years ago, with characterful bears and dolls for her three children. More recently she decided to create as realistic a rabbit as possible given the constraints of yarn and knitting.

At around this time Claire also set up an Instagram account and tried her first bunny out on her small following – an instant hit – so another bunny followed then another and another until she had a positive 'fluffle' of bunnies and a substantial following of knitted bunny enthusiasts. This has now developed into a veritable menagerie: foxes, mice, birds, deer, and there are still many more creatures in the future.

You can follow Claire and her creations on Instagram at @dotpebbles_knits.

SUPPLIERS

YARN
All the yarns used in this book can be bought from woolwarehouse.co.uk, who ship internationally.
For other suppliers, please check the yarn manufacturers websites:
DROPS – garnstudio.com
Rico Design – rico-design.com
James C Brett – jamescbrett.co.uk
King Cole – kingcole.com

TOY EYES
Cello Express – ebaystores.co.uk/Celloexpress
Glasseyes.com – glasseyes.com
Mister Eyes – etsy.com/shop/MisterEyes
Shamrock Rose – etsy.com/shop/ShamrockRose

TOY STUFFING
Habbyboy – ebaystores.co.uk/Habbyboy
Christie Bears Ltd – christiebears.com

WOOL FELT
Etsy – etsy.com

ACKNOWLEDGEMENTS

First thank you goes to my Number One inspiration Beatrix Potter, without whom this book would not be and without whom the idea of dressing a rabbit in a blue coat or a frog in a mackintosh and galoshes would probably never have been a thing.

Secondly a heartfelt thank you to the wonderful, brilliant team at David & Charles, in particular Ame Verso for giving me the honour of knitting the creatures created by one who I admire so much.

Also, a thank you to Penguin Random House for approving it all, especially Thomas Merrington for your kind words on my Mrs. Tiggy-winkle!

Brilliant styling as always, thanks Pru, and superb photography as always, thanks Jason – you've both really brought these fellows to life.

And much love as always to my gorgeous family who let me be, let me play with my yarn and have enabled me to enjoy myself immensely with my knitting!

INDEX

A DAVID AND CHARLES BOOK

David and Charles is an imprint of David and Charles, Ltd
Suite A, Tourism House, Pynes Hill, Exeter, EX2 5WS

First published in the UK and USA in 2023

ISBN-13: 9781446309674 hardback
ISBN-13: 9781446310106 EPUB
ISBN-13: 9781446310304 PDF

This book has been printed on paper from approved suppliers and made from pulp from sustainable sources.

Printed in China by Leo Paper Products Ltd for:
David and Charles, Ltd
Suite A, Tourism House, Pynes Hill, Exeter, EX2 5WS

10 9 8 7 6 5 4 3 2 1

Publishing Director: Ame Verso
Managing Editor: Jeni Chown
Editor: Jessica Cropper
Project Editor: Tricia Gilbert
Technical Editor: Hannah Maltby
Head of Design: Anna Wade
Pre-press Designer: Ali Stark
Technical Illustrations: Kuo Kang Chen
Design & Art Direction: Prudence Rogers
Photography: Jason Jenkins
Production Manager: Beverley Richardson

David and Charles publishes high-quality books on a wide range of subjects.
For more information visit www.davidandcharles.com.

Share your makes with us on social media using #dandcbooks and follow us
on Facebook and Instagram by searching for @dandcbooks.

Layout of the digital edition of this book may vary depending on reader hardware and display settings.